THE
New Mom's
Companion

Care for *Yourself* While
You Care for Your Newborn

Debra Gilbert Rosenberg, L.C.S.W.
with Mary Susan Miller, Ph.D.

SOURCEBOOKS, INC.
NAPERVILLE, ILLINOIS

This publication is designed to provide accurate and authoritative information in regard to the subject matter covered. It is sold with the understanding that the publisher is not engaged in rendering legal, accounting, or other professional service. If legal advice or other expert assistance is required, the services of a competent professional person should be sought.
—*From a Declaration of Principles Jointly Adopted by a Committee of the American Bar Association and a Committee of Publishers and Associations*

Published by Sourcebooks, Inc.
P.O. Box 4410, Naperville, Illinois 60567-4410
(630) 961-3900
FAX: (630) 961-2168
www.sourcebooks.com

Library of Congress Cataloging-in-Publication Data

Rosenberg, Debra.
   The new mom's companion: care for yourself while you care for your newborn / by Debra Rosenberg.
      v. cm.
Contents: Emotional ups and downs — Physical changes — Practical matters — Going back to work vs. staying at home — The marriage — Extended family — Your social life.
   ISBN 1-4022-0014-5 (pbk. : alk. paper)
   1. Mothers. 2. Motherhood. 3. Mother and infant. 4. Mothers—Family relationships. I. Title.
HQ759 .R637 2003
306.874'3—dc21

2002153443

Printed and bound in the United States of America
BG 10 9 8 7 6 5 4 3 2 1

To my husband, Alan, for loving me and making me a mother, and to my children, Jill, Lynn, and Mark, for enriching my life and being the primary reasons that my motherhood has been so fulfilling.

ACKNOWLEDGMENTS

I feel grateful to so many people for their help and support; friends, family, and countless new mothers have contributed to my life and to this book by telling me their stories, offering suggestions, cheering me on, or sharing their professional expertise. These gifts have been invaluable.

Thank you to the women in my groups, and specifically to Elizabeth Davies, Beth Hepburn, Laura Holmes, Beth Sirull, and Elena Vassallo for advice, referrals, encouragement, and kindnesses that went beyond the scope of the group. This book is, in a sense, from and for all of you.

Thank you to Dr. Audrey Bromberger, for your suggestions and comments while reviewing the chapter on physical changes.

Thanks to West Suburban Temple Har Zion, and especially to Harvey Gross and Lucy Matz, for recognizing the needs of first-time mothers and graciously offering space and administrative support for the New Mothers' Groups.

Thank you to my agent, Linda Roghaar, whose optimism and enthusiasm helped me maintain mine. And many thanks to my editor, Deb Werksman, who shared my vision of what mothers want to know and added her wisdom and insight to make this a better book.

Thank you to my friends and colleagues, without whom I could not have done this, and particularly to Edie Balch, Christine Baumbach, Katherine Billingham, Amy Brinkman, Carol Fred, Kitty Hall, Beth Inlander, David Inlander, Michael Klonsky, Susan Klonsky, Debra Landay, Hilarie Leib, Janice Monti, Alice Perlin, Sylvie Sadarnac-Studney, Ann Schreiner, Susan Sholtes, Cindy Tomkins, Judy Weiss, and Susan Weiss. Your unwavering support, advice, useful information, and pep talks kept me going.

A special thank you to Mary Susan Miller, who is both family and friend, for your warmth, wisdom, cheerleading, excellent ideas, and belief in this project.

Thanks to my mother, Dorothy Gilbert, my brothers, Steve Gilbert and Gary Gilbert, and my sister, Kathy Gilbert, for growing up with me, listening to me, sharing your stories, offering computer and legal advice, and your love.

And, of course, I wouldn't be a mother without my husband and children. My gratitude and unending love go to Alan, my husband, and to our children, Jill, Lynn, and Mark. I have been truly awed by the depth of your love, patience, and support. Thank you for making my motherhood such a delightful part of my life, for helping me to balance work and motherhood, and for believing that this idea could truly become a reality.

Table of Contents

Foreword

New mothers enter the world of parenting feeling much like Alice in Wonderland. They are stunned by the overlap of their emotions—joy, fear, guilt, all playing out at the same time in disharmony; they are bewildered by the myriad new tasks they are called upon to perform for this strange new creature they have created; and they feel totally incompetent in their ignorance. Nothing is familiar; nothing seems to make sense anymore. I remember, even in my first job, that I felt more secure than I did when faced with the responsibility of my first new baby. After all, as a teacher, I had lesson plans to follow, clear-cut goals, and, best of all, a mentor to give me guidance and support. No such luck for the first-time mother. I entered motherhood feeling that my education and preparation for this important new role were painfully nonexistent.

Today's first-time mother, finding this new life stage as profoundly confusing as it is delightful, often feels isolated and emotionally uncertain. She is expected to adjust to motherhood easily and instantly, even if she is living in a community distant from her own mother, despite getting little or no sleep, regardless of her comfort with her decision about work vs. staying at home, and whether or not she has any friends or acquaintances nearby who are also new mothers. With no one to guide her, and frequently little or no experience caring for babies, she is understandably worried that her discomforts with all these changes are abnormal, or that her lack of perfect happiness means that she must be a bad mother or an inadequate woman. Her own emotions are intense and unfamiliar, yet she feels that there is no one who would understand what she's feeling.

To be sure, new mothers in our culture have many advantages over their own mothers, grandmothers, and great-grandmothers. A woman planning to give birth in the United States expects, and usually achieves, a positive outcome: a healthy baby and a healthy mother. Women are encouraged to focus on education, self-fulfillment, career, and independence.

In addition, middle-class women giving birth in this country are often well educated and intellectually prepared for childbirth. They have a wealth of knowledge and support for the birth itself. They plan their pregnancies and deliveries; they understand what's happening to their bodies and the developing fetus. They are physically knowledgeable and prepared to have a baby. Socially and emotionally, though, they are unprepared.

Women in developing countries enter motherhood very differently than we do in the United States. The expression, "It takes a village to raise a child," takes on a completely new meaning in a village in a developing country such as Kenya. An entire Maasai village, houses, people, and all, could fit into a typical suburban United States high-school gym. Relatives and friends are only yards away, rarely beyond earshot. Men and women have clearly defined roles, and girls are involved in childcare from an early age. Experienced women surround new mothers. If a new mother has trouble breast-feeding, her sister, mother, or cousin is there to give suggestions. She doesn't agonize over whether or not to return to her career; her role in the community *is* her career, and it easily integrates motherhood. Her relationship with her husband doesn't rely on their ability to spend time alone together pursuing hobbies or mutual interests, nor does it suffer because the marital dynamics change as they embark on parenthood together. She is not isolated in her experience of motherhood. The women and children of her village spend their days together, always available to relieve a recovering new mother from her other duties, to attend to a crying baby, or to offer advice.

New mothers in developing countries don't worry about learning infant massage or playing Mozart to stimulate their babies' intellects. They don't worry about their day-care arrangements or whether their baby will get into the best college. They do not worry about losing touch with their best friends or not being able to pursue their other interests. They are not isolated from other mothers nor are they expected to manage all the changes in their emotions, priorities, and chores without support, as are new mothers here. New mothers in developing countries would find the need for this book totally inexplicable. They don't struggle to adjust to their new lives as mothers because their lives are not dramatically changed.

But the lives of new mothers in more prosperous nations do change, and they change dramatically. Along with our many advances, our middle class has lost the sense of community and connection women in other parts of the world can take for granted. We teach our new mothers how to breathe their way through a difficult labor, how to diaper a baby and take her temperature, and how to childproof a home, but we don't help them handle the emotional and relationship transitions, which are nearly universal in our industrialized world. Without that support and understanding, without the expectation that becoming a mother is a personal challenge and a significant transition, new mothers feel lost and lonely, incompetent, inadequate, and unfeminine. We have heard all too much about postpartum depression and psychosis and its sometimes disastrous results, and not enough about how normal it is to feel weepy for a time after delivery. Women don't have the knowledge or resources to assess if their own tears are indeed normal, or if they should be seeking medical help immediately. They haven't the awareness or access to other new and experienced mothers to determine if their marital squabbles are simply due to lack of sleep, or if they need marriage counseling. And because motherhood is still seen as normal and natural, they are embarrassed to be so uncomfortable with all this uncertainty.

The New Mom's Companion will fill the gap in a first-time mother's adjustment to motherhood. My experience as a parenting educator makes it clear to me that the best mothers, those who are well able to provide a loving, nurturing home with appropriate expectations for their children, are those who know who they are and are comfortable with their choices and their roles as mothers, partners, daughters, coworkers, and friends. I also know that in order to make a comfortable adjustment to motherhood, a woman must face her feelings and reassess how motherhood will fit into her life. She must be able to ask questions and share other women's ideas and experiences; she must be able to integrate motherhood into the rest of her life. It is much easier to be a good mother if you are a whole person, at ease with yourself and your various roles; becoming a good mother and a fulfilled person demands much more than simply learning to care for your baby.

The New Mom's Companion is not about becoming a better parent; it is about becoming comfortable and confident as a mother. First-time mothers want straight answers. Here is a resource to turn to when you question your own attitudes and reactions, a companion to reassure you when what you are feeling is perfectly normal, and a guide to tell you when to seek professional help. With *The New Mom's Companion,* a new mother no longer has to find her way on her own. Enjoy your journey into motherhood and take advantage of this companion, which is here to shine a light along your way.—Mary Susan Miller, Ph.D.

Introduction

This is the book I wish I'd had when I first became a mother. This is the book I wanted to consult when I was horrified to find myself angry with my beloved baby because she was wide-awake and wanting to play (again) at 3 A.M.; when as an intensely modest woman, I found myself walking around my apartment, sometimes all day long, unshowered, in my nightgown, with the flaps of my nursing bra down, raw nipples exposed to the supposedly healing air and any visitors; when it seemed that my neighbors and friends found motherhood so much easier than I did; when I felt exuberant, powerful, full of love, and bored, lonely, and incompetent all at once; when I was annoyed with my husband for not fully appreciating how important and successful I was as a mother because I'd kept both our daughter and myself alive for another day and I hadn't burned down the house. I wanted someone or something to reassure me that most new mothers, bleary-eyed from lack of sleep, novices at child care, physically and emotionally in transition from young womanhood to motherhood, feel all of the things I was feeling.

I have loved being a mother from the first days of my motherhood, but I also recognized early on that *becoming* a mother, not just *being* a mother, was more work than I'd anticipated. I talked with friends who had become mothers shortly before I had, and they mostly agreed that this transition to motherhood was more than any of us had bargained for. While we all welcomed certain aspects of the shifting priorities and pounds, there were other changes, in relationships, lifestyles, and focus, and in our very souls, that we hadn't been expecting, let alone prepared for.

Many pregnant women have an idea of what they hope their childbirth experience will be like. Some women plan for home births, some are determined to have drug-free deliveries in a hospital, and others want to be anesthetized as soon as possible. Some write detailed birthing plans and invite best friends to join them, while others want to leave every decision to their doctors. When you talk to new mothers after their deliveries, though, it's clear that once labor begins, it rarely goes as planned. Your labor and delivery may have been longer and more difficult than you'd ever imagined, or so fast you hardly had a chance to think, but no matter how much you plan and prepare yourself, childbirth is rarely just as you expected.

Similarly, there seems to be no great way to prepare yourself for the emotional rawness you feel when you become a mother for the first time. I'm convinced that even if you read every book written about becoming a mother you can only absorb or believe a limited amount. I was certain that I knew more than enough to adjust to motherhood easily, and I know I wouldn't have believed anyone who told me that becoming a mother was going to be as emotionally challenging and physically demanding as it was. Besides, I think that kind of preparation would have been like the birth plan: minimally helpful, but not really anywhere close to preparing me for the real thing.

Even as a clinical social worker who had lots of nieces and nephews, who had worked with teenaged mothers and adoptive families, and who had read nearly every book available about pregnancy, I was still unprepared for the impact motherhood had on my life. I knew my life would be different once my baby arrived, but I didn't have a clue as to what extent. I figured we'd add a person to our family, not become different people.

This tiny baby's birth seemed to change not just my body, but also my ability to think clearly, my relationship with my husband, and my feelings about my own mother and other family members. Motherhood changed many of my friendships, my attitudes about work, my sense of myself as a woman, just about everything that made me *me*. You name it, it changed, and if it didn't actually change, its relative importance in my life changed. All of these changes weren't bad at all; in fact, becoming a mother was mostly delightful. But there were many aspects of the process of becoming a mother that really caught me by surprise. Few women talked about these changes until I initiated a conversation, and then they seemed thrilled and relieved to share how motherhood had changed them. We all seemed to believe that motherhood should be a natural and positive experience, *that we shouldn't find it stressful.* As first-time mothers, it was sometimes difficult to admit that motherhood had put us on an emotional roller coaster, and we usually felt as though we didn't have the seat belt securely fastened. Out of shame or embarrassment, we couldn't admit to ourselves or to other new moms that we found becoming a mother emotionally challenging.

But while I discovered that lots of other new mothers also felt almost everything I did, I couldn't find resources that focused on *my* concerns, on my adjustment to motherhood. I found books on breastfeeding, books on becoming an excellent parent, books on how to get my baby to sleep, books on how to massage the baby, and books on how to get into shape after childbirth. I found groups with similarly baby-centric topics. Nothing on the bookshelves or in the community attended to my particular needs and questions about the emotional and relationship changes involved in becoming a mother.

Starting in 1989, after my third child was born and I was thoroughly immersed in motherhood (and, importantly, a whole lot more efficient, confident, and casual about my own motherhood), I began my New Mothers' Groups, meeting with first-time mothers to discuss the universal experiences and emotions of becoming a mother in our society. I've been meeting with new mothers of all ages and backgrounds ever since, and they agree that while motherhood is wonderful, and almost every new mother loves being a mother, most also struggle with adapting to the changes in their identities, bodies, relationships, work situations, and lives that this new role demands.

But not every new mother has access to a group, and so this book was born to offer all the support that new mothers need from a companion who's been there and discovered that she was not alone. This is the book I would have grabbed when I wasn't sure if it was normal to feel lonely or bored, or when I worried that my husband and I would never figure out how to divide the household tasks equitably. I would have consulted it when my mother appeared suddenly far wiser than I had ever before noticed, or when my former best friend didn't seem to understand or care about what my life had become. This book takes your exhaustion, concerns, and anxieties seriously and focuses on *your* transition as a person trying to integrate motherhood into the rest of your life.

This book is to help all first-time mothers adjust to becoming a mother, whether you are the first or the fourteenth among your circle to have a baby, whether you are twenty-two or forty-two, whether you live two blocks from your mother or two thousand miles away, whether you have lived in your neighborhood for ten years or ten days. It's for any new mother who has questions about mothering. It's for you.

How to Use This Book

The material in this book is presented in a question-and-answer format to allow you to find the topic you are concerned with easily and get a quick answer. You can either read the whole chapter or just the specific question, depending on whether you need some quick support or you want broader reassurance. The chapters are organized according to the specific areas of a woman's life that becoming a mother alters, from the internal, most personal emotional changes, to the countless adjustments in your most important relationships and work life. Occasionally an example or quote from a real new mother is included, although never using her real name.

Sometimes topics overlap. For example, your sex life has questions and answers in both the chapter on physical changes and in the chapter on marriage, but the aspect of the question determines its placement. When you are concerned with your husband having a different level of desire than you do, that's in the marriage chapter. When you wonder about the mechanics of sex after childbirth, look in the chapter on physical adjustment.

Part One focuses on what happens to you as an individual when you become a mother and is divided into four chapters. The first is about your emotions, the second, about physical changes, the third, practical concerns, and the fourth, the life-choice issues of working outside the home or staying at home. Part Two is devoted to how your primary relationships shift to adjust to your new role and has three chapters, one about your relationship with your baby's father, one about the extended family, and one about your social life. The Appendix is a bit of a catchall. It includes questions that are increasingly common, but less universal than the first two sections (for example, questions relating to adoption).

The heart of this book comes from all the women who have trusted each other and me enough to share and compare their stories about becoming a new mother. It includes the wisdom and experience of hundreds of mothers, women who have embraced motherhood with all its trials and treasures. Always remember you are not alone. Motherhood is a challenge and a privilege and you're going to be just fine.

Being a mother is one of the most rewarding jobs on earth and also one of the most challenging.

Section One
Your Personal Transition

Nothing else in my life has changed me the way motherhood has, not going away to college, not getting married, not losing a loved one. Becoming a mother is forever and irreversible and consuming: it involves your body, your soul, and how you spend your time. It changes how other people perceive you and how you perceive yourself. I had never changed a diaper before my first child was born, but I knew a lot about child development and parenting, so the things that worried me about becoming a mother had to do with practical issues. I worried about breast-feeding, losing the pregnancy weight, and whether or not I would return to work. I didn't really think twice about how my personal life would change once I had a baby.

While this entire book is dedicated to how motherhood changes a woman and her life, this first section focuses on the personal, individual changes a new mother undergoes, and it's divided into four chapters. The first chapter examines emotional identity changes, the second chapter discusses the physical changes childbirth and early mothering create, the third chapter is devoted to how having a baby impacts the way you spend your time, and the fourth addresses work and life-choice issues.

While what a new mother experiences physically often spills over into what she feels emotionally, what she *does* certainly affects her feelings in both the physical and emotional arenas, and her *work* impacts her emotions and self-image, I've attempted to keep these separate for the sake of convenience and clarity. When your emotions seem out of control, you can find the answer to your question about mood swings in the first chapter. In the middle of the night, when you find yourself wondering if there is something medically wrong or if it is normal that your hair seems to be falling out, you'll find that in the chapter on physical changes. When overwhelmed by large piles of tiny but dirty clothes, you can turn to the chapter on the practical changes motherhood brings and get some tips on how to get you through with minimum fuss (from you or the baby). And when you feel torn between a job you enjoy and a baby you love, the chapter on life-choice issues will be the resource you need.

In the next four chapters, you'll find answers to your questions about all things affecting you as an individual.

Motherhood is a process. Learn to love the process.

Chapter One

Emotional Ups and Downs

I loved being a mother, but I was caught off guard by the intensity and range of my own emotions. I would alternate, sometimes from one minute to the next, between feeling cranky and calm, from insecure to confident, from morose to joyous. My moods were unpredictable and my concerns were unfamiliar. I hadn't expected to feel bored and lonely; I hadn't counted on the power of my love; no one warned me that my previously clear ideas about working outside the home would become so cloudy. In a matter of a few short months, I went from wondering how the hospital could possibly have released my daughter into my care (was I *really* grown-up enough to be a mother?) to feeling like I'd been a mother forever. Becoming a mother was nearly as consuming as taking care of my baby was, and just as interesting a metamorphosis as pregnancy had been.

I had so many questions about this personal transformation for my friends and relatives who had already had babies. Often, other new moms were thrilled that I brought up the topic and wanted to compare literal sob stories. But almost as often, particularly among the more seasoned mothers, women talked first (and glowingly) about how wonderful those early days of mothering had been. It wasn't until we chatted for a while, and I had disclosed some of my own moments of uncertainty or emotional meltdown, that the other woman would tentatively admit that she had spent her first year of motherhood in a fog, and not always blissfully so. There seemed to be real discomfort, if not amnesia, about admitting how hard those early days had been.

I was shocked that I couldn't find books that looked at what happens to a woman's identity when she becomes a mother, because it was so obvious to me that having a baby was a much bigger deal than I'd ever thought before. It also amazed me how relieved most new mothers were to have me open the conversation to the less savory sides of early motherhood. We all felt better knowing that most, if not all, new mothers in our culture struggle in the process of incorporating motherhood into their lives.

This chapter answers your questions about the emotional journey into motherhood. Most new mothers reevaluate many areas of their lives when they become mothers for the first time, and most experience reactions and emotions they hadn't anticipated. This chapter looks at how a new mother sees herself in her world, at what it means to be a good mother, and at finding a way to hang on to who she was before motherhood. Even though becoming a mother challenges most women in ways they never expected, these challenges are extremely common.

There is a tremendous amount of learning that takes place in the first year of your baby's life; the baby learns a lot, too.

**I thought I was well prepared to become a mother.
Why am I so stunned by what it's *really* like?**

You may be as well prepared as humanly possible, but after becoming a mother myself and then working with hundreds of first-time mothers, it is very clear to me that no one fully understands what it feels like to be a mother until she becomes one. As Alissa, one new mother, said, "Before my baby was born, I thought I was well prepared. I had a good marriage; I read lots of books about pregnancy and child care; and I couldn't wait to become a mother. But nothing prepared me for how I *feel,* which includes amazingly in love, sore, incompetent, powerful, exhausted, and overwhelmed. What makes this so hard?"

Reading everything you can get your hands on about childbirth and child care can help you enormously through pregnancy, labor, and delivery, and teach you the basics of taking care of a baby. Painting the baby's room and buying baby clothes, a car seat, and a stroller will help you ready yourself to care for your baby, but those books and all the child-care equipment you'll ever need can't prepare you for your own personal, emotional, and day-to-day adjustments to motherhood. Just as no one can adequately describe what your labor and delivery will be like, no one can teach you how you will experience motherhood.

Change is difficult, and so much about your life changes when you bring that baby home. Many new mothers describe feeling unrecognizable, physically and emotionally, even to themselves. Your body looks different, emotions run amok, efficiency and competence plummet, and your priorities and interests are suddenly so narrowly circumscribed that you worry you've become boring. How you spend your days (and nights) changes suddenly and dramatically, particularly in those first several weeks. The most significant relationships in your life must compete for attention with a new baby who has few obviously redeeming qualities, yet is also the object of a love so intense it brings tears to your eyes. While all of these aspects of the transition to motherhood are nearly universal, there wasn't anything you could have done to become better prepared.

Despite having thought, before the baby was born, that you would just adore every facet of motherhood, getting comfortable in your new life doesn't come automatically or easily, and you can't adapt to all those changes in a matter of days. The birth of every first baby is the birth of a new mother, too—just take one day at a time and don't be too hard on yourself. Your efforts will slowly begin to pay off and you *will* find life easier; with time, patience, and experience, you will recover physically and settle into motherhood, learning how to balance your various roles and develop confidence and competence.

It is sometimes difficult to reconcile the fantasy of what you thought motherhood would be like, and what you thought you would be like as a mother, with reality.

Why didn't anybody tell me how hard it is to be a mother?

Most women find motherhood a challenge, but few are willing to admit to themselves, let alone share with others, just how tough it can be. New mothers enter motherhood anticipating the joy of caring for an adored newborn, never expecting to find the transition so stressful. In public, women describe motherhood as blissful and beautiful; in the media, mothers are depicted as natural and womanly. Real new mothers rarely divulge the less-than-lovely parts: the struggle to sit comfortably, chronic sleep deprivation, or the repetitious tedium of taking care of a baby all day. When your personal reality falls short of what everybody else seems to be experiencing so easily, it is difficult to accept.

While most first-time mothers eventually confess, at least to themselves, that the challenges of motherhood come as a shock, finding motherhood difficult is exactly what I think keeps them from sharing their feelings with others. Some new mothers have a sort of "motherhood machisma." They don't want anyone else to know that they are not experiencing the happiest time in their lives. Believing motherhood to be natural and therefore easy, they feel flawed and inferior for not finding motherhood a breeze, for not being perfectly content, perfectly organized, and perfectly gorgeous. Others, isolated and exhausted during those rough first several weeks, develop a sort of "motherhood amnesia"; the early adjustment goes by in such a blur that they honestly don't remember the mood swings and mayhem.

There's no conspiracy to keep non-mothers ignorant of the trials of motherhood. But it takes courage to be the first one to acknowledge how difficult it is to become a mother. If you think that everyone else handles it better or more easily than you, it's not surprising that you are reluctant to tell people you're floundering. But trust me, most women agree with you; if you initiate a conversation with other new mothers about your struggles, you will undoubtedly find that you are in good company.

Why do I feel like such a mess?

Terri, an attorney and new mother, felt the same way. "I see women having babies and just weeks later, they look great, seem energetic and in control, while I am still a slob," she said. "I can't even seem to manage to look nice enough to go to the grocery store. Why can't I?"

Because you are a real person and a real new mother, you are going through a normal period of adjusting to motherhood. Perhaps you have unrealistic expectations and role models. The new mothers in magazines and on TV look great because that's part of their job. If your career depended on your appearance, and you had the opportunity to have a full-time personal trainer, cook, makeup artist, and live-in nanny, you might be able to devote hours each day to getting back into shape and looking glamorous, too. It is too bad that more people, including the gorgeous and famous, don't let on about how hard it can be for a typical new mom to take care of herself while taking care of a newborn.

Certainly some women do seem to handle the adjustment to motherhood with tremendous grace. Some need less sleep to function well or truly are hyperefficient. Some are biologically blessed with bodies that return to their non-pregnant dimensions shortly after childbirth. Some have a lot of help. And some new mothers are just so uncomfortable when they feel disorganized or sloppily dressed that they find ways to make sure they look good, at least when out in public. But they are truly in the minority.

If you are just a regular person, it is perfectly normal to take some time, maybe a whole lot of time, to get adjusted emotionally and physically to your new life. Don't belittle yourself because you aren't what you imagine these other women to be. Enjoy and accept who you are, and don't expect that you should look like a supermodel unless you already do. As time goes on and your baby becomes more independent (and he will, I promise you!) you'll slowly be able to begin adding back in some of the things that help you feel "pulled together." For now, either take a very accepting attitude toward your appearance, or try to find one easy thing that you can do to help you feel better. Put your baby in a sling carrier while you brush your hair or put on a little lipstick. Terri, the attorney, discovered that just not wearing sneakers and sweats all the time made her feel more like her old self. Above all, remember that you are great just the way you are.

My labor and delivery did not go at all the way I had planned. How can I get past the disappointment?

It can be difficult to come to terms with your disappointment when your real life experience falls short of your fantasy. Whether you planned to have your best friend assist in the delivery only to discover that she had to be out of town, or you wanted an unmedicated delivery and found yourself begging for drugs after thirteen hours of pushing, it's difficult to accept having a life-changing event turn out to be so far from your ideal.

Unwittingly, some childbirth preparation classes and books seem to set women up for disappointment. Pregnant women get the impression that they will be able to control both their labor and delivery and are then crushed when things progress too rapidly or slowly, complications arise, or, in the frenzy of the moment, all their plans go awry. A maternity floor nurse I know once told me that she cringes whenever she sees a couple in labor come in with a birthing plan, as she knows that disappointment often accompanies their high expectations.

Having a baby can be delightful, but it can also be a struggle. If your delivery didn't meet your expectations, your anger and disappointment are normal. Face your disappointment head on; accept that your birthing experience was not what you had wanted, and focus instead on your new family and new life. If talking with your doctor, midwife, friends, and trusted family members doesn't help you come to terms with your feelings, consider talking with a qualified therapist. Your feelings are real and valid and deserve to be attended to.

My pregnancy and delivery were so difficult. How can I be a good mother if I had so much trouble giving birth?

I like to think of pregnancy and childbirth as akin to engagement and marriage. When you become engaged to be married, you are consumed with planning. You spend hours preparing for the big day, getting in shape to look your best, trying to anticipate and control each detail. You want the day to be perfect, and you imagine that the perfection of the day will foretell the success of your marriage. Similarly, while pregnant, you focus on getting physically and emotionally ready to give birth; every ache, twinge, or thought commands your attention. You hope that your careful preparation will guarantee you excellence at motherhood.

But both a wedding and a delivery mark only the beginnings of these new life stages. Your marriage might be totally satisfying even if it rained buckets on your wedding day and the flower girl vomited on your gown. Much the same, medication, bed rest, and medical intervention do not doom you to a difficult motherhood. Both motherhood and marriage involve long-term commitments and evolving relationships. Your motherhood isn't determined by your ability to give birth without a whimper, and needing medical intervention doesn't make you any less of a woman.

The birth experience may have been a disappointment, but your labor and delivery are not related to your future ability as a mother. Isn't the goal of a pregnancy to deliver a healthy baby to a healthy mother? Then you have not failed at all, and you can certainly still be an excellent mother! Labor and delivery, despite feeling like they go on forever, represent only the tiniest fraction of your motherhood. You can be a great mother no matter how your baby and you begin this together. Thank goodness you are both okay now, and let yourself enjoy your new baby. You are already a success.

The goal of pregnancy, labor, and delivery is to end up with a healthy baby and a healthy mother. If you achieve that result, whether you need medication, in vitro fertilization, a cesarean section, adopted your baby, or gave birth after ten minutes of labor in your own bedroom without breaking a sweat, you have achieved a successful outcome.

What if my baby and I didn't have the first few minutes to bond?

The bond you develop with your baby doesn't depend only on those first few hours after your baby is born. It grows and deepens over the course of your lifetime together. You are not sentenced to a cold and distant relationship even if you were unconscious for the first few *days* after delivery, if your baby was in an incubator and you couldn't hold her constantly, or if some other problem kept you apart for weeks.

There are many reasons why a new mother and baby may not have the ideal beginning, from a premature infant needing intensive care for several weeks to a mother's postpartum depression. More often than not, little (and occasionally, big) things happen to put a kink in your childbirth plan and those first hours aren't what you'd anticipated. Women who, for a variety of reasons and time periods, are unable to care for their newborns immediately are definitely capable of developing excellent relationships with their babies. Try not to worry, and take your time; relax, recover, and get to know your baby.

Establishing a bond in the first several hours of your baby's life is wonderful when it happens, and it's true that researchers believe that being able to hold your baby immediately after birth is ideal. But the specialists in maternal-infant bonding never intended their findings to become a burden to new mothers; they just wanted you to have the best opportunity for a good beginning with your baby. The relationship between a mother and her child grows and deepens over the course of many years and is far too complex to be determined in only the first few hours.

Sometimes even new mothers who have easy birthing experiences are surprised that they don't feel that instantaneous rush of love the minute they look at their babies, but that doesn't prevent them from developing warm and nurturing relationships. You and your baby will fall in love with each other before you know it. Don't allow your disappointment that you couldn't "bond" with your baby in his first three hours (or even days or weeks) of life to lead you to despair that the bond will never develop.

You can create the bond. Spend time focused on your baby. Hold her whenever you can; look into her eyes when you feed her; keep her in a sling carrier so she is close to you; nurse her on demand. Attend to her when she cries, talk to her, dance with her, and pay attention to what she likes and doesn't like. With a little time and attention, the bond will develop naturally. You and your baby can most definitely have a wonderful life together.

How can I do everything I should for my baby, and am I hurting my baby if I don't?

There is such an enormous range of acceptable parenting styles and so much information about early infant development available that many women, particularly the most highly educated, worry that their babies will fall behind if they aren't properly stimulated every day. Nan, an artist, fretted that she wasn't doing enough for her baby. "When I look at all the books and classes on child care," she said, "there is always something else I find I 'should' be doing." I'm certainly not going to tell you to ignore your baby, but it may help to assuage your guilt to know that Albert Einstein and Mother Teresa were both probably raised without the benefit of infant massage, black-and-white mobiles, car seats, or educational videos.

Despite the tendency to make new parents believe they should be offering constant stimulation, what babies really need is *optimal* stimulation. If your baby is developing well, reaching social and physical milestones at appropriate ages, and isn't fussing all the time, it is likely that you are stimulating him adequately already. Keep in mind that every baby needs a different level of stimulation, and some babies need less than others. If your baby is easily irritated or fretful, it may be that you're stimulating him *too* much. Rather than worrying about doing enough, pay attention to your baby's cues, play calmly and lovingly, soothe him when he fusses, and he will be fine.

Don't let experts create problems where there are none. As long as you spend time each day relating directly to your baby, chances are you are stimulating him enough. Being responsive to your baby's needs and emotions is every bit as important as providing a stimulating environment.

If you are convinced that you aren't doing enough for your baby because you just don't know how to interact with him, though, that is easily remedied.

- Talk to your baby whenever you are together. Tell him what you see and what you are doing; recite the names for each body part and all his surroundings. I remember feeling a bit silly telling my daughter all about the sheets I was folding, but talking to your baby while you are doing chores can soothe him as well as improve his vocabulary.
- Do what you enjoy with your baby. If you love to sing, make up songs. If you adore going to museums, put your baby in the stroller and head on out. Your enjoyment will be contagious and will help introduce your baby to a variety of experiences naturally and enjoyably for you both. He may not fully appreciate Monet, but he will be fascinated by the array of sounds and sights.
- Play baby games like patty-cake and peekaboo. If you don't know any baby games, don't worry, neither does your baby. You can make up your own, ask a friend, or get a book, video, CD, DVD, or tape from the library to help you.
- You may have heard that there's evidence that playing Mozart can be good for your baby's brain development, but it won't hurt to play show tunes or bluegrass if that's more to your liking. Music is good.
- Show your baby old photo albums, clang pie tins together, or demonstrate how to toss socks into the hamper. Your baby wants your involvement. If you are enjoying being with your baby and doing things together, you will be stimulating. A trip to the grocery store with a mother who enthusiastically points

to the apples while saying "apples" is every bit as valuable as listening to genius tapes day in and day out. Maybe better.

Although these are tips to do more with your baby, don't assume that you aren't doing enough. If you feel you are already doing everything you can for your baby, then trust those instincts, and give yourself a break. The experts who urge new mothers to stimulate their babies are offering suggestions, not trying to undermine your confidence.

Don't worry about not stimulating your baby enough. It's your relationship with your baby, not what you do to or at him, that matters most.

Can I still be a good mother when I feel so frustrated and still want so much for myself?

Being a good mother does not require a woman to give up everything for her baby. As lovable as your new baby might be, spending every waking minute unselfishly caring for her does not fulfill all *your* needs, and it is not selfish, in the pejorative sense, to still want to do things you used to enjoy or to want to be coddled yourself occasionally. You can be a stupendous mother while still making sure your own needs are being considered.

Good mothers are real people, and real people get bored, feel frustration, and need entertainment and adult stimulation. Certainly good mothers often put their baby's or family's needs ahead of their own, but there is no benefit to you or your baby if you don't also take care of yourself. Helen, a new mother in one of my groups, said that she'd heard that "a happy mother is a good mother" and it is true. You can't give unselfishly to your baby if you don't give to yourself as well.

Not only is it important to make sure you take care of yourself emotionally so you can be generous and loving with your baby, but taking care of yourself also provides a good role model for your child. Women in particular need to learn to strike an appropriate balance between caring for others and caring for themselves. If you keep everyone's needs in perspective, if *everyone* in the family, including you, has time alone as well as time together to pursue their interests, to rest, and to enjoy themselves and each other, then your baby will grow up feeling loved and respected. He will also love and respect you as an individual.

So, when you are feeling like you can't be selfless for one more minute, pay attention. Call a friend, find a baby-sitter, read a book, go for a walk, do whatever it takes to be emotionally replenished and renewed. Don't feel guilty or embarrassed; take care of yourself so you can take care of your baby. It is not selfish to treat the person in charge of your baby well, especially when that person is you.

Take care of yourself. If Mommy isn't happy, no one else in the family is happy either.

How can I keep up with all these roles I'm responsible for and still do a good job?

Many new mothers have told me that they feel guilty all the time, that they're not being a good enough mother, a good enough wife, a good enough friend, a good enough housekeeper, a good enough worker, or a good enough daughter. It sounds as if you expected that when you became a mother you would continue to do everything you did in your pre-baby life in addition to learning to manage the new duties of motherhood, and that you would immediately do it all well. That's not possible!

When I asked a close friend and wise mother what the most important piece of advice she would give a first-time mom was, she said without hesitation, "Lower your expectations." Try to be realistic about what you can and can't accomplish. *Lower your expectations and don't feel guilty.* Guilt comes from doing something you know you shouldn't; there's no cause for guilt in being unable to meet your own impossible demands.

Juggling all of a mother's roles takes a lot of energy, both physically and emotionally. If, before you had a baby, all your time was filled with work, your marriage, friends, and family, how can you expect to keep up with all your various old roles and responsibilities when you've added such an important and time-consuming new one? Make a conscious effort to realign your priorities.

- Make a schedule for yourself of absolutely required activities (bathing, eating, sleeping, baby care, etc.) including how much time each demands.
- Determine what optional activities matter most to you and how much time you need to devote to each. Cleaning the bathroom or seeing a friend may be a daily necessity for some women, a weekly chore for others. Put the jobs *you* value on your calendar.
- Figure out what connections are most important to you. Consider which relationships are most satisfying and/or need

more frequent, face-to-face contact to maintain, and which can be sustained through phone calls or email.

- ❧ Schedule less important or not-so-enjoyable people and activities less often or eliminate them altogether.
- ❧ If you are worried that you are neglecting someone you care about, communicate that your diminished attention isn't personal; you don't have enough time for *anyone*.
- ❧ Do not include or worry about the unnecessary and unpleasant (people or tasks) at all. Be generous to yourself when sorting through who or what to avoid or let slide.

When you have a new baby in the house, those who love you will understand that you are learning how to manage your new life. It is perfectly acceptable and normal for new mothers to feel pulled in many directions as they try to be everything to everybody, including themselves. Of course you feel bad letting some things go, but your time and energy are limited by reality. The best solution is to reassess your priorities and lower your expectations. When you are realistic about what you can handle you will feel and be more successful. Don't feel bad; you're doing great!

New mothers generally need to lower their expectations.

I love my baby, so why am I crying?

A certain amount of mood swings and tears is pretty normal. As Cassie, a first-time mom, said, "My baby is a few weeks old and I still feel so emotional all the time. I seem to have little control over my emotions. It's gotten so bad that we wonder what's wrong when I *don't* cry." If you are like most new mothers, tears and mood swings are a part of life for the first several weeks. The dramatic and abrupt hormone shift, sleep deprivation, and role adjustment after childbirth sometimes turns mild-tempered women into temporary shrews and easygoing, lighthearted women into blubbering sensitives. The range of normal postpartum emotions is broad and often difficult to tolerate.

The most successful "cure" for this early motherhood personality transplant is time. Most women who experience the typical, non-pathological "baby blues" notice that their more familiar level of emotional self-control and flexibility returns after several weeks or months. The physical contributions to your mood swings settle down—the hormone upheaval subsides, the pains and discomforts from childbirth disappear, and you get a little more rest. The unexpected feelings and relationship changes become more familiar as well, so you feel more like your former self.

Most of the time, the mood swings are unpleasant and surprising, but not dangerous. It's often just a part of the normal transition to motherhood to find that you dissolve into tears watching a TV game show, argue with your mother over when to bathe the baby, or just feel stupid or confused. If you can describe yourself as happy between bouts of emotion, if you are able to feel pleasure, eat normally, and sleep when you have the opportunity, and you are getting through each day without causing harm (and without constantly fearing that you will), you are probably experiencing the typical highs and lows that follow childbirth.

A small but significant percentage of new mothers *do* develop postpartum depression or psychosis, which is noticeably more debilitating and difficult to manage and requires medical attention. If you worry that your emotions are beyond your control or outside the norm, ask yourself the following questions:

- Do you feel sad or anxious *most* of the time?
- Do you have trouble eating or sleeping?
- Do you feel suicidal or homicidal?
- Do you fear that you will harm yourself or your baby?
- Do you or your husband worry that your judgment is faulty?

If you answered yes to any of these questions, or if you feel that your emotions are out of control too much of the time, you may have a more serious problem, and you need to be evaluated by a doctor or mental-health professional. Don't suffer needlessly: seek help immediately. Go to someone who understands and has successfully treated postpartum depression or psychosis, or to someone who will make an appropriate referral. You, your baby, and your husband all deserve for you to be able to function more comfortably and healthfully, and there are now ample treatments available.

I'm with my baby all the time, so why do I feel so lonely?

A first-time mother is often confused when she recognizes that because she's always taking care of the baby she is never alone, yet she is lonely. Whether you are working outside the home or not, you are likely spending many hours with your baby. Being alone with a pre-verbal baby is exactly what you describe; you're never *really* alone, because you are constantly attending to your baby, but you're lonely because you have no one to talk to: your baby is a baby.

The real issue is this: you love and adore your baby, but being with her is not always enough. You are never literally alone anymore, so you miss that, yet you are starved for adult companionship. You enjoy being with your baby for all her important (and unimportant) milestones, but because babycare is a nonstop activity, you have no time to yourself. This ambivalence, though unwelcome, is normal.

Be honest with yourself about what you are truly missing. If the babycare allows you too little solitary time, you might need to find a sitter or trade baby-sitting with a friend so you can take the time to be on your own. If you miss being with other adults or being involved in non-baby related activities:

- Plan outings or visits with friends who will welcome, or at least tolerate, your baby tagging along.
- Go back to work, for even a few hours a week.
- Join (or start) a group or class for new moms.
- Do volunteer work.
- Go to a museum, coffeehouse, or zoo with your baby. Talk to the adults there.
- Read.
- Connect with people on the Internet.
- Strike up a conversation with that friendly looking woman with a baby you see at the park.

Most importantly, don't feel bad that your baby isn't enough for you. Most women who become mothers still enjoy being with adults and need some time to be alone. Ambivalence is normal.

Since my baby was born, I feel like a lioness. Why have I become so demanding?

Pretty impressive what nature can do, isn't it? It is a natural instinct to protect your baby. Leanne would have been too embarrassed to send back the wrong soup at a restaurant, but soon after her baby was born, she unashamedly accepted nothing less than perfection for her baby. She said, "I used to be so meek and tolerant and accepting, but I know I'd do anything to protect my baby or to make sure she gets whatever she wants." She found herself doing things and approaching people on her baby's behalf that seemed out of character, and although she worried that people would think she was too forceful, she also enjoyed being able to protect and take care of her baby. It's perfectly acceptable and appropriate to stand up for your baby's rights and best interests.

Many women were raised to believe that asking for special treatment or requesting others to accommodate personal wishes is not polite or feminine. Assertiveness is confused with aggression, and women have not traditionally wanted to be seen as aggressive. Although you may want what you want as much as anyone else does, you might have been socialized to feel like a demanding witch if you asserted yourself. But once you become a mother, it is not only acceptable to take care of your baby, it is instinctive. While you might not bother to ask someone to move out of *your* way, you would now ask that mountains be moved for your baby.

Your lioness qualities may ultimately help you be more assertive for yourself, and that is good for both you and your children. When you've had the experience of asking for what your baby wants and making sure your baby is well treated, you may feel freer to ask for what *you* want. When you make sure that you get what you need in a kindly and firm manner, your baby will learn to do so as well; your newfound assertiveness sets an excellent role model. Treat others well and expect that you are treated well, and you and your children will benefit.

Why do I feel almost invisible now that I'm a mother?

When you're pregnant, you get all sorts of attention. Once the baby is born, though, it seems like no one notices you or cares how *you* are doing. The new-mother "invisibility" can be hard to take, especially if you enjoyed the attention pregnancy brought. Pregnancy is one of the few times of life when we are actually encouraged to be egocentric, and it can feel rather nice. More than one new mother has sheepishly confessed that she misses her obstetrician, as even the health-care focus switches from mother to the baby.

But just as pregnant women draw a lot of attention, new babies tend to draw even more. Strangers at the mall who only weeks ago might have stopped to regale you with stories of their own pregnancies now stop to admire your baby. Relatives want to know if the baby resembles them; strangers want to hold the baby; and it seems that no one even notices you. The contrast is striking, and many women feel a surprising emptiness when the enormous concern and interest formerly focused on them seems to disappear. You feel ignored just when you need support and confidence the most.

In the early days of being a mom, it is difficult to feel appealing, confident, or competent, so the loss of attention can be particularly painful. You go from being treated like a queen to feeling like a hand-maiden to your baby. To bridge the attention gap, you may need to learn to reach out to others more directly. Tell your husband, mother, sister-in-law, neighbor, friends—whomever you love and trust—that you still need some time with them, not just with your baby, and be clear about wanting to focus on adult topics.

In addition, try to recognize that the fascination with your baby may be an extension of the love people have for you. Learn to ask for what you need emotionally when you feel neglected or lonely, and recognize that your baby's magnetism hasn't diminished yours. And be reassured that many other new moms experience the new-mother invisibility with disappointment, too.

If you want or need some attention or support, ask for it. Even the most loving husband or friend may not know what you need or that you need help.

My head tells me that the baby is fine, but sometimes I find myself checking to see if my baby is still breathing. Am I totally nuts?

You are not even partially nuts; most new mothers check on their babies "unnecessarily" at times. You care about her so very much that even when you know she's fine, your heart needs the reassurance that checking on her provides. It is scary to have the full responsibility of caring for this new person you love so much, and scary to realize just how little power you have. So you comfort yourself every so often that she is still breathing. If that makes you feel better, and your baby is not disturbed, no harm done.

Occasionally fearing for your baby's life when she sleeps three hours longer than she ever has before is one thing; being paralyzed with worry about your baby's safety at all times is another. If you check on your baby only occasionally, that's fine, but you want to be sure that you are not overly anxious.

If you or you husband are concerned that your anxiety about your baby is beyond the norm, consider these questions:

- Are you so uncertain about your baby's ability to stay alive that your constant checking on her wakes her frequently?
- Does your worry prevent *you* from sleeping at night?
- Are you unable to take a shower (go to the bathroom, etc.) unless there is another adult in the house?
- Are you unwilling to hire a baby-sitter for fear that she/he will kidnap your baby?
- Do others often tell you that your concerns are silly or extreme, yet you aren't reassured?
- Do you feel that no one but you is vigilant enough to care for your baby, and do you worry that you aren't vigilant enough either?
- Do you question your own judgment about your baby?

If you answered yes to several of these questions, it might be time to consider seeking help. While some worry is normal, a doctor or mental-health professional can assess your anxiety and help you through it.

Many new mothers (and fathers) I've known have checked on their baby's breathing at least once. As long as your anxiety is not running or ruining your life, your concern is based on an unexpected change in your baby's routine, and you know that it's a bit silly, go ahead and reassure yourself. Watch her chest gently rise and fall, admire her unbelievable beauty, accept your good fortune, and go back to bed.

Is it normal to be so worried that I won't always be able to keep my baby safe?

In an effort to help young parents avoid unnecessary tragedies, women's magazines, newspapers, and talk shows have pointed out so many potential dangers to babies and young children that many a new mother is terrified that something awful will happen to her baby unless she does something to prevent it. Poor Cynthia, an especially nervous new mother, wouldn't allow even her *husband* to take care of their baby alone, which I believe is extreme and unhealthy. While I definitely advocate being a careful and conscientious parent, I also think it important to recognize that your concerns with safety should not get in the way of your ability to enjoy life. Educate yourself thoroughly, be prudent about who cares for your baby, and maintain a safe dwelling, but also try to relax and help your baby enjoy the world. *It is as important to teach him to feel good about his world as it is to keep him safe.* If you are immobilized or consumed by your concerns for your baby's well-being (as in the previous question), you may need to get help.

As a loving parent, it's natural to want to protect your child from any discomfort or crisis. And there are certainly some things you can do to minimize risk to your child, including never letting your little one ride in a car without a car seat, and checking references on all baby-sitters. Follow your pediatrician's advice about feeding your baby and how to put him to sleep. Don't leave a baby unattended in the bathtub, and so on and so on.

Your home can easily be made a safer place by taking advantage of the abundance of resources available to help parents minimize the dangers in their baby's life. A whole industry has blossomed to provide childproofing to homes; the Internet, bookstores, and your library have plenty of materials to show you what products are safest, which products to avoid, and how to make your baby's environment as safe as possible. You can hire a professional childproofer to safeguard your home for you, but you can certainly do an excellent job yourself. (Children's furniture and toy stores and many hardware stores carry childproofing products for do-it-yourselfers.) You can pay attention to product recalls and talk to other mothers about their experiences. As long as you are doing what you can to maintain your baby's safety, you need not experience constant anxiety.

Creating a safe home for your baby is obviously important, but keeping your baby *forever* out of harm's way is a daunting responsibility. First, no matter how hard you try, you cannot predict or plan for every potential problem. Second, many perfectly healthy adults walking around today spent their first years sleeping on their stomachs in cribs with slats too far apart to be sold today. And third, the vast majority of the time, children somehow grow up safely. In other words, as a parent, do the very best you can, hope that that is enough, and try not to get too crazy about your role as protector.

You can't protect a child from every conceivable danger, and your baby needs to know that you believe the world is a good and safe place to live. Teach him what is safe, how to trust in others, and how to trust in himself.

Why do I sometimes get so angry with my baby?

You get angry because you are human. As Marcia put it, "I love this baby more than I ever thought possible, more, maybe, than I've ever loved anything else, yet, once in a while, say when he's fussing at 3 A.M., I want to throw him out the window." Many women feel guilty if they admit that they get angry at their newborns, but it is not inconsistent or abnormal to be frustrated or annoyed with someone you love. Unconditional love doesn't require the elimination of all other emotions. It is perfectly normal to resent anyone who keeps you up all night, and when you are sleep-deprived, it is even more likely for your emotions to be somewhat exaggerated. *As long as you don't act violently on your anger, as long as you aren't worried that you might actually do something dangerous, it is OK to feel it.* Not pleasant, perhaps, but normal.

You love this baby just because he exists, and because he is wonderful, intelligent, sensitive, beautiful, and charming. When you feel the enormity of your love for your baby, and know that you would do anything for him, you also feel good about yourself, and about your capacity to love and be an excellent mother. Your adoration of your baby is very important, as it helps you get through sleepless, cranky nights, teething, and temper tantrums, while still believing that your baby is inordinately special.

That you are able to love this baby regardless of the inconvenience he's introduced into your life can make you feel somewhat saint-like. When you love your baby simply for being, despite the trouble he occasionally causes, he feels worthy of that love, and that is very good. The immense love you feel for your baby contributes to your baby's self-esteem.

Accept, though, that you will sometimes feel extremely irritated with your baby, and do as Jill does. Whenever she feels that anger well up, she takes a break: she takes a quick shower, has a cup of coffee, or calls her husband for support. Sometimes she even gets a friend to watch her baby for a few minutes. It's wise to take the time to calm yourself so that when you go to your baby you're able to greet him with a (reasonably) sincere smile and say (and mean it), "It's so good to see you!"

As long as you don't act on the anger, rest easy knowing that *feeling* it is unpleasant but normal. Don't ever forget that love and anger aren't mutually exclusive. Just do your best to *show* the love and *manage* the anger. And again, if you worry that you can't manage the anger, get professional help immediately.

It's all right, even natural, to feel angry with your baby at times. It's never OK to hurt or abuse her.

What happened to the intelligent and interesting person that I used to be?

You are interesting *now*. If you think about it, survival is very interesting, and your baby's survival is what has you so captivated right now. If you were drowning in shark-infested waters, your interests would be pretty limited, too. So now you are immersed in motherhood. Sure, discussing the struggle to get to safe ground sounds more exciting than the struggle to remove banana stains from your favorite shirt, but that's just because drowning is less commonplace. Diapers, spit up, and teething are just as compelling to a new mother as air is to a drowning victim.

Before your baby was born you may have thought that you'd never be one of those mothers so totally consumed by the minutiae of your baby's life, but now nothing seems to interest you as much as her burps, poops, and other new tricks. Yet when you are with other mothers of new babies, you may notice that your conversation sparkles. You see, it isn't that you aren't interesting anymore, it is simply that what interests you is deep and narrow and consuming. Other new mothers are similarly engrossed by the details of their babies' lives. These details are what keep you and your baby alive and thriving, and that's why they are so engaging right now. Your topics of conversation may have less appeal to non-mothers for awhile, but that makes them no less important, and you no less charming.

When you are certain of your baby's survival, when you can get through the day more efficiently, and through the night with more sleep, you will begin to have room in you head for things beyond your baby. You will regain your old enthusiasm for whatever you used to enjoy, and you will become able to focus your attention elsewhere as well as you did before your baby was born. You needn't be so harsh with yourself; if you weren't a boring person before your baby was born, you probably aren't one now. You're just totally involved in taking care of your baby, and that's an enormous task.

I can't seem to concentrate on anything; I can't read or stay awake through a whole movie. Does childbirth cause maternal brain damage?

No, it only seems that way. The early weeks of motherhood do seem to turn your mind to oatmeal. You are physically and emotionally exhausted and you have no opportunity to recover. You are working twenty-four hours a day, seven days a week, and there is no predictable schedule or even time to relax. Of course you're having trouble concentrating!

This is temporary. I remember Natalie, when her first baby was six weeks old, worrying that she would never be able to read another novel for the rest of her life. Only weeks later, the baby was sleeping through the night, and Natalie's ability to concentrate improved. Every woman adjusts to motherhood at her own pace. Your physical recovery from childbirth and your ability to handle sleeplessness affects your powers of concentration. Your attention span, anxiety level, and ability to tolerate frustration will impact your ability to focus. Even the temperament of your baby may influence the recovery of your mental capacity, as a needy or fussy baby takes more energy and attention than a calm or self-soothing sweetie.

Keeping your newborn alive, reasonably clean, and content is a full-time job. When you learn how to do it more efficiently, and the baby becomes less demanding, you will notice that your mind has just been on stand-by, patiently waiting for a chance to be used for something not baby-related. Over the next few months, you will regain your ability to concentrate for longer periods of time. You will graduate from catalog reading to magazines, and from sitcom reruns to the movie of the week. Before you know it, you will be able to read a book cover to cover (other than *Good Night Moon*). Maybe not all in one sitting, and maybe not *War and Peace,* but your brain will return once you are well rested, more confident, and more efficient. Your intelligence is not diminished; it's just sleeping while you aren't.

Now that I'm a mother, why does it make me cringe every time someone asks me, "What did you do all day?" What do they think I do, sit around eating bonbons?

Most likely, someone who asks you that question doesn't have a clue how you fill your time. Most likely your friend, husband, or mother-in-law sincerely wants to know how you are spending your day now that you have a baby because they care about you. They are not accusing you of slothfulness. Your reaction, though, shows that you aren't too comfortable with the answer yourself.

What's stressful about that dreaded, frequently asked question is that even though you're busy all day and exhausted by noon, there is little to show for all your efforts. Somehow, the day disappears with seemingly nothing accomplished. Unlike working outside the home, where work has a distinct starting and stopping point and specific tasks to tackle and complete, motherhood is an all-day, less-quantifiable experience. It's not surprising, then, that when someone asks what you did all day, you sputter and fume, getting angry or defensive, because you're wondering the same thing. It takes awhile to learn to fill your baby's needs, figure out how to go to the bathroom without your baby (or you) dissolving into tears, and get anything other than mothering done.

Recognize the value of what you are doing all day. You love your baby; you keep her comfortable, do her laundry, feed, amuse, and cuddle her, bathe, soothe, and talk to her, teach her about the world, and otherwise help her grow up to be healthy and emotionally well adjusted. Your days overflow with essential mothering activity. When you look at it all like that, you have no need to be embarrassed or defensive. Babycare is exceptionally valuable and time-consuming work of which you have every right to be proud.

Why don't I think that my baby is perfect?

It can be very stressful when your pre-birth fantasies about your baby are far removed from the reality you now confront. Disappointment in your baby is difficult to admit, although it's common that real-life babies often bear little resemblance to your dream baby. Babies come with their own personalities and body types, and sometimes the baby you get doesn't appear to have the traits you expected or wanted.

It's OK to be disappointed, but it is also extremely important to learn to love the baby you have. Sure, it would have been nice if your baby had your eyes instead of your husband's Aunt Fanny's, and you would have preferred for him to have the temperament or activity level you'd anticipated. But even real babies that more closely resemble what you were hoping for are occasionally cranky, smelly, and less than enchanting. Your baby is the kind of baby he is meant to be, and you must learn to love him as he is and to enjoy his unexpected personality.

- Try looking at your baby with an unprejudiced eye. Rename what you don't like too much. What you see as hyperactivity may be reinterpreted as intense enthusiasm. A passive baby may be highly observant. A clingy baby may be an especially loving baby.
- See your baby's real qualities as positives and they will become positives.
- Remember that your job as a mother is to help your baby grow up to become the best person *he* can be, to be independent, kind, and capable. *It is not to change him into what you want him to be.*
- Focus on your baby's strengths, and as he grows up, encourage and love all those parts of him that he loves about himself. If you keep an open mind to his uniqueness, you will learn to love him for who he really is.

If these ideas don't help you overcome your disappointment, it would be wise to make sure that you aren't suffering from postpartum depression. Being mystified or secretly disappointed by a child who looks and acts differently than you'd hoped is one thing; it is altogether another to feel hateful or angry or wish to hurt your baby. Talk to your doctor or midwife and get a professional opinion if you are worried that you can't care for or love your baby adequately. Although accepting some disappointment when reality doesn't meet your expectations may be necessary, you and your baby are entitled to be as pleased with each other as possible.

A good mother learns to love her child as he is and adjusts her mothering to suit her child.

How can I regain some sense of control in my life?

Jane, who needed routine and structure, said, "I was always a person who liked to plan ahead, to know what was happening when, to be organized. I can't stand how much my life seems to be so discombobulated, all because of a little baby!" Anna lamented, "I was always a person who liked to be spontaneous, do things on the spur of the moment. Now that I have a baby, I feel so tied down. How can I get my go-on-a-whim life back?" Such a small baby has such an enormous impact!

Whether you preferred an organized, predictable life or one where you could stay out until dawn if the spirit so moved you, a baby may make your old style hard to sustain. Clearly, a baby doesn't know how to be anything but spontaneous, but spontaneity in a baby doesn't mesh well with either a well-scheduled routine or a drop-everything-

and-go-out-for-ice cream approach to life. Even the most predictable baby will still occasionally surprise you by sleeping for only ten minutes when, at the same time yesterday, she slept for an hour and a half, and some babies of free-spirited mothers demand regular feeding and nap schedules. Happily, neither of these situations need to be permanently painful.

If you enjoyed maintaining a schedule, it may be simpler for you to relax, at least temporarily, your need for order as your baby becomes more integrated into your life. That means you will do well to learn to accomplish tasks in segments, develop some comfort with jobs left momentarily unfinished, and begin to enjoy your baby's detours from routine more. But while the routine-loving mother may adjust to the needs of her baby, her baby can also learn to fit into her lifestyle. If you are the structure-loving sort, you may find help in one of the many books on child care that promote methods to regulate your baby's feedings, naps, and nighttime sleep patterns. Some babies thrive on having a schedule introduced early on, and then they are more likely to fit your need for structure. As you and your baby adapt to each other's needs and quirks, your days will acquire a more comfortable rhythm, and order will return. It really will.

The more spontaneous woman can similarly establish ways to hang on to her more flexible attitude. You may need to learn to delay some of your adventures or cut them shorter to accommodate your baby's style. If you are a follow-the-wind sort of woman, you will benefit from figuring out which naps can be delayed without mother-baby meltdown, learning how to be packed and ready to go as soon as your baby takes her last slurp, and appreciating that your baby can be as impromptu as you. The baby's spontaneity may not always coordinate with yours, but a baby doesn't have to tie you down like a ball and chain.

Once you and your baby adjust a little to each other, you will enjoy motherhood more. Bear in mind that babies don't try to upend your life; they just do. Your baby is being the best baby she knows how to be. Pay attention to her needs as well as your own, and she will learn to fit into your life as you learn to fit into hers. Babies are totally demanding and helpless for a very brief time, but they are also surprisingly portable and content to be almost anywhere as long as they are with you. You don't have to relinquish your favored approach to living to be a very good mom.

I love being a mom, but lately it seems that I've lost my identity. Who am I?

Kathleen put it this way, "I expected that having a baby would *add* to my life; I didn't anticipate how much he would *change* not only how I lived my life but also how I thought about myself." Before you were a mom, your identity was probably composed of a variety of roles and relationships with which you felt quite comfortable. You were a daughter, a friend, a sister, a wife, and a worker, as well as a member of several groups, including your race, ethnicity, family of origin, religion, alma maters, community, and profession. Your identity probably also included your age, physical stature, energy level, habits, hobbies, intelligence, appearance, clothing style, and socioeconomic group. All these pieces of you added up to make you who you were and how you saw yourself. You knew exactly who you were.

Many women feel, at least initially, that the role of mother wipes out all their other roles. If a major source of your identity and self-esteem was derived from work, and you've diminished your involvement in the work place, then it follows logically that your identity needs some refurbishing. If your appearance was very important to you, then your changing body and clothing styles may make you question who you've become. Further, if becoming a mother means to you a total commitment and dedication to mothering, and you have forsaken your other roles and pursuits to be the best mom you can be, then you may feel empty on those rare times when you don't have your baby around to define you. With all of these changes, it shouldn't surprise you that you don't know who you are anymore.

While it is unsettling no longer to have a clear picture of who you are, it is not unusual for a new mother to wonder what's become of her former, familiar self. It takes time to sort out how to be a great mother and maintain your sense of self, figure out where motherhood fits into your life, and figure out how you will integrate all the most important aspects of your past and future. When you feel like you've lost your "self":

- ❧ Plan a weekly baby-free outing in which you do something completely for yourself.
- ❧ Start (or resume) an exercise routine once you get your doctor's go-ahead. Even if you need to bring your baby along on a power walk, make sure you choose a workout program you enjoy and will continue.
- ❧ Make an effort to see, not just email, pre-baby friends or coworkers.
- ❧ Join or organize with other new mothers a group that is related to some area of interest to you (books, bicycles, art, stock market, etc.).
- ❧ Start a new hobby (gourmet cooking, woodworking, or watercolors, for example).

- ❧ Do volunteer work.
- ❧ Return to a favorite pastime of your youth, even if it is finger painting.

Give yourself time to make the adjustments to motherhood, and try to tolerate the discomfort while you adjust. Allow yourself to be at loose ends for a while so you can rediscover who you are. Remind yourself about what you've enjoyed in the past and let yourself be who you are now. Your life has changed dramatically; have patience for yourself and you will once again become comfortable with who you are.

Becoming a mother changes your life. It doesn't have to become your identity, but it contributes to it, shows you who you are and what you value, and allows you the opportunity for tremendous personal growth and satisfaction.

My mother made it all too clear how much she sacrificed for her kids: how can I avoid burdening *my* children with my regrets?

The easiest way to avoid burdening your children with your regrets is to live your life in such a way as to minimize having regrets and to take responsibility for the choices you make. To that end:

- ❧ Make choices that are well considered.
- ❧ Once you've made a decision, accept it. If you made the choice

with good intentions, whether or not it worked out, then no apologies or regrets should be necessary.

- ❧ If something isn't working for you as a mother or as a person, recognize your discomfort and *seek a solution to your problem*. If you don't enjoy staying home with your baby full-time, find a job or hobby that gets you out of the home. If you are working hard to provide your baby and family with the comforts of a larger income but find that you want to be home with your baby more, find a way to do that.
- ❧ Don't complain about the choices you've made. If you are unhappy, make appropriate changes. If you want credit for how hard you work or how much you've sacrificed, be proud of yourself in private; no one wants to be the cause of a loved one's martyrdom. There's no value in sharing all the pains or disappointments suffered on your child's behalf.
- ❧ Do the best you can because you want to and don't do or say those things to *your* children that made you feel like you were a burden to your mother.
- ❧ Above all, recognize that every choice made necessitates making the choice to not do or be something else. Be comfortable with the choices you make so you don't need to bemoan the lost opportunities.

Being a good mother doesn't require sacrificing yourself, and, in fact, self-sacrifice isn't a good idea. Be a good mother by being a fulfilled person who is also a mother.

Motherhood is so permanent and such a huge responsibility. Will it always feel so overwhelming?

Fortunately, motherhood lasts forever, but the overwhelming sense of responsibility and the level of constant involvement diminish as the baby grows up. Kerry described panicking when she realized that she was alone with her baby for the first time; she worried she couldn't possibly be the one expected to take care of her daughter, to teach and nurture her for the rest of the baby's childhood. Heather described feeling like she'd been given a part in a play without a script. Many women have described reacting similarly, wondering how they ended up as somebody's mother.

With a little more time and experience under your belt, the relentless aspect of motherhood will feel more normal. As you become more efficient and at ease about your mothering, the panic and exhaustion will be replaced by confidence, and the fear of not being able to meet the challenges of parenthood will give way to the many joys a baby can bring. Although you may always feel responsible for (or at least concerned about) your child's well-being, taking care of her will become second nature. Eventually, of course, she will take care of herself.

This is one area where you need to have faith: faith in yourself, faith that you will become a competent and wonderful mother, faith that your baby will blossom, and faith that this period of adjustment is transitory. You will meet the challenges of motherhood and you will shoulder this responsibility, and, most likely, you will eventually look back at this period of your life with fondness.

Chapter Two

Physical Changes

While you are pregnant, the universe seems to be devoted to your uterus. At your fingertips, you have concerned health-care providers, any number of books explaining how you and the baby are developing, and an approximate date when the pregnancy will be over. Pregnancy is different for every woman, delightful for some, uncomfortable for others, but either way, most first-time pregnant women spend nine months focused on how their bodies change and feel. Whether you feel great or terrible, you know that, in a matter of months, the pregnancy will be over and you will be rewarded with a beautiful baby.

Once you give birth, all that attention shifts surprisingly abruptly to the baby. You are fully in charge of keeping the baby alive and content, despite the fact that your body has undergone an enormous and sudden change. Your hormones may be all over the place, you get little or no sleep, and your body is trying to return to "normal." You spend your days lifting and shifting the baby, bending and reaching in ways you never have before. And that beautiful baby you imagined, while still quite charming, is usually not nearly as cooperative as you'd hoped.

While you're taking care of a newborn, it can feel as if your personal needs are being ignored. When childbirth has gone well, you get a six-week postpartum checkup and then you're really on your own. Even with more complicated deliveries, you are expected to take care of your baby and get on with your life. All this after you've lost twenty or thirty pounds in twenty-four hours, are getting no sleep, and are adjusting to a new identity as well.

The questions and answers in this chapter are devoted to the concerns new mothers have about their bodies after delivery. Sleep deprivation has very real consequences, hormones do not simply or immediately return to a prepregnancy state, and other body parts react and balk at your new life. Every new mother I've known has had some uncertainty that her normal recovery was really normal, and many have worried that their back pain, hair loss, and other common but unplanned physical changes meant that something was terribly wrong.

This chapter is intended to help you know which symptoms indicate that you may need a bit more patience and which symptoms require professional attention. Most of the time, fortunately, you'll find that your recovery is going just fine, just at your own pace, and that your pace, while normal, may not be the same as your sister's or the women in your books. Try to remember that there is a wide range of normal in the physical changes that childbirth initiates, take it easy, and call your health-care provider whenever you are worried.

I seem to be losing a lot of hair. Is this common, and will my old hair ever return?

Temporary (notice the word "temporary" here) hair loss occurs much more commonly than most women realize. So, yes, it is common, and yes, your formerly lovely locks are likely to return. Major stress or a change in hormones (e.g., giving birth) can cause a change in a new mother's hair growth cycle resulting in temporary hair loss. As many as two-thirds of all women suffer perceptible hair loss at some point in their lives, with childbirth being one of the most frequent contributors.

Some women notice shocking amounts of hair shedding when they wash or brush their hair, while others experience a more subtle change in texture or shine. Elsa knew about many of the changes her body would undergo with childbirth, but she never anticipated that her hair, which had always been thick and lustrous, would seem thinner and have less body. She agonized that pregnancy and childbirth had left no part of her unchanged. Fortunately, the problem is transitory in most women; Elsa's hair returned to its original glory about the time she celebrated her son's first birthday.

There is little you can do to counter postpartum hair change. There are medications that purport to help regain hair. Certainly, you may consult a health-care professional to rule out more complex health concerns and ask your favorite hair stylist for suggestions to flatter your altered tresses. But be reassured that although few women expect to have even their hair go through an identity crisis, hair loss occurs fairly often, is generally only temporary, and is only problematic cosmetically.

My skin isn't as clear as it was before my pregnancy. Will it get better again?

Some new mothers notice that their skin improves in pregnancy and early motherhood, but others definitely experience more blemishes. Just as hormone fluctuations are blamed for adolescent acne, so can they be held responsible for childbirth-related skin problems. Often new mothers frequently get less sleep and eat differently, which may also contribute to the problem. Fortunately, skin problems in new mothers do not seem to last as long as during the teen years. As your hormone levels, sleep, and eating patterns restabilize, so will your skin.

If your skin irritations are intolerable, by all means see your doctor. Otherwise, take good care of your skin, wash regularly with mild soap, eat healthfully, drink plenty of water, get as much sleep as you can, and try to be patient. Your pregnancy and delivery caused a major upheaval in your body. When your eating and sleeping habits and hormones return to your non-pregnant state, so will your skin.

I am still so tired all the time. Will I ever feel well rested again?

Of course you are still tired, and yes, you will, eventually, feel well rested, but don't hold your breath. Many new parents are surprised by just how long it takes new babies to learn to sleep through the night. And after weeks of being awakened every two to three hours every night, many new parents are willing to consider an uninterrupted stretch from midnight to 4:30 A.M. cause for celebration. Compared to night after night of fragmented sleep and unwelcome playtime at 3 A.M., four and a half continuous hours of sleep in the dark are heavenly. But it still isn't enough.

Every baby is different, and it may be completely normal for your baby to wake once or twice during the night for the entire first year. If your baby is a night owl, you will be tired until she begins to sleep for longer periods of time. Sleep deprivation not only makes one tired, it can also be quite disruptive, causing impaired judgment, poor reflexes, and inefficiency, not to mention serious crabbiness.

Naps will help, but they are not generally enough to allow you to feel truly refreshed. Besides, many moms find it difficult to follow that sage advice to "Sleep whenever the baby sleeps," either because they need time awake to unwind, or because they feel they should be accomplishing something. Nap when you can, but if you need to stare out the window or read a novel, that's fine; you don't need to add guilt to your exhaustion. Do what seems most likely to make you feel better. Be patient with yourself and your baby, though: you will be less tired once your baby's sleep patterns allow you to resume yours. Until your baby cooperates, try some approaches used by other new parents:

- Fran and Tim, the chronically worn-out parents of three-month-old Kevin, decided to divide the nighttime child care. The bedtime ritual began every night at 9 P.M. Fran went to bed, by herself, by ten, sleeping undisturbed for at least four hours. Tim would sleep next to Kevin, feeding him breast milk that Fran had pumped or comforting him when necessary, until Fran would come back on duty, around 2:30 A.M. Then she was in charge, letting Tim sleep without interruption until he had to get up around 7 A.M. Although they slept separately for several weeks until Kevin got the knack of sleeping through the night, they were each guaranteed to sleep several hours a night. Once the baby slept predictably for at least six hours at a time, they were back to sharing a bed.
- Other couples make sure each gets a full night's sleep on a regular basis, switching off who's on baby-duty according to what works for them. For some couples, it's every other night; for others, one parent is "on call' weeknights while the other takes

weekends. If one of you requires less sleep, he/she can be on call more often. Work together to find a way to maximize sleep and you'll both benefit.

- ❧ There are a number of well-respected books on how to help your child sleep through the night. Ask your pediatrician, best friend, librarian, or bookstore clerk for suggestions. Be sure that your baby is old enough to try the methods suggested, and that the approach is comfortable for you. Some experts advise leaving the baby to cry for increasingly longer periods of time and many new parents are not willing to do that.

Although it is well within the realm of normal to be exhausted all the time, it's difficult. It *will* get better. You will become more efficient even without enough sleep, and eventually your baby will become civilized and you'll get the sleep you desire. Do your best to sleep when you can, and remember how chronic sleep deprivation feels so that you can be more compassionate to other new (and not-so-new) haggard parents.

A baby who needs very little sleep or cries a lot isn't being "bad," he is being a baby. It will get better.

I don't know whether to breast-feed or bottle-feed. I prefer one method to the other but all my friends and family did the opposite. What should I do?

Fortunately, at this point in time, women have choices about how to feed their infants. Unfortunately, having the choice means you may choose to do something that no one else you know would have chosen. Feeling confident about deciding to (or not to) breast-feed your baby when your friends and family have all chosen differently can be tough. Either choice is reasonable, but the choice is yours, and you must learn to feel confident about it.

Your baby needs to be fed and nurtured, and even though this is an area in which everyone else has an opinion, whether you breast- or bottle-feed your baby is ultimately up to you. The goal here is to provide nutrition and love to your baby. That can be successfully accomplished by breast-feeding or bottle-feeding. Even though new mothers find confidence hard to come by, as long as your baby is thriving, no apologies or explanations are necessary.

There is ample evidence that breast-feeding a baby for the first few months of his life is advantageous for both baby and mother. Although I am personally a big advocate of nursing, I also know that breast-feeding is not for everybody. Some women can't breast-feed for physical reasons (for example, the mother's medication for a medical problem would enter the breast milk and harm the baby) and some just find it too awkward or distasteful. Some have work situations that make it too stressful to nurse for more than the first few weeks. A very few babies are allergic to their mother's milk, so bottle-feeding is necessary for the baby's health. There are good reasons to choose the breast or the bottle, and there are many excellent formulas available now so all babies should be able to be well-fed.

If you have considered carefully whether or not breast-feeding is right for you, then you are making a reasonable choice. Your decision about how to feed your baby may go against what the women in your family or social circle have done, but that doesn't make it wrong. If you breast-feed, go to a LaLeche meeting or find a lactation consultant who can help you meet other breast-feeding moms. If you bottle-feed, you are actually in the majority of new mothers in this country. Either way, it is your personal choice and no one else's.

Whether you breast- or bottle-feed your baby, make sure you spend some of the feeding time holding him and looking into his eyes. Talk to him, sing to him, or simply exchange loving glances. If you breast-feed amid bottle-feeders, make sure you are discreetly covered (a strategically placed receiving blanket usually covers well), and if you bottle-feed among breast-feeders, just relax. As long as your baby is healthy, then how you feed your baby is between you, your husband, the baby, and your health-care team. You are doing the right thing, whichever you choose.

Everyone says that breast-feeding is "natural." I really want to be able to breast-feed my baby, but it seems like it isn't going at all well.

Breast-feeding *is* natural, but that doesn't mean it always comes naturally or easily. I've known many women who confess that it was *weeks* before they were confident or proficient with breast-feeding. If you are a first-time mother, breast-feeding is new to you and to your baby. You are both learning a new skill, and that can take time.

Successful breast-feeding relies on more than simple determination, although determination is crucial. Your ability to nurse effectively depends on many factors including your baby's sucking style, the size of your baby's mouth, your milk production, the shape of your nipples, your diet, and your patience. When you're not feeling confident, you may break into a sweat just trying to figure out if the baby is hungry, yet you must find a comfortable position, relax enough to allow the milk to flow, and drink lots of fluids. It's hard to manage all that; you need time to develop your own nursing techniques, to allow your breasts and nipples to adapt to these new demands, and for the baby to learn how to suck efficiently.

Talk to a lactation consultant or your doctor if you are worried that there is something actually wrong with your breast-feeding. Do *not* listen to your mother-in-law or neighbor who suggests that "the baby isn't getting enough," unless your baby cries constantly and is not gaining weight or growing properly. Patience, persistence, and tenacity are essential; a little grit and self-confidence, so hard to muster at this point in one's motherhood, come in handy, too. If you are dedicated to learning to breast-feed, and there are no physical or medical reasons why you shouldn't, it will get easier. Chances are that in a few more weeks, you and your baby will have become nursing naturals. Take a deep breath; allow yourself the time to learn. Accept that you may not feel like the LaLeche mother of the year just yet. Nursing your baby can be a wonderful experience, but for most women, it takes time, commitment, and effort before it becomes "natural."

And if breast-feeding just doesn't ever click for you, no matter how much you wanted it and no matter how briefly or valiantly you tried, that's OK, too. The goal of breast-feeding is to nourish your baby, not to make you feel guilty or inadequate as a mother.

*Just because something is normal or "natural"
doesn't mean it is easy or always pleasant.*

Is breast-feeding supposed to hurt this much?

That depends a bit on how much is "this much." If it hurts briefly when the baby is latching on, or in the first several weeks as your breasts are toughening up, or when your infant unknowingly chomps down on your nipple, that's unpleasant but normal. Keep going; the pain should ease up as your breasts become more accustomed to nursing and your baby becomes more adept.

Many new mothers have been told by supposedly reliable sources that breast-feeding should not hurt "if it's being done correctly." That comment not only makes a breast-feeding woman in pain feel like a failure, it is clearly wrong. Especially in the early weeks, breast-feeding can often be very painful, and there is some logic here. Before you gave birth, chances are that no one had ever nibbled on your nipples for twenty minutes at a time, several times a day, day after day. Even though your nipples are intended for this purpose (and even if you followed that somewhat deceptive advice about rubbing your nipples with a towel every day for a few weeks before giving birth), they need to toughen up before breast-feeding becomes painless. Please don't feel embarrassed or ashamed because it hurts you to breast-feed—*it hurts most women for at least a little while.*

However, if breast-feeding causes you more pain than you can tolerate, you need to discover why. Sometimes pain is caused by your baby latching on incorrectly, sometimes by a clogged duct, sometimes just an overfull breast. If you have a fever and flu-like symptoms, you may have a breast infection, or if you notice a white, curd-like substance in your baby's mouth, you may have thrush; call your health-care provider, as these are problems that may need to be treated medically.

Ask an experienced friend, lactation consultant, midwife, or LaLeche League leader to watch you breast-feed, and then follow her suggestions, or refer to a book on breast-feeding to help you diagnose the problem. You need to determine if the problem can be solved by adjusting how your baby sucks, by getting more rest, or if you need medical intervention. No matter what, drink plenty of fluids and above all, get more rest, doing nothing more than resting in bed and breast-feeding until the pain is gone.

In addition to the problems mentioned above, it is common for breast-feeding women to experience unexpected discomforts in their breasts. "Let-down," the sensation when the milk in your breasts comes in for nursing, is sometimes accompanied by unfamiliar or uncomfortable sensations. Some women feel a tingling, some a cramping, some a fullness, and some a stinging. Let-down can occur not only when you're ready for a feeding, but also when you just think about your baby or hear a baby cry. Some women have a more generalized pain or discomfort when the baby latches on, or just for the first few seconds of nursing, and sometimes women have dripping from the non-nursing breast. These are all normal and sometimes inconvenient, but not worrisome.

Any experienced breast-feeding mom will tell you, whether you are in pain or not, to take very good care of your nipples and breasts to avoid infection or discomfort. Make sure you wipe off any excess milk or the baby's saliva with a clean, damp cloth after each feeding, get as much rest as you can, drink lots of fluids, and leave your breasts exposed to the air whenever possible. Yes, you might feel like a cross between an exhibitionist and a cow, but the results will be worth it. And always, if the pain is severe, or if you are still uncertain, call your lactation consultant or health-care practitioner for help and advice. You need not suffer pain or shame.

With breast-feeding, I feel as if my breasts are no longer my own and they are no longer sexual. Will I ever feel the same way about them again?

Once you have weaned your baby and your breasts are no longer at the service of a demanding infant, they will become yours again. Nursing breasts seem to become something altogether different than they used to be, and it can be worrisome to think that such a sensual part of your body might be so strictly utilitarian. When body parts that used to be both private and sexual become "working boobs," as one new father calls them, often in full view of anyone within spitting distance, it's difficult to imagine that they will ever resume their more personal, sensual place in your life. But they will.

As your baby gets older and begins to take more and more nourishment from solid foods, your breasts will no longer have lives of their own. They won't leak or get engorged, and they may even return to their previous shape and size. You will not have to organize your wardrobe, your diet, or your schedule to accommodate your nursing. If you nurse up to and beyond one year, as more and more mothers are doing, you will find that breast-feeding no longer controls every aspect of your breasts' lives. After you wean, they will become private again, and will most likely regain their sensual sensitivity. Your "working boobs" will simply be your breasts again.

I've heard that breast-feeding helps a woman lose the excess pregnancy weight sooner. Is that true?

A new mom should not worry about her weight, especially if she's nursing! Truly, how much you weigh is so much less important than that you are nourishing your baby. Breast-feeding is good for your baby and it is good for you. Breast-feed because it benefits you both, and don't even *think* about your weight.

The reason people believe that a breast-feeding mother will lose more weight comes from the idea that the calories taken in by the baby outnumber those the mother consumes while breast-feeding. Nursing mothers need to eat healthfully to nurse successfully and stay healthy themselves, and those should be your top priorities. Breast-feeding actually requires more calories than pregnancy did, and your energy level will certainly be affected if you stint on calories.

A strict diet-exercise routine may be hard or even unhealthy to maintain while nursing. And I'm convinced that some women don't lose those last several pounds either because their bodies need the extra caloric consumption or body fat to support the breast-feeding, or they have babies who don't use as much milk as the mother produces.

You have no control over which scenario will be yours. No techniques or diets (including breast-feeding) work for everyone. You aren't doing something right if you lose your pregnancy weight sooner, and you're not doing something wrong if you don't. Breast-feed your baby because you want to—just don't count on nursing to be your weight-loss program.

Breast-feeding women need to consume lots of calories to support the milk production. Please don't worry about your weight while you're breast-feeding!

My breasts are so much different now. What can I expect to happen to them?

While pregnancy clearly changes your breasts, your breasts will generally return, more or less, to their former size and shape within a matter of weeks or months whether you breast-feed or not. How quickly and how closely they resume their previous appearance depends on heredity, your age, how much weight you gained in pregnancy, and how much your breasts enlarged during pregnancy. Some women feel that their breasts have completely returned to normal after a few weeks, while others find that their breasts are either a little larger or smaller, a little less firm, more or less sensitive, or their nipples are different than before they became pregnant. It is unusual for a woman's post-pregnancy breasts to be dramatically different than her prepregnancy breasts, but it does sometimes occur. Mostly, the changes are subtle and noticeable to no one except you, your husband, and your doctor.

If you breast-feed, it is not uncommon for there to be a minimal amount of milk expressible from your breasts for up to a year after weaning. Nipples may become either temporarily or permanently more protuberant, particularly if your nipples were flat before nursing. Some women experience changes in their sexual response to breast or nipple stimulation. These are all common, normal, and minimal changes.

You may have an emotional reaction to even subtle changes, though. A formerly large-breasted woman whose breasts decrease in size may feel pleased, but a previously small-breasted woman who enjoyed her bigger breasts while nursing may be sad to see them go. Similarly, it may be disappointing if your breasts were very sexually sensitive before your baby was born if they lose some of that responsiveness, but a pleasant surprise if you gain some sensitivity.

Whatever changes your breasts endure, try to remember that only you and your husband will actually notice or care, and that breasts are actually just another body part, albeit one that gets an inordinate amount of attention. Your breasts will continue to change subtly over the course of your life, with or without subsequent pregnancies. It will stand you in good stead if you can accept them for what they are; enjoy the positives and adjust to the rest.

I've lost almost all of my pregnancy weight, but my old jeans still don't fit. Is it my imagination, or are my hips wider and my tummy bigger since having this baby?

This might not be what you'd bargained for, but many women notice that their bodies are different after childbirth. Your hips definitely may be wider and your belly rounder than before you had your baby. Even when you return to your normal pre-pregnancy weight, the pounds may be redistributed. Broadening hips are a particularly common experience, as the pelvis often widens and loosens to accommodate the birth of the baby. Lots of new mothers notice they no longer look like teenagers; they have more womanly bodies now.

Some women find that over time their former shape does come back. Others will discover that these new curves are more lasting. Pregnancy involves your whole body, but keep in mind that bodies change as you age whether or not you have children; having babies makes changes that are dramatic, apparent, and abrupt.

The best thing you can do is take care of yourself, both during and after your pregnancy. Eat healthfully, exercise regularly, and your body will become familiar again, either because it resumes its former shape or because you become used to the new you. And recognize that although your new body may or may not be welcome, this is the body that helped you have this baby you now love so much. Wider hips or not, that body is pretty impressive.

My appetite is incredible since I've given birth. I eat all day. Is that OK?

This is also not unusual. If you are nursing, you need to take in five hundred more calories per day than when you were pregnant. Of course you are hungry; you need to eat more to support the breast-feeding. In addition, if you are like many new mothers, you find yourself at home much more of your day than ever before. You are tired. You are cranky. You are bored. Your body looks and feels different. You are busy all the time but you feel you aren't getting anything done. If you are typical of many new moms, when you feel especially exhausted or lonely, you will not say to yourself, "I need to eat right and exercise more." You are more likely to grab a box of chocolate chip cookies and eat every single one yourself.

Although this is not necessarily good for you, it is (almost) logical. Sugar gives you energy and chocolate gives you pleasure, and you definitely need energy and pleasure. Although those cookies won't help you feel perky and fit for long, they may give you the boost you need to get through these weeks without sleep or adult companionship, and that makes some sense. It's a lot easier to watch what you eat when you are not so exhausted.

It's difficult for many new mothers to eat properly in those early weeks. There doesn't seem to be time to prepare nutritious dishes, so snacking all day may be taking the place of more balanced meals. If you are concerned about your eating (or weight) getting out of control, first check with your doctor to rule out any medical problems. Once you determine that your constant eating is strictly behavioral, there are some things you can do to improve your food intake quality and quantity.

- Make sure you buy only nutritious snack foods, including raw fruits and vegetables, so the temptations around you are healthful. Store fruits and vegetables washed and ready to grab and eat.
- Do something physical whenever the urge to overeat comes upon you. Go for a walk or even run in place (your baby will find that highly amusing) before you open that bag of candy.
- Try cooking. Sometimes being involved with food preparation can satisfy your desire to eat without you actually eating so much. Prepare more elaborate foods, but don't lick the bowl.
- Drink lots of fluids. Make yourself a fresh pot of tea or coffee (decaf, if you're nursing) every morning. Drink it hot or iced. Drink lots of water. You will be less hungry if you are full of liquids, and you need to drink if you are breast-feeding.
- Satisfy your oral craving by calling a friend before you resort to the snack cabinet.
- Chew gum or eat hard candy if you really need the sweet. Both stay in your mouth awhile with fewer calories than other candies.

In time, when you have caught up on your sleep and created a routine that suits you, eating won't dominate your day, and when you have weaned your baby your appetite will naturally diminish. You will become accustomed to having access to food all day and you may even begin to have enough energy to exercise instead of grazing when you get a little droopy. Until then, give yourself a chance to settle into your new life.

My baby is six months old already. Is there something wrong with me that I still look vaguely pregnant?

There is nothing wrong with a rounded belly, and some people even find their rounded contours more womanly. It is true, though, that pregnancy can be really tough on a number of different body parts, and the stomach is certainly one of them. Depending on your resolve, delivery, and genetics, getting a teenager-like flat stomach again will be more or less difficult for you. If you are determined and genetically so disposed, it is certainly possible to have a flatter tummy within months of delivery.

Time, determination, and self-acceptance are your biggest allies in regaining a figure you are satisfied with after pregnancy, and many women don't anticipate how much effort it can take. Your weight may be redistributed, your eating habits different, and exhaustion and nursing may make exercising and dieting nearly impossible. But absolutely, if you are ready and willing, you can do a few things to improve your shape.

First, make certain you have the medical go-ahead before you embark on an exercise program after delivery. Women who deliver by cesarian section should know that their recovery and return to flatness will take longer. You must make completely sure that all incisions are fully healed and that you are physically prepared for any new exercise regimen before you start. A flat stomach is not worth the potential pain, infection, or exhaustion from overexertion.

When you are adequately rested and have recovered from childbirth you can start to do exercises for your abdominal muscles. Check with a local gym, ask your health-care provider, or borrow a book or movie from the library to find appropriate routines. With a consistent and conscientious workout, you can retrain muscles loosened and stretched by pregnancy and childbirth to return to a more familiar, taut state.

Be tolerant of yourself, and accept the body you have. It was this body that brought your wonderful baby into your life; it deserves praise, not disapproval.

Your body created and nurtured your baby.
Don't hate it; treat it with respect.

Is it normal that my sense of smell is different now?

Lots of women experience a new-found tolerance for the formerly intolerable when they become mothers; it's a normal part of the body's adaptation to motherhood. Sarah, a new mother who had previously lived a conspicuously child-free life, commented on how weird this was. Suddenly she felt completely natural to sit in a group of moms and babies, one mother with her nose near her baby's bottom, another with a finger down a diaper, and Sarah herself happily sniffing her own spit-up covered bundle! This casual acceptance of the least sweet-smelling human functions must be nature's way of helping you through what might otherwise be an unbearable necessity of parenthood.

The scents your baby emits help you know what he needs. While most women don't mention actually *liking* those smells, many women enjoy the closeness and intimacy that accompanies caring for a new baby. Your sense of smell may be different now, but it is far more likely that love and tenderness allow it to adapt so you can take excellent care of your baby.

Interestingly, as your baby gets older, those smells may become unpleasant again. When your baby is eating mostly solids, and especially when he is ready to be toilet trained, you will be amazed to discover that your old, familiar revulsion of those bodily odors will resume. When it isn't so charming to be changing that toddler's diapers, both your body and the baby's will tell you that he is ready to move on. Your nose knows.

I've developed a backache in the last few weeks. Is this related to my having a new baby?

It certainly could be. You may have back pain from not adjusting adequately to the abrupt shift in weight from carrying your baby on the inside during your pregnancy to having a live, growing, and sometimes squirming baby to carry around on the outside now. Do not worry that you are carrying him "too much," but you might be carrying him incorrectly or in such a way that causes your back strain. If your back has bothered you only since your baby was born, you may need some assistance. Ask your doctor to suggest some exercises to help your sore back and to assess if you need any more intense intervention. Many women find relief from occasional or regular chiropractic adjustments or massage.

You may also do well to find another method to keep your baby close while keeping you *both* comfortable. There are a number of slings and baby carriers on the market now designed to help you carry your baby without undue back strain. Ask your friends and neighbors to borrow theirs for an hour, as different designs suit some mother-baby pairs better than others. Front packs work well for some mothers while backpacks are better for others. Keep in mind that your baby will likely grow rapidly; you may want to find one that adjusts as the baby grows.

Be careful how you lift your baby. Make sure you lower the side rail on your baby's crib before you lift him out. Remember those suggestions to lift heavy objects with your back straight, using your legs? This applies to picking up your baby, whether it's off the floor, out of the car seat, or from the bassinet. When you bend to lift, it strains the back.

As your baby gets bigger and heavier, there will come a time when you just won't be able to carry him around nearly as often without overtaxing your back. It is absolutely OK, and even good for you both, for your baby to find other ways to soothe himself. When he needs to be close to you, hold him while sitting in a rocking chair, lying in bed, or snuggling together on the sofa. Talk to your baby, sing to him, and take him for a walk in the stroller or a drive in the car to calm him without putting excess strain on your back.

When your baby is needy, it's appropriate to hold and comfort him. It is equally appropriate, though, to take care of yourself. If you are unable to tote your baby around all day, don't. You can hold and comfort him without hurting yourself. If you don't take care of your back, you could end up with more serious problems, and then be unavailable to hold your baby at all. Neither one of you will be happy with that.

Will stretch marks ever go away?

It depends. About half of all women who give birth develop stretch marks, or "striae," and in general, the extent of striation is proportional to the weight gain of the mother. Stretch marks are thought to be genetically or hormonally determined. Your skin type, color, and elasticity seem to contribute to how noticeable and permanent your stretch marks will be. Many people who go through growth spurts also have stretch marks on their knees, thighs, or breasts, wherever their bodies grew fastest.

Keep in mind that most women see a dramatic improvement over the first several months after giving birth. As your shape returns to normal and you regain some muscle tone, the striae become less visible. Typically, the color fades to normal, although some stretch marks maintain a shiny appearance. Sadly, there is little evidence that over-the-counter products either prevent or remove striae, although creams certainly can't hurt, and some women swear by them. My personal guess is that the creams that "succeed" likely "work" for those women who wouldn't have developed particularly noticeable stretch marks anyway.

While stretch marks are not one of the most enjoyable side effects of pregnancy, they are medically harmless, and are easily kept as a private reminder of your motherhood. Penny, a new mother and marathon runner, considers them her "badges of honor." She purchased a great one-piece bathing suit, saying, without too much regret, that her bikini days are over. True, you and your husband will see them, but generally no one else will, as, fortunately, stretch marks are usually completely hidden under clothing. The best advice I can give you is to accept them, knowing you are not alone.

My baby is a few weeks old, and I'm still spotting a bit. Should I be worried?

There is tremendous variation in how easily and quickly women recover from childbirth. While you probably have nothing to worry about, you will only know that for certain by checking with your doctor or midwife. The six-week time frame that many doctors give for the first postpartum checkup is based on the *average* recovery time. That means it can be perfectly normal to be healed in four weeks or not until eight weeks. Likewise, the length of time normal women continue to spot after delivery varies.

As you probably know, the recovery time for women who deliver vaginally is different than women who have c-sections. It is also logical that your recovery may be compromised if you had an extensive and exhausting labor, or if you have no help after delivery. Having a colicky baby, leading to you walking the baby long hours every night and diminishing your hours of sleep, may also contribute to the delay in feeling back to your old self.

Ask your health-care provider what's normal for you. It seems that women who are on their feet a lot after delivery bleed a little bit longer, and getting more rest always helps. Pay attention to how you feel and always, *always* ask the appropriate professionals if you are worried. If your doctor or midwife's practice isn't supportive of and responsive to your concerns, find a practice that is. You are new to this, and you are entitled to be reassured if you are fine and assisted if you need help.

No question is too silly or too stupid. If your health-care provider, friends, or relatives belittle you, or make you uncomfortable asking, then you're asking the wrong person. Find someone who will be gracious and helpful and will treat you respectfully.

When will I get my period back?

Women resume menstruating again anywhere from a few weeks to over a year after giving birth. Ovulation may also resume at any time. By three months after giving birth about 90 percent of nonbreast-feeding women and about one-third of breast-feeding women have gotten their periods back. Some women describe having a feeling that their cycles are returning, but still don't menstruate for months. Others return to regular cycles before they are even sure they are done bleeding from delivery. What's normal for you may be totally unlike what's normal for your sister or best friend. Your periods may come back and instantly resemble your pre-pregnancy cycles, or they may be quite different. Your cycles may be heavier or lighter, more or less predictable, than before you had your baby.

Typically, nursing mothers do not have their cycles return to normal as soon after delivery as mothers who don't breast-feed, and sometimes menstruation doesn't restart until after they have completely weaned their babies. Since mothers sometimes breast-feed for extended lengths of time, they may go for a year or more, postpartum, without a period. However, please note that breast-feeding does not guarantee that your periods will not return. And just because you haven't begun menstruating again doesn't mean you can't get pregnant, so don't rely on this for birth control.

We've been given the go-ahead to have sex again, but it seems I'm not lubricating the way I used to. Is this very common?

Definitely. Many new mothers experience a decrease in vaginal lubrication during lovemaking, particularly in the first several weeks postpartum. Hormone changes, decreased desire, exhaustion, or anxiety may cause this generally temporary problem. Time often solves it.

If you're experiencing vaginal dryness or discomfort during intercourse, first consult with your health-care provider. Once the unlikely possibility of a medical problem has been eliminated, she might suggest a vaginal lubricant (most are available without a prescription). This might be all you need to make your sex life a lot more comfortable until your hormones and life settle down.

If a lubricant is unappealing or doesn't seem to be enough, you might need just a little more romance, sleep, and time to get your lovemaking back to your pre-baby level of enjoyment. It takes at least weeks (or months or even more for some women) for those tender tissues, ovulation, and hormones to return to normal. Being perpetually tired or worried that you'll wake the baby also adds to the difficulty many women have getting in the mood. Lots of women find that sex just isn't the priority it used to be, and without the pre-baby time and energy you were accustomed to being able to devote to lovemaking, lubrication can be a problem. For the near future, you may require more creativity, romance, candlelight, music, a baby-sitter, a lubricant, and, bluntly, more foreplay, to become physically ready. It will improve.

I'm afraid having sex again is going to hurt—is it likely to be painful?

The prospect of having sex when you feel very tender is understandably frightening. If your fear of the pain is overwhelming, it will influence how tense you get when you do try to make love. That emotional tension will likely make you more physically uncomfortable, possibly making sex more painful than it would otherwise be.

But sex is not all in the mind; physical factors are, of course, also involved. If you had an episiotomy or c-section, or are still sore from giving birth, your fears may be based in reality. Pain and the possibility of infection if you have sex before you are fully healed are the concerns doctors have when they suggest you wait about six weeks to resume having intercourse after delivery. If, however, you are six *months* past delivery, feeling fine, and able to go horseback riding with abandon, it may be time to figure out where the problem really lies.

Once your doctor or midwife has given you the lovemaking go-ahead, if you are still fearful of pain (which is completely understandable and extremely common), try to understand the fear. Some women do experience discomfort or pain the first few times they have sex after delivering a baby, but others do not. Those who find lovemaking uncomfortable usually describe feeling "tight" or a bit raw. Usually it isn't too bad, and gets increasingly better each time. There's no way to know whether you will be pain-free until you try.

The likelihood of pain, though, often increases with the fear of pain. You are more likely to tighten all your muscles and less likely to become fully relaxed and sexually aroused if you are terrified of suffering. Also, some women are afraid of getting pregnant again or of waking the baby, so they don't become wholly involved in the lovemaking, also making the process less comfortable. Of course, telling you not to worry about the pain isn't much help, but if you could do so, that would be great.

Work with your husband on this. Share your fears with him. He may worry about hurting you, too! Take time together to relax and snuggle. Realize that the first few times you make love after having a baby may feel different—it may be great, it may be uncomfortable, and it will almost certainly get better over time. Just take it slowly in the beginning.

Remember, couples often have more than one baby, which proves that they continue to have sex after having their first child. Even parents, even you, can continue to have enjoyable sex lives. If your sex life was pleasurable before you gave birth and you are physically ready, your lovemaking can and will be satisfying, and not painful, very soon.

Couples often have more than one baby, which proves that people do have sex after having their first child.

My *forearms* hurt. My doctor says it's from carrying the baby around all day, but I've never heard of this before. Is this true?

It is very likely. Think about how differently you use your body since giving birth. You spend hours a day feeding, carrying, lifting, and otherwise holding your baby; it should be no surprise that your body reacts in unexpected ways. The different and increased use of your hands and arms since giving birth may easily cause aches, cramps, and pains. In time, your muscles will strengthen and the pain will diminish. Until then, try these suggestions:

- ❧ Pay attention to your posture when you feed your baby. Try using different positions at different times when you feed her, allowing strained muscles a rest.
- ❧ Use pillows to help support your baby or your arms whenever you're feeding her.

- Make sure you are relaxed and comfortable before you begin a feeding. If you aren't comfortable, shift around until you are; feeding should be a pleasant and comfortable experience for you both.
- Use good posture whenever you lift or hold your baby. Use your legs, rather than your back or arms, when you lift anything.
- Change positions frequently when holding your baby.
- Use a baby carrier to relieve your arms.
- Rest you arms whenever possible.

If making these minor adjustments doesn't give you enough relief from the pain, once again, contact your doctor. He/she might suggest specific exercises to do on your own or visits to a physical therapist. Although hand, wrist, or arm pain is not life threatening, it can be very unpleasant and there is usually an easy way to lessen it. Think about how you handle your baby, make some necessary adjustments, and be reassured that this is both common and usually temporary.

I developed some varicose veins during my pregnancy. Are they permanent?

No one really likes them, but many women develop varicose veins (swollen, colored, and visible veins) during pregnancy, mostly on their legs, and they are sometimes permanent. Varicose veins cause a wide range of discomfort and disfigurement, from hardly noticeable flat purplish veins (often called "spider veins") with no soreness, to ropy, swollen, deeply colored, and very painful veins. Since varicose veins are usually caused by weakness in the vein walls, the increased flow of blood to support the fetus and uterus in pregnancy can cause the varicosity. Nearly half of the women with visible varicose veins have a hereditary predisposition to them, so if your mother or grandmothers had them, chances are you will, too.

Fortunately, many women do experience a significant decrease in both the visibility and the discomfort in their varicose veins within the first several weeks or months after giving birth. If you are just a few weeks postpartum, wait a bit to see if the veins retract on their own. As your weight, blood flow, and hormones return to their non-pregnant state, those "road maps" may soon disappear.

There are a couple of noninvasive approaches that may minimize your vein problem. While you were pregnant, your doctor or midwife may have suggested that you rest and elevate your legs periodically or wear maternity support hose, and these continue to be useful treatments even after you've given birth. Some women benefit from the more supportive support hose available only by prescription; ask your health-care provider if these would help you. Often this is all that is necessary to decrease both the appearance and achiness associated with varicose veins.

Women respond to their own varicose veins in a variety of ways, some depending on the physical discomfort, some on the level of disfigurement. I knew three women who gave birth within a few weeks of each other, all of who developed quite obvious varicose veins on their legs. Barbara was in constant pain from her enlarged veins, so she sought relief from her doctor. Jennie didn't like the looks of her legs, but didn't have any physical distress; she simply vowed never to wear shorts or short skirts again. And Kate decided that her veins, although not at all welcome, were just part of her new look.

It is reasonable to seek help if your veins are painful or unbearably embarrassing, and it is equally reasonable to decide simply to accept your body's changes. No matter what, if anything, you ultimately do about your varicose veins, give yourself time to heal, become well-informed, and handle the varicosity the way that is right for you.

The reality is that some women, despite taking very good care of themselves, do not see much improvement even months after child-birth, and while some women barely notice or care about their varicose veins, others desperately want to have them disappear. Thankfully, there are numerous medical methods now available to eliminate, or at least improve, both the appearance and comfort of your legs, and some of them, depending on your diagnosis and policy, may even be covered by insurance. If the physical pain and your emotional distaste with how your legs look persist beyond your comfort level, ask your health-care professional for options available to you.

I have hemorrhoids. What can I do to feel better or to get rid of them?

Hemorrhoids are relatively common; they're just varicose veins of the rectum or anus. They feel itchy, swollen, or painful, and occasionally they bleed. They often develop in the last months of pregnancy and the first weeks postpartum because of the increased pressure on the rectum, and they are aggravated by constipation. If hemorrhoids weren't a problem for you before your pregnancy, they usually resolve within the first few weeks after delivery.

Over-the-counter creams or ointments and sitz baths may provide temporary relief and aid healing. Drink plenty of fluids and eat lots of fiber to regain regularity, use cold compresses, sit only on a rubber or inflated doughnut-shaped tube, and get enough rest. Usually one of these remedies will do the trick.

As with all things medical, if the discomfort is relentless or if the hemorrhoids show no signs of healing, call your health-care team. *Some hemorrhoids require medical attention.* Of course, it's always difficult to take care of yourself properly when you're caring for a new baby, but you don't need any extra aches or pains right now. And hemorrhoids are a relatively easy problem to solve.

Life is difficult enough when you have a new baby; you don't need any extra aches or pains.

Even my shoe size is bigger now. Can this really be happening?

It sure can. Some people's feet may keep growing slightly for their whole lives, mostly undetectably, but occasionally enough to warrant some adjustment in shoe size after a number of years. It is not at all unusual to discover that your feet have swollen or actually grown during or following a pregnancy. Increased blood flow and added weight contribute to the small but discernable change in shoe size.

Were you bloated during pregnancy? Did you move up a shoe size for comfort? If your larger size resulted from water retention, your feet may return to their former delicate proportions when your other body parts do. Did you switch from high heels to wearing flat shoes to avoid awkwardness? If so, you may find that it is your newfound comfort in flatter footwear, rather than actual foot growth, that leads you to wear a bigger shoe than before your baby was born.

Please do not worry about this. You are not some freak of mother-hood, just a woman who is aware that her feet now feel better in larger shoes. Your foot enlargement may be unwelcome, but it is not dangerous, harmful, or indicative that you will be wearing clown shoes before your childbearing years are over.

Chapter Three

Practical Matters

⌣

"What did you do all day?" I always hated that question, partly because in those early weeks of motherhood I felt that I needed somehow to justify my existence, and partly because I wasn't so sure myself what had kept me so busy yet gave me nothing to show for all my effort. This chapter will help you have an answer to that question, become more efficient, and become more adept at accepting your inefficiencies.

This is probably the most practical chapter in the book. It includes tips on cooking and paying your bills, ideas for keeping your baby cheerful while you're trying to finish a project, and ideas for shopping more effectively. By no means are these the only ways to streamline your life, and by no means should you take these suggestions to mean that your life *should* be more efficient. But if there's an area you'd like some help on, I've included tried-and-true methods, many recommended by new mothers who also wanted to feel better about the way they spent their time.

Use any ideas that appeal to you. Relax and enjoy the new pace and structure of your life when you can. There are lots of "right" or "best" ways to do things. Figure out what is important to you and to your family, and you will develop your own rhythm and skills over the next several months.

Whenever you don't quite know what to do, just listen. Listen to yourself, your husband, and your baby. You will find your answer.

Am I a bad mother if I can't seem to keep up with the clutter?

Of course not! In those early months, it's almost impossible to tidy up as easily as you and your baby can generate a mess. How neat and clean do you think your home needs to be? Caroline, a mother of two, said that she always tells her friends who become mothers to lower their standards. Most women I know who have been mothers for a while feel they have had to learn to expect less of themselves and to tolerate more chaos; some women even learn to feel cozier surrounded by their family's belongings. The truth is, as long as the health department hasn't been summoned to condemn your home, chances are your concern about your sloppiness is more uncomfortable than the mess itself.

If you worry that external disarray is a sure sign that you're a bad mother, that you'll never be able to invite friends over again, or remember the color of your bedroom carpet, be patient with yourself. You'll get more organized when you are fully recovered from the birth and getting enough sleep. Until then, your baby doesn't mind that she's a slob, and fortunately, she doesn't care if you are, too. Besides, housekeeping and motherhood are not the same thing. You can be an excellent mother and be a terrible housekeeper.

If you're concerned about the disorder for fear that your husband, mother-in-law, or neighbors will think less of your mothering, then you might need to work out your sensitivity to their opinions of you. In the beginning weeks and months of your new baby's life, it is difficult to get everything under control; you don't need the added burden of meeting what you assume to be other people's expectations. If they truly love you, they will understand.

Try not to pass judgement on yourself; your ability to conquer clutter isn't necessarily a reflection of your mental health, your character, or your ability as a mother. If you feel better when your life and living space are orderly, that's fine; if you don't care or notice, that's fine, too. Develop better organizational skills (or ask, beg, or hire someone to help) *if that will make you feel better.* In time, you will become more adept at keeping up with the disarray, and you will know that you don't have to pass the "white glove test" (or even know what that is) to be a spectacular mother.

Your baby will grow up to become a person who remembers the time you spent together, what you value, and who you are as a person—not how tidy the house was.

How can I get showered every day with a new baby in the house?

It's a rare new mother who is able to get showered or bathed on a daily basis, especially before noon. But, ultimately, every new mother finds a way. You might need to develop an entirely new approach to personal hygiene, but you will eventually discover what works for you. Here are a few tried-and-true methods:

- Get up when your husband does every morning (or before) and let him take care of the baby while you shower before he goes to work.
- Shower during your baby's nap time.
- Put your baby in her infant seat or bassinet, and place her on the bathroom floor near you. Then you can easily talk to her, hear her, and peek out at her through the curtain while you are soaping up.
- Take a bath with your baby.
- Shower at night, when your husband is home and in charge of the baby.
- Invoke the "36 Hour Rule": you need to have a shower only every 36 hours.
- Be pleasantly surprised when you get to shower after only 35 hours.
- Shower faster.

I promise you, you will become more efficient about this over time. You will learn your baby's habits so you instinctively know when your baby will stay content while you wash and rinse. You will get more sleep on a regular basis so you no longer value napping more than cleanliness. In the meantime, take heart in knowing that this may be the single most frequently asked question by new mothers.

It is extremely difficult, and a major accomplishment, for a new mother to take a shower and get dressed before noon.

How can I figure out what to do first when I feel pulled in so many directions?

First, you need to set new priorities. It's hard to know what to do first if you haven't sorted out what matters to you most. Consider what you and your husband value. Amy is uncomfortable when her home isn't sparkling, neat, and clean, so cleaning is crucial for her. Janet can't live without seeing her friends weekly, so she has set up a weekly girls' night out. If a sit-down family dinner is essential to *your* emotional well-being, then you must find a way to secure that. Whatever matters to you or your husband, and eventually to your baby, needs to become an honored priority in your life.

Second, you need to be clear about what is absolutely essential to family survival, such as keeping your family fed, clothed, and clean enough to prevent disease or embarrassment. Then consider what gives you pleasure, because being rested, nurtured, loved, and entertained are important, too. Each family enjoys these things in different balances. You get to decide what matters most to you. Obviously you must make sure that survival needs are met, but you can clean and decorate every square inch of your home, if that's your passion, or keep housekeeping to a bare minimum, buy prepared meals, and devote more time to your family, friends, or favorite hobby.

Once you've clarified what you and your husband care most about and what is absolutely essential, you can set about trying to accomplish those things first. What you used to be able to do without thinking needs careful consideration when there's a baby in the picture. You may need to adjust your standards a bit and give up the idea that you must take care of everything, every day, perfectly. A family dinner doesn't have to be home cooked every night, thank you notes may be less lengthy or eloquent, and your TV may temporarily replace the multiplex. But you needn't give up what you most value.

Prioritize and organize, reduce perfectionism, and do what you need and want, all in good time. Take care of your personal essentials first, and attend to the rest as either the need or whim allows. You will get better at all of these tasks, and learn to care less about the things that really don't matter. Then, even if you aren't that much more efficient, you'll feel better.

There's so much to do now, and my mind is fuzzy. How can I keep track of everything?

Make lists. It's a challenge to keep track of everything when you have a new baby around, and writing things down serves two purposes. Listing what you need to do or buy gives you a visible, concrete record that remembers for you. You can hold it in your hand, add to it, and cross things off as you accomplish them (the best part). And, for many people, the act of writing or seeing something written helps secure it in the memory, so even if you lose the list—which will, of course, happen occasionally—you'll be more likely to be able to reconstruct it.

To-do lists should be brief and manageable:

- Be clear about what requires immediate attention, what can wait, and who is responsible for each task.
- Whenever possible, break jobs down into separate parts: list "clean the sink," "vacuum," and "laundry," rather than "clean the house" to avoid being overwhelmed by your own expectations.
- Try to be realistic about what you can accomplish in a given period of time.
- Estimate how long a certain job might take, and be sure to include jobs that can be done in ten-minute bursts of energy.

Shopping lists work best if they are comprehensive and specific:

- Keep separate lists for grocery, hardware, or drugstores, depending on your shopping habits.
- Maintain running lists: when you polish off the last bowl full of Cheerios, write down "Cheerios"; when you notice that there's only one more roll of toilet paper, add "toilet paper" to the list. That way you won't have to go through your cupboards or memory bank to figure out what you need when you're ready to go to the store. (And a ready-to-go list makes it a lot easier to delegate the shopping to someone else, which is always a nice idea.)

Use daily, weekly, and monthly lists:

- Specify what needs to be done every day, every week, every month, or just when you get around to it.

Denise, one of the most organized people I know, keeps lists of people to call, thank you notes to write, household tasks, important birthdays, and the like, and suggests keeping all your lists in a spiral notebook or on a clipboard too big to misplace. Audrey, an artist and new mother of twins, prefers separate lists magnetically fastened to the refrigerator, with a pen attached. Work out the number, format, and location of the lists to suit your style and help you regain a sense of control.

Don't allow your lists to make you a slave to them; discard them if you feel pressured to do more than you can handle. Their purpose and value is to help you, and when used properly, lists can be invaluable to help you set priorities, keep track of your life, and see how much you are actually accomplishing each day. When you finish a task, cross it off your list with a flourish. You will feel almost as good as when you finished the jobs.

I make lists and am pretty clear about what needs to get done first; what else can I do to be more efficient?

Every mother develops tricks to help her get through the chores of life. Making lists and setting priorities are certainly two important ones. Undoubtedly you will come up with many of your own over time. Here are a few tips some new mothers find helpful. Use the ideas that seem comfortable to you:

- Be flexible and creative. Try a different approach to solving a problem or managing a difficult task.
- If you're having trouble getting something done, leave it for another time. You might be better able to handle it with a clearer head or in a different mood.
- Some women like to do many things at once. If that's you, save

time by doing some things together. For example, time your laundry so it is ready to be folded while you watch your favorite television show. Use a cordless telephone or a cell phone with a headset so your hands are free and you can make important calls or talk to a friend while setting the table or tidying up the living room. If you combine physical labor with intellectual stimulation or entertainment, you may enjoy your efficiency more.

* Other women prefer to devote their full concentration to one task at a time. If that's more to your liking, assign yourself one task a day, and give it your full attention until it is done, even if that means taking a break once in awhile to care for your baby.

* Invite a friend to do errands with you.

* Realize that what may be a chore to you is an adventure for your baby. Explaining in a dramatic voice how you are scrubbing out the tub or writing a report can be outrageously entertaining to a six-month-old. Grocery shopping, with all the colors, textures, smells, not to mention other shoppers to admire your baby, may be the highlight of her week, instead of the drudgery it is to you. Seeing things from your baby's perspective will make them more fun and you more efficient.

* Sheila, an especially organized new mom, set up workstations around the house. Jobs that were not completed in one sitting could then be left partially undone, ready to be continued when she had the chance. This eliminated setup and clean-up time and allowed more immediate transitions from task to task. When she had a free moment, she could go to that station and pay another bill, write a thank you note, or paste four more photos into an album.

* Use small increments of time wisely. Sometimes you may have only five or ten minutes until your baby is likely to wake up.

Instead of exclaiming in frustration that that's not enough time to do anything, *use* that time. You may be surprised at what you can accomplish in five to ten minutes. You can clean a bathroom fixture, write a note, make a call, or start a bigger project. Chipping away at a big job (like cleaning the basement) one section at a time can make the prospect less daunting and you will feel more efficient.

- Develop your own style. Embrace your talents and quirks. Ask your friends for ideas and trade skills with them. Above all, be tolerant of yourself. You are new at this and you are getting more efficient all the time.

My baby is four months old already; how can I get my thank you notes done?

Thank you notes can be tough to get to with a new baby around, but I think you have several weeks or months before you are considered to be totally ungrateful or rude. People usually understand that as a new mother you don't have a lot of time or the ability to focus on writing a response that adequately reflects the extent of your gratitude or fondness for the giver. Here are some things to consider that might make it easier to get thank yous out of the way sooner.

- When you receive a baby gift or card, put the card in a specific box or bag until you are ready to write the thank you note. Write the date you received the gift and a description of it so you won't forget who gave you what.
- Some women find it easier to write the thank you note the day a gift arrives, while others prefer to do several at a time.

Figure out and do what works for you. You still might need to do several all at once in the beginning, as the bulk of new baby gifts arrive shortly after the birth. Of course, that's when it is hardest to formulate complete sentences, let alone write legibly or coherently, so be kinder with yourself about those early notes.

- Not every thank you note has to be a literary masterpiece. You need only about three or four sentences: "Thank you so much for the thoughtful (fill in the blank, and be specific). We really love it; it fits our (color scheme, taste, baby). We can't wait to (see you, have you meet our baby, use it). We really appreciate your (generosity, humor, thoughtfulness). Love, you." And it's done.

- Buy postage stamps and note cards in bulk (you can even do this over the phone or Internet), and store them with a pen and your address book. Write one a day. Or two. Before you know it, you'll be caught up.

- Have your husband write thank you notes to his side of the family and friends. Seriously.

The people who love you know you're busy. Make sure you at least tell the giver when you receive a gift, so they don't worry it got lost in the new baby shuffle. Take care of yourself and your baby and get to the notes when you can.

Thank you notes do not need to be literary masterpieces.

Paying the bills has become a challenge; what can I do to stay better organized?

Here are six ideas that can make your bookkeeping easier:

- One way to make bill paying easier is to use fewer credit cards. You can easily eliminate several bills a month by using just one of several major credit cards honored in just about every department, grocery, and drugstore as well as at restaurants, hotels, and gas stations around the world. If you consolidate your credit using the one card, it not only results in fewer checks to write each month, but also allows easier monitoring of your spending habits. If you have one of the airline mileage cards, you get the added bonus of accumulating extra miles every time you spend. If you do make all of your purchases with a credit card, *don't buy anything you wouldn't buy otherwise, and be sure to pay off the entire amount each month.* Otherwise, the often-astronomical interest charges on any unpaid balance will be far worse than any late fees.

- Some bills can be automatically charged to your credit card. Newspaper subscriptions, some utilities, some Internet servers, and other monthly payments then get added to your major credit card. One check allows you to pay many bills at once, and again, be sure to pay off the entire balance each month or it will end up costing you a lot more.

- Alternatively, you may choose to use credit cards for absolutely nothing, eliminating some monthly payments altogether. This works well for people who have easy access to cash and who need an external control on their spending. When you pay cash, you know what you've spent on a daily basis.

- If you pay for many purchases by personal check, deduct the amount of each purchase immediately to be sure you have sufficient funds. Keep your record of deposits and withdrawals constantly up to date for the same reason. Bounced checks can be as costly as late fees.

- Some regular bills can be paid automatically from your checking account. Often utility companies, mortgage lenders, and some other companies with monthly billing will, with your authorization, automatically deduct what they are owed. Just as some employers allow for automatic check deposit (also a great idea, as the money may go into your account faster, especially if you don't get around to depositing your paper check immediately), these companies pay themselves from your account. Check each of your monthly bills for automatic payment set up. Each automated payment is one less for you to think about.

- If you don't like to have the bills pile up, keep your checkbook, some envelopes, and stamps in an accessible spot, and pay your bills as they arrive. The advantage of this method is that you don't have to be organized enough to keep track of them all until you are ready to pay, or remember which are due when. The disadvantage is that you lose some of the interest accrued in some accounts over those several days between when you are sending out the checks and when they are actually due. (Of course, you could write out the checks and hold them until you need to put them in the mail, but that involves thinking ahead.)

- If you prefer to pay your bills less often, or if you worry that you will misplace a bill waiting until check-writing day, try what Mandy did. With a few phone calls, you can generally arrange to have all your bills due at the same time each month.

Just contact the creditor and ask firmly for a payment due date of the first (or fifteenth or thirtieth, whatever) of the month. Then, when the bills arrive, you put them immediately into a file or folder or drawer designated for currently due bills. Seven to ten days before they are due, depending on the mail where you live and your anxiety level, you pull everything out, along with your calculator, stamps, and checkbook, and you sit there until you are finished. File the receipts and you're done for the month.

When you've gotten into the habit of paying the way that works best for you, you will have less anxiety, fewer late payments, and more time. Maybe you can use the extra time and money to go out.

Are there things I should be doing that I might not know about?

Four things come to mind that new parents don't always think about when a new baby is born:

- If you have health insurance, your baby needs to be added to your policy. Sometimes this can be done by telephone or over the Internet, but to receive coverage, it must be done, and often there is a time limit within which to do it. Call your employer or your insurer to find out how to proceed.
- Request a couple of official copies of your baby's birth certificate. Your baby's birth is generally registered in the county in which he was born, at the Bureau of Vital Statistics, and each official copy costs a few dollars. Your baby's birth certificate is

required to apply for a passport (and even babies need passports to travel out of the country), to enter school, and for many other legal or financial matters. Note that when the official copy is necessary, a photocopy of the official one won't do, so ask for a few and keep them in a safe place.

- If you didn't apply for a social security number and card for your baby when you delivered, do it now. In order to declare your baby as a dependent for tax purposes, you need a social security number. You can request an application in person at your local social security administration office; you may request an application by telephone and submit it through the mail; or you can apply online at www.ssa.com.

- If you have a will, update it, and if not, it's time to create one. You and your husband should consider who you would like to become your child's guardian if anything should happen to you, and make sure the people you designate are willing.

Although I know you don't really want more to do, these suggestions will save time, money, and aggravation in the future.

I can't seem to keep up with all the stuff we need in our house; we're always running out of something. How can I become a better "supply clerk"?

Whenever storage space and money permit, buy in bulk, especially when bulk prices are better. Make a list of all your household staples. A typical list will look something like this:

- Dry goods: toilet paper, paper towels, dishwashing soap, laundry soap, toothpaste, deodorant, diapers
- Non-perishable groceries: flour, sugar, cereals, frozen and canned foods, rice, pasta
- Perishable groceries: milk, juice, bread, fresh fruit, vegetables

Your personal list may also include contact-lens solutions, Tabasco sauce, and frozen waffles, but the idea is to know what you use on a regular basis and to buy often-used items and non-perishables in bulk whenever possible, before you run out of an essential. Check prices. Occasionally, the family sized, thirty-two-ounce container actually costs more than two sixteen-ounce boxes of the same item. But buying in bulk should lead you to fewer shopping trips and a few pennies saved as well.

A note of caution: don't buy too much of an item that your baby will outgrow (newborn diapers, for example) or that you will become sick of before you can use it all up. Check your supplies before you go shopping, and keep a running list of what you need so you don't have to rely on your sleep-deprived memory. And consider having things delivered, especially in the middle of a storm. A well-designed shopping list, storage space in the basement, the Internet, and a credit card make a frazzled new mother's life more livable.

I miss the order my days used to have. What can I do to create some of that structure again?

Look for structure in your baby's spontaneity; your baby probably already has a little routine going, and you are his designated assistant. When your baby is tired, you recognize his signals and help him calm down enough to nap. When he is hungry, you feed him, and so on. The structure is there; it is just quite a bit looser and less predictable than you are used to—it is very soft and flexible, like your baby. You may come to depend on patterns in your baby's behavior, which then disappear as quickly as you've identified them, but that doesn't mean you were wrong. It means your baby is growing and changing again. But you will continue to discover and develop patterns in the pandemonium.

Jane, a first-time mother who missed the structure and excitement of her job as a nurse, started writing down in a notebook what she did all day. When she looked at her daily logs after a week of baby care, she felt a whole lot better; she had not even been aware that her baby was on a schedule of sorts. Once she recognized that her baby napped every morning and every afternoon at nearly the same time, and that she had spent literally hours a day involved in breast-feeding and dia-per changing, she felt reassured that she was spending her time more wisely and well. And she was better able to find time to herself once she recognized that there was some predictability to her day.

Some mothers introduce a schedule to their babies earlier than oth-ers, insisting on naps at a designated time, working hard to establish a predictable and organized pattern of feeding, sleeping, and playing. You can certainly try to get your baby to sleep and eat according to a schedule, but be aware that while some babies respond well to such routines, others resist even the most insistent mother's attempts. Your baby will let you know how much structure works for her; if her resistance is strenuous, you may need to wait a little longer before a schedule will be tolerated.

Until your baby is ready to agree with your idea of how to spend the day together, you may have some adjusting to do. If you always enjoyed structure, living with a baby can feel like you're being shaken out of a comfortable routine. But take comfort in the knowledge that your baby will be this demanding, needy, and unstructured for a relatively short time. True, you may now have nothing more tangible to show for how you spent your day than piles of dirty diapers, toys, and laundry, but these are extremely important "accomplishments" for you and your baby. Your best bet is to try to get used to the ebb and flow of living from need-to-need instead of from project-to-project, and to get used to the fact that your schedule will be more changeable for awhile.

When you are living with an infant, life is really just a series of interruptions.

Sometimes when I'm on the phone or immersed in some project, my baby clamors for my attention. How can I keep her happily occupied for just another ten or twenty minutes?

After the first several weeks, as harsh as this may sound, it is at least partially up to you, not your baby, to decide what is important and necessary, what to attend to immediately, and whether it is the baby or the project that can wait. Of course you must drop everything for a baby in pain, distress, or danger, but when your baby is just sitting next to you, you decide whether or not to go to her. You must learn to assess the baby's needs effectively and how to help your baby amuse herself so you can happily accomplish all that you each want to do.

Some babies are peaceful from a very early age simply watching you take care of business, but others need to mature a bit before they are willing or able to entertain themselves for more than a couple of minutes. Many babies aren't able to sit contentedly until they have some head and hand control so they can manipulate toys, observe your every move, or just admire their own body parts and ability to wiggle. If your baby is still very young, your wish for her to develop more patience may not be realistic. You may simply need to wait a few more weeks for her capacity for solitude to catch up to your needs.

Once your baby is old enough to be content for brief periods of time without your active involvement, you can try a few tricks to keep her amused a bit longer. (Of course, if you are the only adult in the house, she must always be in a safe place, preferably within view as well as earshot of you.)

- Use the Ten Minute Rule. Often, if you devote your full attention to your baby for about ten minutes, she will then be content to stare at her toes or watch you work for half an hour or more. Playing with her *before* starting that project, giving her your full attention, may stretch the time until she again falls apart from missing you. A snuggle in time saves whine.

- Have designated toys for special situations. Marla has a bag of specifically designated "telephone toys"; when she is on a phone conference, out come those telephone toys. Her baby actually looks forward to playing with them, and she is able to complete her call in peace. These toys should have high appeal, be totally safe and intended for solitary use, and, to remain special, should not be available to your baby except when you want to keep your baby occupied. You will need to change the toys as your baby matures or if they no longer seem novel.

- Whenever possible, talk to your baby while you work. Babies often experience your talking to them as involvement enough. You can read to her from the document you are composing or describe in detail the blue-and-white plate with the bubbly soap. Not only will your baby know you are very interested in her, but you are also helping her develop language skills, identify colors, and enjoy your artful conversation.

- ❧ Hire a sitter or call a friend or relative when you absolutely must finish something within a limited period of time. Even the most cooperative baby has days when she needs to be held or played with, and it is unreasonable and frustrating to you both to try to get through those days without help.

You will learn what works for you and your baby. It is good to teach your baby as soon as she can understand that your work (or life) is important, too, and though you love her very much, you can't always entertain her. Be attentive to her needs and she will eventually be able to let you attend to yours. In time, she will become more self-sufficient and you will get more done.

If you give a fussy baby or toddler your full attention for about ten minutes, it can often soothe and satisfy her enough to allow her to play calmly near you for half an hour or more.

Ever since my baby was born, I have been late to everything. I used to be so prompt. How can I start being on time again?

Plan ahead and simplify. Before your baby was born, getting out of the house entailed grabbing your keys and purse and closing the door behind you. Now you must get you and your baby ready, pack the baby and any necessary equipment, and sometimes change another diaper or take a feeding break before you can confidently be on your way. Many first-time mothers can barely manage to get out of the house before dinner, and that's largely because they haven't yet streamlined their routines.

If you are taking your baby with you:

- Plan your outings ahead of time, considering the baby's likely nap or feeding times.
- Add at least five to fifteen minutes to your travel time to allow you to pack the baby and all her paraphernalia into and out of the car.
- Schedule meetings or dates for times when your baby is likely to be pleasant.
- Pack your diaper bag the night before, throwing out the stale crackers, updating the size of the extra outfit and diapers.
- Do not carry a separate purse; put your wallet and keys and any other absolute necessities in the diaper bag. You'll have one less thing to lug around and keep track of.

If you are not taking your baby with you:

- Have whoever will be watching your baby take over child care at least fifteen minutes (half an hour if you are the anxious sort) before you have to leave.
- If you are breast-feeding, schedule your date so you have plenty of time to feed the baby and tidy up before you must be on the road.
- Organize your baby's things and your purse an hour or more before handing the baby over to the baby-sitter so you can give the sitter a baby update and say bye-bye to your baby.

Whether or not you bring your baby:

- ❀ Suggest a fifteen- or twenty-minute span as the meeting time, as in "I'll be at the north door between 1:00 and 1:15," and then aim to arrive at the earlier time.
- ❀ Plan your route, what you are going to bring with you, etc, at least hours in advance of the outing, writing things down if that helps.
- ❀ Don't plan activities in which promptness is essential.
- ❀ When a precise arrival time is important, plan to get there at least fifteen minutes ahead. If you really do show up early, you can relax, grab a cup of coffee, or check your outfit for spit-up. If not, you'll be on time.

Until everything in your life becomes more predictable and controllable again, you have to rethink what it takes to get you and your baby ready to go. You are still trying to figure out what equipment to bring, and how to organize and carry it all; it's easy to forget just how long it can take to load everything into the car and include that preparation time as part of the travel time. Relax your standards! A few minutes off really won't matter in the grand scheme of things.

Taking the baby out is such a big production. Does this get better?

In a word, yes. It will get better if you let it. That means two important changes may need to take place. First, you must get more efficient and reasonable about what baby items are true necessities and second, you must be more realistic about your baby's behavior.

Some new mothers believe that they are doing their babies a disservice if they leave the house without every toy and blankie in tow. When you are going to the grocery store, do you *really* need Jason's favorite rattle, three pacifiers, five extra diapers, and his rubber bath duck? Probably not. Some outings, like a day-long trip to the zoo, do require snacks, reserve outfits, and diapers, but others clearly do not. You aren't a better mother if you are overprepared, especially if it makes you cranky.

If it's your baby's potential crankiness that's a deterrent to getting out and about, there are ways to avoid this problem, too. First, and this is good advice for the rest of your parenting years, don't expect perfect behavior. All babies cry and fuss, and although you are falsely convinced that nobody else's baby sounds as loud as yours does, other people aren't as upset about this as you might be. Second, you aren't a failure as a mother if your baby cries in public. A little baby doesn't know she's not supposed to be fussing while out and about; she's just expressing herself.

To avoid feeling overwhelmed by all the anxiety of going out with your baby:

- ❧ Follow the suggestions above for getting places on time with your baby along.
- ❧ Pay particular attention to the suggestion to plan outings for when you can reasonably expect your baby to be peaceful.
- ❧ Don't plan more errands or events in one excursion than you or your baby will enjoy.
- ❧ Plan your errands or outings with geography in mind. If you can do all your errands in one mall, eliminating the need for frequent buckling and unbuckling of car seats, for example, you will have an easier time.

- Use drive-through, mail, and Internet purchasing, and home delivery whenever possible.
- Pay attention to other mothers with babies out in public. You'll notice that babies do cry and fuss in public, and then you won't feel as bad about your own.
- When your baby falls apart in public, which she will, do as other great mothers do. Nurse your baby at the park or in the shop's bathroom. Leave the store, shopping unfinished, if necessary, to calm your screaming baby, or try to soothe him by interrupting the errand and talking softly or holding him until peace is regained. Your baby isn't trying to ruin your day, so attend to his needs and then get back to your own.

As your skills as a mother increase, your anxiety will decrease, and taking your baby out will be more fun. You may not get everything done that you had planned, especially with very new babies, but what you accomplish will have been more enjoyable for you both.

How can I take care of the baby, do household chores and errands, and otherwise take care of my family's needs without feeling so bored and lonely?

Some women alleviate their loneliness and boredom by pooling their resources. If you have a friend or neighbor who's also a mom, you have the potential for a "broom and mop (or errand) club." Pick one day a week, or more if you and your friend and kids are especially compatible, and get together to do your chores. Both moms work at one house one time, the other home next time. The tasks get done, and you and your baby each have a social event as well.

Plan to do errands together as well. One of you runs into the bank or the cleaners while the other mom stays in the car to amuse and safeguard the children. This allows you to minimize getting your baby in and out of the car, which slows down your efficiency, and which both mothers and babies find annoying although necessary. Again, both you and your baby have a play date, and errand running is more productive and less tedious.

You might think about swapping services or bartering with a neighbor or friend. If you love to cook but hate to clean, offer meals to your buddy who is a whiz with a scrub brush. If you are good with finances and organizing papers, trade time helping your friend sift through her paperwork for her skills with gardening. Again, this relieves you from doing what you either loathe or have no talent for while gaining some much-needed socializing and the opportunity to share your skills.

As much as you adore your baby, the chores that sometimes accompany child care can be monotonous and solitary. It's a challenge to find emotional gratification or intellectual stimulation when you're folding laundry for the eighteenth time that week. So find a friend or neighbor; discover creative ways to increase your time with what you enjoy and decrease time spent on the mundane. You will achieve increased efficiency and decreased boredom. Not a bad deal.

Some days I'm so busy I forget to interact with my baby. Is there a way I can be engaged with my baby while also accomplishing some other tasks?

Sure thing. You can be engaged with your baby without being constantly joined at the hip. For example, while you are working on something that keeps your hands busy but your baby nearby, keep a running monologue going. Your baby loves to hear your voice, and the chatter keeps you connected. Studies show that babies whose mothers talk to them develop better speech than those whose mothers do not. Your baby is not picky about the topic. Tell him your innermost thoughts, describe what you are doing, describe what he is doing. Keep talking to him.

If you are musically inclined, sing to him or play music while you work. Your baby won't care if you play Led Zeppelin, Beethoven, or polka music. But he will be enriched by it, and you can expand each other's taste by starting when your baby's young. You don't have to listen to baby music just because he's a baby.

Dance with him, and learn to do things one-handed. Your baby is a baby for a very brief time. If you take care of business less than perfectly, it will probably be all right. Cart him around in a sling or soft baby carrier whenever possible, or move him and his favorite perch (infant seat, stroller, swing) from room to room as you go.

Set a timer or alarm clock to go off every hour or two. Use that as a reminder that you need to spend time directly interacting with your baby. Sing to your baby; tickle him; play a game together. Let everything else go for ten to fifteen minutes and enjoy each other.

Buy, borrow, or check out of the library song and game books and videos or DVDs for babies if you're at a total loss for ideas about how to play with your baby. Many adults become parents without ever having any previous experience with a baby. Ask your friends what they do with their babies; watch a children's television show together; take your baby to a museum or on a walk. You may be forgetting to interact because you don't know what to do. Once you know what you and your baby can enjoy together and you've become a bit more at ease with your other responsibilities, your interaction will be fine.

Babies need physical and emotional comfort, nutrition, cleanliness, sleep, and social interaction. So do parents. It is up to you to decide how to get everyone's needs, including your own, met.

Good mothers are supposed to be able to get healthy meals on the table, but so far, frozen dinners are the best I can do. Is there a better way?

At this point in your life, there is nothing wrong with frozen meals, fast food, or peanut butter on a spoon, for that matter. But there are other, slightly more appetizing and nutritious ways to get a meal out without too much effort or skill.

If you would prefer a home-cooked meal occasionally, even if that means you are the one doing the cooking, here are some ideas that can save you time and still turn out as something presentable. Keep in mind that you don't need to be a gourmet chef to be a good mother or to set a lovely table.

When you feel like cooking, several types of entrees serve new mothers well. What you need are dishes that allow for much of the time-consuming preparation to be done hours or even days ahead so the final few minutes can be done when Dad is home to entertain the baby.

- Stir-fries are quick to put together once everything is cut up, and if you're really pressed for time, you can use precut vegetables, fresh or frozen, from the grocery store. If you use meat, cut it into bite-sized pieces, marinate it if you want, and cooking time will be minimal. You can do all the preparation during baby's nap time, so the final steps will take just minutes, while your husband plays with the baby. Or he can do it.

- ❧ Jazz up an otherwise dull or repetitive chicken breast or other meat by marinating. Marinades (make your own, use salad dressings, or purchase ready-made marinades) can be used up to twenty-four hours in advance.
- ❧ One-dish meals such as casseroles, soups, stews, or substantial salads work well because they can be assembled whenever you have the time, and the amount of cooking time is very forgiving. You can often purchase parts of the dish already cooked to save even more time and energy.
- ❧ Adding a delicious salad dressing or homemade-style loaf of bread (purchased from your grocer or baker) heightens the interest level of an ordinary meal at a low cost.

All these types of meals can be put together during nap time or any calm moment, or you can do a little at a time if you want.

On days when time, creativity, and energy are scarce, meals can still be gracious:

- ❧ Get out that tablecloth you love but save for special occasions.
- ❧ Use a beautiful serving bowl to present macaroni and cheese from the box.
- ❧ Garnish plain, broiled chops with a lemon wedge or a sprinkling of herbs, paprika, capers, or raisins to add color, flavor, and visual interest.
- ❧ Many packaged foods have embarrassingly easy recipes to make a simple dish more intriguing. You know, a jar of this, a can of that. Try them.

- Take advantage of ready-made, gourmet-style foods at your grocery store. You can put together a whole meal from appetizers to desserts without spending much more than if you made it all yourself, with a lot less effort.
- Whenever you prepare a dish that freezes well, make it in large quantities, freeze extra portions (packaged and labeled), and save them for those days when cooking is beyond you.

Don't forget that leftovers, ordering in, and dishes created by your grocery store or deli are all great, too. Shop online or call for groceries to be delivered if that will help. Remember, Martha Stewart has a full staff, thirty zillion dollars, and doesn't live with a baby, and your value as a mother isn't based on your abilities in the kitchen or dining room.

Already we are up to our knees in adorable photos of our baby. Where should I keep them until I have a chance to organize them into albums?

Many new parents are faced with thousands of great photos but never have the time or energy to organize them. If at all possible, starting now and for the rest of your life as a parent, when you get the photos developed, immediately place them into albums, date them, and include a written caption identifying everyone and everything in the picture. I know, you think that you will never forget the day that hat fell so charmingly over your baby's eyes, but after the next baby or two, you will appreciate having it all in writing.

As technology changes, there are other choices. If you are computer literate and digitally inclined, you can store your photos on a disk. While this can be enormously helpful, not to mention space saving, there are long-term pitfalls. Some people warn that you will still want hard copies of the best photos. In addition, if technology changes dramatically over the years, or your specific system fails, you may not have access to your favorite pictures. So have a backup system, or print at least your favorite snapshots now.

There are great products available to make putting together a baby's photo album special and fun. In some communities, there are photo-album parties, similar to Tupperware parties, to which party-goers (you) bring loose photos in shoeboxes, shopping bags, or moving vans. During the party, an expert helps you put your album together using (and buying) her company's materials. These items also exist separately, available in some craft and department stores as well as at the parties, so if you are self-disciplined and just want those special scalloping scissors, stickers, and acid-free paper, you can put together an album on your own.

If you want to be extremely organized, you will also get into the habit of keeping extra photographs and all negatives in a file, with names, dates, and places labeled. These are habits it would be useful to develop when your first baby is very young. The older your baby is, and especially if you ever have more children, the harder it is to keep up. With a little bit of effort, though, you could have beautiful, organized photographic records of your child's life.

How can I respond politely to unwanted suggestions?

There are a number of polite ways of responding to unwanted advice. Hannah, who says her loving mother-in-law has criticized or corrected every move she's made since her baby was born, has an arsenal to share. "Thanks, I'll have to consider that," or, "That's an interesting thought," she'll say sweetly. "I'll talk it over with my husband," and, "What a great idea—I hadn't thought of that before," have also served her well. Another young mother's favorite reply is "My doctor says we need to do things this way for now, but thanks so much for the idea."

The beauty of these responses is they inform the self-appointed consultant that you have heard her, appreciated her input, and will think about her suggestion. You sound confident and pleasant, and you're able to hear it when occasionally someone offers a truly useful tip. Of course, you don't need to mention that later, if the advice or advisor was particularly ridiculous, critical, or annoying, you'll be laughing hysterically or complaining bitterly about her comments.

Unwanted advice is hard to hear at this stage of your life because you don't yet have a lot of confidence as a mother. The most useful advice about getting unwelcome advice is to be willing to listen to (and when appropriate, either take or ignore) any and all advice. At best, a suggestion may help you solve a problem, at worst, it can make you doubt your ability as a mother. Chances are you weren't an idiot before you became a mother, so you are probably aren't one now, although you may occasionally feel like one. In motherhood as in life, there are many ways to handle most situations. The trick is to keep your defensiveness at bay long enough to listen to the recommendation and use your own judgement to figure out whether this particular offering will help. Be pleasant when offered advice, consider both the suggestion and the source, and trust yourself to do what is right.

Remember, opinions are neither right nor wrong, they are just opinions.

Chapter Four

Balancing Work and Home

⌒

When you have a baby, you have lots of new choices to consider, and no one can know what is right for you but you. You want to be a good mother, but it's not always clear what that means. Whether or not to work outside your home, how many hours, who should take care of your baby while you're gone, how to come to terms with your choice, recognizing that society doesn't always support your choice, and knowing when you need to change plans are all difficult decisions to make. Often decisions about work need to be made soon after you've given birth, and just as often, you might not yet know what will really work for you.

New mothers often feel pressure from their husbands, from their mothers, from their friends, and from their workplace to know what they want and to be decisive, and they expect themselves to be unconflicted about their decisions. Some women, who were sure before their babies were born that they would never go back to work, find themselves longing to return to a satisfying career. Others who anticipated being bored with caring for their babies realize that they love being at home and dread the idea of leaving the baby for work. Still others take advantage of the break from work to reassess their career plans and consider changing professions.

No matter how certain you may have been before your baby was born how motherhood and a career would be balanced for you, when you hold your baby in your arms, or your paychecks stop, or you investigate day-care options, choices that seemed clear while you were pregnant begin to get complicated. Questions arise that never occurred to you, and trusted coworkers, bosses, and friends react in unexpected ways. Although many women feel blessed to have so many options, and while it is decidedly better that these days, whether you work outside the home or not, you will find respect and like-minded women, choosing is still often difficult. This chapter examines the work-life questions that new mothers face and offers a variety of ways to help you think about the choices you have, and come to terms with your decisions.

You cannot judge how "good" or "bad" a mother is by looking only at specific facts, such as does she nurse her baby, is she working outside the home, or is she a good cook.

I don't *have* to work outside the home, and I'm not sure if I want to or not. How can I decide what's best for my family and me?

You're lucky to be able to make a choice about working or staying home, although having that choice can be difficult, too. To decide if being employed outside the home is right for you, you need to understand what it is about working that appeals to you, what individual and family needs you hope to fill, and how well you juggle conflicting roles and demands. This is an extremely personal decision that no one can make but you; the goal is to find the balance between work and motherhood that best suits you.

First, figure out what employment offers you that staying home doesn't. If you have taken time off work to care for your baby, you are probably already aware of some of the aspects you miss about working outside your home. Do you miss:

- Having a sense of control and accomplishment from working a job with clearly defined time lines and goals?
- Feeling efficient and knowledgeable?
- Working on tasks with specific and concrete goals?
- Wearing makeup and nice clothes?
- Going out to lunch with colleagues?
- Getting out of the house regularly?
- Frequent adult conversation and/or intellectual stimulation?
- Having a clearly defined and active professional identity?
- Receiving a paycheck?
- Clear, objective, and expressed appreciation for what you do?

Once you figure out what you miss about working away from home, consider which of those needs may be met only by being employed. For example, if contributing to your family financially is important to you, not just for the money's sake, but for your own emotional well-being, then you need to find a way to bring in some cash. Similarly, if you miss contact with colleagues or the specific stimulations of your profession, you need your job.

Next, examine what you can do while at home. Intellectual excitement, social connections, and professional development may all be attained through involvement in volunteerism, study groups, conference attendance, the Internet, or trade publications. Home crafts may help you achieve the satisfaction of project completion as will attending adult education classes or following a favored hobby.

Answering these questions honestly and thoughtfully should lead you to your answer to the work vs. stay-at-home dilemma. Use your assessment of your temperament and needs to determine if working outside the home might enhance your life. Try not to be influenced by your friends' or neighbors' preferences; be true to your own desires. Working outside the home maintains some women's sanity while it strains other women's. Take your time, and make an informed and carefully considered decision. But don't forget that you can change your mind if you discover that what you have chosen doesn't suit you. Appreciate the luxury you have in being able to make a choice, and good luck.

Few decisions need to be forever; few choices are irreversible. You can almost always change your mind.

How can I choose between part-time work and full-time work?

There are five things to consider when making the choice between part-time and full-time employment:

- Do you have the financial flexibility to work as much or as little as you like? Some families really need both parents to work full-time to make ends meet, while others can get by on the reduced income. And some women's income is low enough that, when the extra costs of working are calculated, the financial benefit to the family is negligible. If you are working strictly for personal fulfillment, the number of hours you work per week can then be based on personal preference, keeping in mind the next four points.

- Do you have the temperament to work full-time with a baby at home, or would you be happier working fewer hours? Some women want to be home with their babies as much as possible, some like to work a day or two a week, but others need more work outside the home to feel content.

- Some careers and work situations lend themselves to part-time employment more easily than others. If working part-time requires you to give up potential promotions, for example, or if you are in a job that demands you specifically be there full-time, part-time may not be an option. On a positive note, employers are becoming more accepting of part-time, flex-time (adjusting hours to suit your needs), or even job-sharing, so be creative and discuss with your employer what options are available to you.

- Health and child-care benefits often depend upon your full- or part-time status. If your husband's benefits are adequate for your family, you won't need to rely on your employer to provide them. Many companies require a minimum number of hours worked per week by an employee (often in the range of thirty to thirty-five hours) to receive any benefits, including pay for vacation, holidays, or sick days. Be sure to consider your family's needs for benefits and your employer's policies.

✒ Lastly, you need to consider your child-care options. Unless you have a reliable and loving relative or friend who is willing and able to baby-sit as much or as little as you want (and most women don't), you will need to find good child care. Some day-care centers and family day-care providers welcome part-timers, but many require you to pay for full-time care regardless of how many hours you use them. Professional nannies also often insist on full-time work, but many people who baby-sit in families' homes are delighted to find part-time situations or are willing to be "shared" by two or more families with part-time needs. Find out what child-care opportunities are available to you in your community.

Once you figure out your answers to the above questions, it should be clearer to you what balance between work and home will be best for you. Be honest with yourself, your husband, and your employer about what you want and need, and you will figure it out.

I'd like to work from my home. Is that feasible?

Working from home is a godsend for some people and a mess for others. Yvonne loved the freedom of working from home, not having to dress up, and being able to adjust her schedule to meet her baby's needs. But Justine found that she hated it. Her supervisor seemed to want more proof of the hours she worked, she missed her colleagues, and she found herself constantly distracted by her baby.

To sort out whether or not working from home will meet your needs, you must find out what your employer's attitudes and policies are about employees working from home:

- Find out if your employer allows your job, or parts of your job, to be done from home.
- Ask about flexibility of hours. Must you work specific hours and days, or can you adjust your schedule according to your personal preferences or family demands?
- Will your lack of visibility in the workplace affect your ability to move ahead?
- Will there be meetings or times when you will be required to show up at your workplace, how often might this occur, and how much advance notice will you have?
- Will your company be supplying you with all the equipment (computer, fax machine, telephone line, etc.) and technical support you need, or are you expected to use your own?
- How easy will it be to get professional or technical support when you need it?
- Will additional computer security be necessary to allow you to work from home, and who will be responsible for providing that?
- How will your work be monitored?
- Will your health and child-care benefits remain unchanged?
- If other workers in your company have worked from home in the past, talk with them and find out how well it worked for them, both professionally and personally.

You also should assess how well you and your family will adapt to such an arrangement:

- Will you need to have child care (most people do), or can you adjust your work around your baby's needs?
- If you have child care in your home, will you be able to focus on your work if you hear your baby cry?

- Many women feel it is essential to have a separate room that is dedicated to work and has a door that can be closed. Do you have a space where whatever equipment you need can be set up and you can work uninterrupted?
- Will you miss seeing colleagues and clients on a regular basis?
- Will you be too tempted to play with your baby or to take care of non-work projects during your work time?
- If you work at home while your husband works outside, can you come to an acceptable agreement about who is responsible for housekeeping and family related chores?
- Will working from home make you feel freer or more frazzled?

Knowing as much as you can about both your employer's expectations and your own will lead you to make a choice that succeeds for all concerned. Be honest with yourself about your personal needs, your employer's needs, and your family's needs, and make your decision accordingly.

Working from home is a godsend for some women but a disaster for others.

What are some of the financial considerations I should be thinking about if I go back to work?

As any new parent knows, having a baby involves many expenses, and having a baby when both parents work outside the home involves even more. If you are debating going back to work for strictly financial reasons, there are many things to consider beyond just how much money you bring into the family.

- What are the costs of day care? Unless you use your employer's on-site day care or work at home while your baby is cared for at home, you will pay for more hours of child care per week than you work, as your baby will need to be watched while you commute.
- Most two-income couples spend more money per week on clothing (clothing for work tends to be more expensive than stay-at-home clothes and often requires dry cleaning), meals (lunches out, take-out dinners, or prepared dishes from grocery stores all cost more), and transportation and parking, than couples in which one partner stays at home.
- Two-income families often are in a higher tax bracket than one-income families; two incomes may require that you pay a higher percentage of your income in taxes.
- If you have in-home day care you need to consider the costs of paying taxes and health-care benefits for your caregiver.
- Depending on your agreement, you may pay for child care while you are on vacation or on sick or personal days, regardless of whether or not you get paid or whether or not you use child care on those days.

Some new mothers find that it helps them to justify their working when they recognize that child care and all the other costs are incurred because *both parents* are working; *your* specific income doesn't need to exceed the costs of your working to make your working outside your home make sense. If you want to work for personal fulfillment, future job security, or professional advancement, rather than strictly to increase your spending power, how much money you clear after all these expenses may be irrelevant. Remember that you need child care because you are a family and because neither of you will be home to take care of your baby.

What should I know about health and child-care benefits?

First of all, be sure to enroll your baby in your health-care plan as soon as possible after delivery. Many policies require you to enroll your newborn within the first fifteen or thirty days after birth to receive coverage. It would be a shame, not to mention very expensive, to overlook this relatively simple demand.

Once your baby is covered, you need to know about the specific coverage; you will want to be aware of which expenses are covered, which are not, and which charges require a co-pay. Do you have a deductible and how much is it? Are prescriptions covered? Are well-baby visits included? Will you have to pay out of pocket if your doctor charges fees above the limit set by your insurer? Is there a maximum amount of benefit dollars allowed per year? Are there any special inclusions or exclusions of care?

Health-care coverage varies widely from policy to policy, even within the same company; familiarize yourself with your personal insurance plan. Be sure to ask for details so you aren't caught by surprise as Melody was. She had been assured that well-child care was covered, and it was. However, she didn't know until too late that routine inoculations were only covered up to a limited amount, after which all charges must be paid out of pocket. Needless to say, even with a healthy baby, Melody's expenses reached the limit before the baby was six months old, so she had to pay for several vaccinations unexpectedly.

Many benefit plans offer flexible spending accounts for medical expenses, which can be wonderful with a new baby in the house. This benefit sets aside a predetermined amount of pre-tax income, which is then reimbursed to you for out-of-pocket medical expenses. Co-payments for medications and doctors' visits, as well eye care and dental fees, are generally included. Most of the time you choose the amount you want put into your flex account, so calculate how much you are likely to spend. Call your pediatrician and ask what their usual protocol of visits and inoculations might involve. In figuring out your annual total of likely out-of-pocket medical expenses, remember to add on whatever you might expect to pay for all co-pays, doctors' visits, and prescription drugs.

Also ask about day-care coverage. Some health-care plans offer flexible spending accounts for day-care services. These expenses may be covered only when both parents work a specific number of hours per week, but, again, using non-taxable income to pay for a large expense like day care can save you money.

Benefits are often linked to full-time employment status, so be sure to keep that in mind if you are considering cutting back your hours at work. If both you and your husband have health or child-care benefits, look into which package has the better coverage. Knowing what your health-care benefits are can help you make good financial decisions, get the medical care your family needs, and might even influence your decisions about how much each of you will work.

Should I be thinking about any particular career-track issues?

Not that many years ago, women who wanted to work only part-time often struggled to find acceptable positions, and women who didn't devote themselves fully to their careers justifiably feared earning less, being passed over for promotions, or both. Although employers respect women who return to work after having a baby more now than in the past, allowing for more advancement from part-time positions, job-sharing, flex-time, and the like, there are still career-track considerations to keep in mind as you sort out your plans to return to work.

- What are your company's policies? In general, though not always, female-dominated professions and companies are more accommodating to working parents. Examine both the written statements and the day-to-day realities of how your employer supports or thwarts families in the work place. For example, some companies say formally that they do not allow full-time workers to switch to part-time, yet are known to bend the rules for valued employees who become new parents.
- Ask both administrators and coworkers how the company responds to requests for time off to care for a sick baby, to leaving work early for emergencies, or to the needs of breast-feeding women.
- Find out if workers have been passed over for promotions when child-care issues have come up in the workplace.
- Assess your specific job. If you feel that your company or current job description now demands more than you are willing to give, you may want to think about changing the company for which you work, your position within the company, or reevaluating your plans for advancement.
- How flexible is your family situation? For example, if your baby were suddenly to need a parent at home, can either your husband's or your work schedule accommodate emergencies? Is there a relative or close friend nearby who could come in to

help out in a pinch? Don't assume that it must be the mother who must deal with child-care problems when the father, grandmother, or brother-in-law might be able to step in more easily. Tell your employer if your husband will be the child-care backup parent.

- ❧ If you do need to leave work more often or earlier than before you became a mother, find out if you can work from home or make up the hours later. Again, different employers have different abilities to tolerate your new responsibilities at home.
- ❧ If you want to move ahead in your organization tell your supervisor and ask what steps you need to take to do so.

If career advancement is important to you, you need to evaluate all of these variables. Some occupations are simply more conducive than others to balancing work and motherhood according to your own personal needs, and it is reasonable to change companies, job title, or even professions if doing so will help you achieve the level of involvement and satisfaction in each area of your life that you want. Many mothers have been able to go back to work, move ahead professionally, and continue to manage everything at home successfully, too.

Will my coworkers and boss take me as seriously now that I am a mother?

When you take yourself seriously at work your coworkers and boss will take you seriously. Unless your workplace is known to be extremely mother- and baby-friendly, assume that while at work you need to conduct yourself as professionally as you did before you became a mother. Keep your home-life at home and your work-life at work if you want to maintain a strong professional presence while on the job.

This does not mean that you should never mention your baby to your best friend at work, nor do you have to hide photos of your baby if everyone else proudly displays their family snapshots. When on a break, of course you are allowed to talk about your baby, ask other parents for advice, call your baby-sitter, or even take a quick nap. But when you are supposed to be working, if you want to be taken seriously now that you have a baby, you must continue to be a good worker. To be a good worker:

- Be on time and stay for your entire shift.
- Do your work promptly, efficiently, and well.
- Do not complain about being tired or overwhelmed to anyone at work except your most trusted and trustworthy friend.
- Dress appropriately. If none of your pre-pregnancy clothes fit yet, buy at least a couple of pieces that make you look and feel professional.
- Attend all required staff meetings, even if you are one of hundreds of employees, to show that you are serious about your job.
- Keep emergencies to an absolute minimum by planning ahead and having a backup. Know in advance who can take care of your baby at the last minute if your sitter becomes ill and alternate with your husband who attends to at-home conflicts to minimize your time away from work.
- If there *is* an emergency at home that interferes with your job, tell your employer immediately, solve the problem, come back to work, and let your boss know that the problem has been solved.
- Pay attention to the culture of your particular workplace. If

workers never call home while working, then don't you call either, except on your breaks. And limit calls *from* home to emergencies only.

When you show your commitment to being a good worker, your employer and coworkers will appreciate you and respect your work, regardless of whether or not you have a baby.

If you take your work seriously, you will be taken seriously at work.

Both my husband and I will be working full-time. How can I decide between the various types of day care?

There are many different child-care situations available, and each type works well for some families. You need to figure out what you want and what you need. Consider whether you want your baby to be cared for in or out of your home; there are advantages to each.

If the baby is cared for in your home:

- Your baby will receive more individualized attention.
- Some baby-sitters or nannies are willing to do light housekeeping, prepare meals for the family, or run errands when they have the time.
- When your baby is sick, most in-home caregivers will still take care of him.
- Most caregivers will adapt their work hours to yours.

- You don't need to transport the baby or his paraphernalia to day care.
- The baby will be in a familiar setting.
- Usually the baby and caregiver develop a very warm bond.
- There is little exposure to others' illnesses.

If the baby is cared for outside your home:

- No one will be at home during the day to create more mess.
- A different environment may offer a variety of stimulation.
- Day care outside your own home is usually less expensive.
- Your home remains private.
- Caregivers are usually trained, licensed, and experienced.
- Babies can socialize with other babies and children.
- If the caregiver becomes ill, she generally provides a substitute to care for your baby.
- You don't need to worry about paying taxes or providing health-care benefits for day-care centers or family day-care homes.

Often what's most important about this choice is what's available and how you feel. A well-run, cheerful day-care center may be much better than a mediocre nanny. If one setting or situation seems right to you, it probably is.

I've decided I want in-home child care. What should I be looking for?

Fortunately, there are wonderful people who want to take care of young children. You just have to know what you are looking for and where to look. In general, an in-home caregiver falls into one of three categories: a friend or relative of the baby, an individual who baby-sits for a living, and a formally trained nanny, often registered with a nanny service. Most of these caregivers live separately, but some families enjoy live-in care.

Some new mothers prefer to have a close relative or friend care for their babies; they feel more comfortable that the person is well-known to the family and likely loves the baby already. With a relative or close friend, it is essential that both the mother and the sitter feel they can be honest with each other about their distinct roles, the expectations each has about the position and responsibilities, their attitudes toward discipline, eating, and sleeping habits, and how to handle disagreements. They should be able to treat the position as a real job, whether or not pay is involved.

Other new mothers prefer to hire someone so they feel no qualms about telling the sitter exactly what to do and how to do it and don't have to worry about hurt feelings or differences of opinion. If this is your choice, you can find reliable child care for your baby by checking your local newspaper ads and college bulletin boards, calling nearby churches or synagogues for referrals, or checking out nanny services in the phone book. In addition, ask friends and neighbors if they know anyone looking for a child-care job; word of mouth is often the best way to find highly recommended child care.

Live-in caregivers may fall into any of the above categories. In addition, some college students choose to live in a family's home, exchanging child-care services for room and board. Some nannies and au pairs will live in as well; the financial arrangements for a nanny or au pair often include a weekly salary in addition to room and board. Consider your need for privacy, the setup of your home, and talk with

other mothers in your community or with a nanny or au pair placement service to see if this situation would work for you.

Ideally, you will find several possible caregivers for your baby, and
you will need to meet at least a few in person to find the one that's
right for you. Once you have a few prospective candidates in mind,
you need to interview them, even if one is a friend or relative. If you
don't already know, make sure you find out the following:

- How much experience has the caregiver had, and with what
  age groups?
- How long was she in her previous position and why did she leave?
- What other kinds of work has she done?
- What does she enjoy about taking care of babies?
- Does she have a favorite age to care for?
- Does she have training or education in child care?
- Why is she looking for child-care work?
- What are her plans for the future?
- Does she smoke?
- Does she have a valid driver's license? Her own car? If driving
  will be required, will she be using her own car, and does she
  have insurance? Does she need a car seat or can she use yours?
- Has she had CPR and/or first-aid training?
- Does she have any health problems that might affect her work?
- What kinds of things does she like to do with children of vary-
  ing ages?

In addition to the above questions, you'll want to:

- Discuss salary and fees, including whether or not you must pay
  for holidays, vacation, or sick days, and how you will handle

taxes. Nanny services usually determine the financial arrangements, while other sitters may be more willing to negotiate.

- Observe the candidate with your baby and gauge out how well
  you, your husband, and your baby might get along with her.
- Assess her problem-solving ability. Pose hypothetical situations,
  asking such questions as, "What would you do if you took the
  baby out for a walk and got locked out of the house?" "How
  would you handle a baby who won't nap, or won't eat, or who
  cries a lot?"
- Spell out clearly what, if anything, she is expected to do besides
  babycare, such as housekeeping, shopping, laundry, or cooking.
- Make sure you check references, listening to what each former
  employer liked and didn't like about the sitter, keeping in mind
  your different personalities and needs.
- Trust your own instincts. If a person comes highly recommended, but you don't like her, for whatever reason, *don't hire
  her*. If an inexperienced person seems perfect to you, she may be
  the best one for the job. One of our least successful sitters came
  with glowing reports from former employers; for us, she had
  far too little energy and enthusiasm.
- Although many new parents want long-term commitment
  from a caregiver, it may be better to have a fabulous sitter for a
  year than a barely passable sitter for three years.

You must be comfortable and confident about your child care, and
the personality and style of interacting must be compatible with yours.
If you are not satisfied with the people you've found, keep looking, and
if you hire someone who doesn't really satisfy you, be willing to look
for a replacement. You and your baby deserve to have a caregiver you
feel good about and who enriches your life. You can and will find her.

Do what feels right, trust yourself, and you probably won't go wrong.

If I don't want someone in my own home, how can I decide between a day-care center or family day-care home?

If you want to have your baby taken care of outside your home, the decision-making isn't over yet. You now must choose between a family day-care home and a day-care center. In a family day-care home, the caregiver cares for children in her own home. Family day-care homes are supposed to be licensed by the state and must then meet health and safety standards. Often some educational courses and early childhood CPR are required of the providers as well. A family day-care home will generally serve a small number of children, sometimes of varying ages. Generally, they provide necessary equipment, age-appropriate toys, and food.

A day-care center, though, has a larger staff, generally more children (although the baby-teacher ratio remains quite small), and is in a more school-like setting. Because day-care centers have more providers and children, they frequently offer broader opportunities for social and educational development. Equipment, toys, and food are also usually provided, and there is usually a good variety. Day-care centers are generally the least expensive child-care arrangement.

Once you've decided on the type of day care that will work for you, you need to choose the specific person or program:

- Whether you choose a home or a center, get references from both current and former parents and *check them!*
- Discuss charges and fees, including whether or not you must pay for days when your child doesn't attend.
- Ask if sick children are allowed to go to day care, whether or not they are isolated, and under what circumstances you would be called to pick your baby up from day care early.
- Discuss hours and whether or not there are fees for late pick-ups.
- If possible, have your baby spend time in the day-care setting and observe the interaction.
- State your position on smoking, taking your baby out, feeding habits, maintaining a schedule, letting the baby cry, toilet training, or anything else that is important to you.
- Tour the facility. Find out if you can visit during the day or call from work to get an update on your child's day. Make a surprise visit to see what is happening when you are not expected.
- Find out the baby-adult ratio. Often there will be fewer babies than older children per adult.
- In a day-care home, ask what provisions are made for a substitute if the caregiver becomes ill.

Both day-care homes and centers can be excellent. Again, trust your instincts and choose a program that makes you feel confident that your child will be well cared for, safe, and content.

What should I do if my child gets sick while I'm at work?

The answer to this depends on many factors. If you have in-home child care, you should negotiate from the beginning what to do if your child becomes ill. If he has a simple case of the sniffles, it is reasonable to expect your sitter to care for your baby at home, as usual. If a more serious illness or accident occurs, and a parent is needed, the parent with the more flexible schedule or understanding employer should be called first, and he or she can then decide what to do. For example, Alexandra traveled a great deal for her job, so her husband was always the first to be called if their baby became sick.

If you have opted for either a day-care center or family home, there is probably a policy already in place. Generally, children must be fever-free for twenty-four hours to go to day care, so you will need to find a back-up plan on those days that your baby can't go. You will need to find a baby-sitter (or a loving relative, friend, or neighbor) or either you or your husband will need to stay home from work. If you have the sorts of jobs that lend themselves to working from home at least occasionally, ask your employers if you can work from home when there is an emergency.

Fortunately, most new parents and babies make it through the first years with few serious illnesses. Although this is an important concern, if you know in advance whose schedule and work situation is more flexible, and you have a reserve baby-sitter in mind, you, your baby, and your jobs will make it through.

I'm working outside the home full-time. Am I ruining my baby's life?

No, your baby will be fine if you are fine. Babies are resilient and trusting creatures. It's so much more complicated than "To work or not to work." To ruin your baby's life you have to do so much more than simply go to work full-time; you must deny him the physical essentials for living and emotionally break his spirit. Luckily, as long as their own needs are met, babies are pretty accepting and understanding, and a baby's needs are surprisingly straightforward once you get the hang of it. Mothers who work full-time can easily provide well for their babies. No one says the same person must attend to your baby twenty-four hours a day, or that that person has to be you. You may sometimes *want* to be that person, but you and your baby can do nicely even if you aren't the designated full-time nurturer. In fact, your baby might do better with it than you do.

I've found that women who work because they enjoy it and sorely miss their professional lives when they stay at home sometimes have a harder time being certain that they aren't hurting their babies. They feel guilty that they have chosen to work rather than be the one home with the baby full-time. If that's what you're feeling, it is no wonder you feel so bad! It seems to you that by choosing to work, you are intentionally abandoning your baby, or putting him as a low priority. But everyone deserves to spend the bulk of their lives doing what suits them, if at all possible. If you love your work and you are unhappy at home full-time, and if you have good child care, then you might actually be a better mother (as you will be more contented and happy to be with your baby when you are together) if you *do* work.

If you are working strictly for financial reasons, then trust that your decision to work is in his interest as well. If the income from your employment provides a more comfortable life for you and your family, if you clearly love your child, and your child care is excellent, this story has a happy ending. Sometimes women who, without a doubt, must work to keep the family afloat financially have an easier time coming to terms with their decision; if they feel that their working is essential, they may feel some sadness at leaving the baby, but less conflict over the rightness of their choice.

Regardless of why you are working, feeling guilty about it, although common, is neither a requirement nor productive. Studies show that babies who receive good child care when they are not with their mothers do just as well as babies whose mothers stay home with them. Babies who are well cared for do not necessarily, as their mothers usually fear, have trouble figuring out who their real mother is; they do not lag behind their peers in any significant areas; and they do not grow up hating their mothers or having low self-esteem. If they do, you can be reasonably certain that it wasn't the mother's working that caused the problems.

Even mothers deserve to spend the bulk of their lives doing what suits them. If you provide good child care, and are happy yourself, you can work full-time and your baby will have a wonderful life.

How can I have a close bond with my baby if I am working full-time?

With a little time and effort, you can easily maintain a close relationship with your baby while you are working full-time outside your home.

- Show your baby how very much you love him by cuddling him before you leave for work and when you return.
- Make certain that his child care is appropriate to his age and personality (see questions on child care).
- Maximize the time you have with your baby by scheduling

your personal appointments (for example, haircuts, visits with friends, or dental appointments) during your lunch hour.

- ❧ Devote a specific amount of playtime to your baby every day.
- ❧ When you feed your baby, maintain eye contact.
- ❧ If possible, hire a housekeeper or have your child-care provider do light housekeeping so when you are home you can focus on your baby. If not, relax your housekeeping standards a bit, and do what's necessary while your baby is sleeping.
- ❧ When you must do errands on weekends or evenings, take your baby along, and make the chores into family outings.

When you spend time each day enjoying your baby, even if that time is limited, he will have a great life, whether or not you work outside the home. When a baby is well-nurtured, physically and emotionally, he thrives. Relax and accept that your decision to work will not cause your relationship with your baby to suffer. If you understand that your working benefits you and the people you care about, so will your baby.

I'm a full-time, stay-at-home mom. Without work and a paycheck, will I feel unappreciated?

If you have chosen to stay home with your baby full-time because you enjoy it, because you believe that is how you will provide your baby with the best childhood you can, and if those who love you are in support of your decision, you will *feel* appreciated because you will *be* appreciated. Sadly, in our society, personal value seems to be tied to status and income. We don't pay child-care workers or teachers very well, and mothers do not receive paychecks at all. But whether or not you feel valued will be determined by your own attitude toward staying at home, your husband's feelings, and those of your friends and extended family.

Whether you solve the work-home choice by working outside the home full-time, part-time, or not at all, you deserve to feel good about your contribution to your family and to society, and being a stay-at-home mother certainly can be honored and respected. Not every woman has the temperament or opportunity to be a full-time mom. Taking care of a baby full-time is a tremendous responsibility, and one that deserves to be appreciated and honored.

Your appreciation will be shown, though, not in dollars, but in the relationships you develop with your baby and husband, from the satisfaction you get from watching your baby grow, and the belief that staying home with your baby was right for you. You will need to understand that your husband's paycheck is his contribution to your family, your taking care of the children is yours, and both are highly valuable. If you accept your own importance to the family, you will need the external proof less acutely, and you will also be able to ask for reassurance more easily on those inevitable days when you need it.

Not getting paid for what you do doesn't mean you are not appreciated, nor does it mean that what you do isn't important.

Now that I've taken some time off work to be with my baby, I realize that I'd like to change careers. How can I move into a new field?

Taking time off of work and having a new baby leads many new mothers to reevaluate their professional goals. Paula had been trained in business, had worked in hotel management, and had been quite successful, but once she had been home with her new baby for several weeks, she realized that the only thing she missed about her job was the prestige. With more time at home, she rekindled her interest in music, and determined that she would go back to work only if she could find a job that allowed her to exercise her skills on the piano. Within a few months, she found part-time jobs accompanying budding musicians, teaching piano, and playing for dance recitals, and she was happier than she'd been in years.

In order to change careers, you need to know what skills you already have, what skills, education, and experience you might need to acquire, and what the job market is like in your new field.

- Consider what expertise, talents, and interests you have, what jobs hold appeal for you, and how you might get paid for doing what you most enjoy.
- Think about both what you liked and didn't like about your old job. What kinds of occupations will allow you to have what you've always enjoyed while minimizing what you didn't?
- Some positions require training or degrees; if you have the talent but not the credentials, is it possible for you to work as an assistant to get the training you need, or will you have to return to school?
- If you do need advanced training, investigate the opportunities in your community.
- If money is an issue, to eliminate the financial strain, find out if you can continue to work part-time in your old job while getting training for a different line of work.
- Consider doing volunteer work in the kind of place you might ultimately want to be employed. This way you will get some

real experience under your belt and develop contacts and references in your new field of interest, and occasionally, volunteer work can be parlayed into paid work.

Changing careers can be terrifying or thrilling, financially stressful in the beginning, but ultimately rewarding. If you are serious about wanting a change, go for it. Your happiness is important, and your willingness to make changes in your life in a thoughtful way provides a good example for your child.

I work part-time, and I don't have time to chat with my work friends or have access to other mothers. Why don't I feel like I fit into either group?

Even though part-time work can be ideal for a new mom, it can make having a peer group even more complicated. It would seem that you'd have lots in common with both working and stay-at-home moms, and you do. But finding a way to get to know people in each realm can be a challenge. Lynn, who worked in the city but lived in a suburb, also felt that while she belonged to both groups, she had time for neither.

Many part-time arrangements allow little room in the schedule for socializing with colleagues, and because you aren't home as often during the week, signing up for classes or even going for walks with your baby can be tough to manage. Although I have seen enormous progress in recent years in employer accommodation to women who want to pursue careers part-time, women who work part-time typically devote a higher percentage of their working hours to work, sacrificing lunches and "schmooze time" in order to get home to their families. Once home, part-time workers want to focus on their husbands and babies and keeping up with family projects, and have little access to other mothers. If you want to maintain your sanity and both your professional and mothering identities, you have to work harder at each.

- If at all possible, schedule a regular lunch meeting with coworkers you enjoy.
- Join or start a weekly or monthly group at work with the people you like. This could be work related, as in a study group in which you read and discuss trade materials, or something totally social, like a cooking or movie group.
- Join a committee at your office, again, either professionally focused or social, to get to know others better.
- At home, go for walks with your baby in parks, malls, or just in your neighborhood; take your baby to the grocery store or to baby-friendly coffeehouses and strike up conversations with the other mothers. Introduce yourself to other mothers you see in your neighborhood. Be friendly and exchange phone numbers or suggest meeting again if you seem to hit it off.
- Sign up for baby-related classes or organize your own play group. Ask your doctor if you can put up a notice in his/her office to alert potential members, check your local newspaper, and ask at your place of worship or park district if there are programs or groups for new mothers.
- Reconnect with old friends with whom you've lost touch.

If you make an extra effort in both spheres of your life, you will feel more connected to each. You are both a worker and a mother, and you mustn't allow your part-time status in either area to make you feel less a part of either aspect of your life. You belong to both.

I love my baby and I love my job, but when I'm at work, I think about home, and when I'm home, I think about work. What can I do?

In my experience with many new mothers and as a mother myself, I've found that this is an ongoing dilemma. You may be feeling guilty, or you may not have the setup in your life that you really want.

Start out by paying attention to whether you feel the pull equally in each direction. Sometimes that ambivalence is an indication that you're not all that satisfied with either one position or the other. When you're feeling pulled toward your work, for example, ask yourself if it's because being home bores you, because your workload is too heavy to accomplish your tasks in the time allotted, or because work is so exciting for you that you want to be there more. If you miss being home more, would you be happier working fewer hours?

If your work-home balance is not the problem, try to sort out what sours each experience for you. Are you uncomfortable with your child-care arrangement, so you are not letting go of your mother role while at work out of anxiety for your baby? Is your work uninteresting, so your mind wanders? When you're home, are you isolated and lonely? Do you feel uncomfortable or incompetent while taking care of your baby? It's hard to feel fully committed to either activity if you're not suited to it.

Remember that if your work-home choice becomes intolerable, you can change it. Even if you still must work for financial reasons, you might be able to alter the schedule, find a new job, obtain different child care, or work from home.

If your work-home choice is genuinely satisfactory, learn to appreciate what you have. Try to live more in the moment, devoting yourself fully to whichever endeavor you are involved in at the time. Whenever you feel that tug toward your other responsibilities, stop and appreciate where you are; teach yourself to enjoy your work while you are there and enjoy your baby when you're together. Develop confidence (which often comes with experience) that all will be fine both at work and at home.

Accept that some ambivalence and frustration is absolutely normal. Some days and weeks will feel more comfortable than others, sometimes because of situations at work, and other times because you are more adept at switching roles or you've gotten enough sleep. As your baby gets older, he will be more independent and you will know that he can survive without you. You will both become more accustomed to being together and apart.

Become more comfortable with the idea that you cannot be in two or more places at once, nor should you be. Your workplace will manage while you are at home and your baby will thrive while you're at work. If you're a good worker, your boss already knows, and your baby will never mistake the child-care provider for his mother.

Ambivalence is normal. When you're at work, try to focus on work, and when you're at home, focus on home. Practice being in the moment, wherever you are.

Will I be able to continue breast-feeding if I'm working full-time?

The answer is yes. If you are determined, you can find a way to make breast-feeding work for you. Fortunately, many more women are breast-feeding their babies after returning to work, so businesses are becoming more mommy friendly and your wish to pump or store breast milk will meet with less disapproval than in previous years.

Some tips may help:

- You may need to rearrange the feedings per day to early morning, evening, and bedtime. There is no need to limit the number of feedings, just fit them into the time you're with the baby. You can let the baby regulate how often she nurses, and your body will respond to the baby's demand by regulating your milk supply.
- Check with your employer about finding a time and place to pump milk and keep it chilled. If a refrigerator is unavailable, you might be able to bring your own mini-cooler to the workplace.
- If your breasts leak, use breast-feeding shields or pads (bring extra so that you can change them if they get soaked).
- Wear two-piece clothing (not dresses) to facilitate pumping.
- Some mothers prefer to keep their nursing schedule the same seven days a week, (on days off, not nursing the baby during the hours they would normally be at work). On the other hand, nursing as much as possible when you are with your baby encourages bonding, and for many women, the extra closeness is worth any minimal inconvenience. Pumping your breasts while at work at the time you would likely be nursing at home on your off days will help regulate the milk production.
- If your nursing schedule changes dramatically, or if you know you are one of those women who leak often and visibly, give your work wardrobe some extra thought. Wear layers on top

(or keep an extra sweater at work). Many a time, a jacket or vest has kept the telltale wet spots of a leaky nursing employee hidden from view.

If you want to continue nursing your baby, even though you are working full-time, you can and will find a way.

Many working women successfully continue to breast-feed their babies.

My mother doesn't understand the conflict I feel about work vs. motherhood. How can I help her be more supportive?

You might be able to help your mother understand your work-motherhood dilemma better by understanding the options she had when you were a baby. Was she well-educated, but chose to stay home to raise you? Was motherhood always her career plan, or was paid employment her preference? Did your father insist that she work or stay at home? Did she work outside the home? Did she have lots of help? *Ask* your mother what her early adult life was like. Question her opinions about education, work, motherhood, and her role as a woman.

When generations have very different choices available to them, it can be difficult for one to understand the feelings and conflicts of the other. Your mother may be jealous that she didn't have the options that you are struggling with. Women of your mother's and grandmothers' generations lived in a less tolerant social climate; many had to choose between having a family or working, and many felt that they had no choice at all. Engage your mother in a discussion about how women today have a variety of options open to them that she may never have been able to consider.

Help her recognize that, while having a choice is certainly preferable to feeling compelled to live your life to meet some outside expectation, making that choice is often stressful. Let her know that you need her wisdom and support. Recognize that some women of older generations are resentful or envious that their adult daughters have opportunities that weren't possible for them, and others, not too confident that they made the best choices themselves, feel threatened or rejected by their daughters making different life decisions. Open the communication between you and you might get the encouragement that you are seeking. By talking together as two mothers making challenging choices and adjustments, you might become closer as well.

I'm a stay-at-home mother, but I miss my pals from my old job. How can I stay connected to my work friends?

If your decision to stay at home is firm, remaining connected to work friends takes a little effort. To maintain work-related friendships:

- Don't be shy about calling up colleagues to keep up with the latest news.
- Send a birth announcement to your workplace and include a brief but heartfelt note about missing your coworkers.
- Bring your baby to visit the workplace if the job permits.
- Hire a sitter and meet colleagues for lunch or dinner without your baby.
- Invite work friends to your home for a visit.

- Maintain email contact and telephone chats. Ask about important work projects and new developments in the job as well as social events.
- Attend staff events (like holiday parties) when appropriate.

When the context in which your friendships developed changes, the relationship may take extra effort to sustain, but it's worth it.

I plan to return to work in a couple of years; can I keep up my professional skills if I'm staying home?

Of course you can. Try one or more of these suggestions:

- Join or start a group that would focus on your professional interests. When my first baby was born, I joined a study group, which met monthly to discuss social work readings and cases. It kept me reading material related to my job and kept me in contact with other social workers.
- Find or create a newsletter for people in your profession and work on it. Whether you write for it or work on distribution, design, or advertising, you'll stay connected.
- Volunteer for an organization related to your career. A musician could teach music classes at a community center or church. A dentist could work at a free clinic. Volunteering allows you to do good work for people who need it without always requiring regular hours. Often you can even bring your baby along.
- Subscribe to and read pertinent journals and follow media coverage of topics related to your career.

- Attend conferences, seminars, or classes for people in your field. If money is a problem, ask if you can volunteer at the event, as volunteers often get free or reduced admission.
- Talk to people in your field. There might be all sorts of opportunities to stay connected as a volunteer, part-time worker, or mentor.
- If your career allows, work from your home. Although this doesn't provide face-to-face contact with colleagues, working from home, even part-time, keeps your professional skills current.

Women who stay at home are not necessarily doomed to the so-called mommy track. With a bit of effort and creativity, you can be a stay-at-home mom and still nurture your professional interests.

I love going to my women's group (or study group, book group, needlecraft group, etc.), so why do I feel guilty taking time out for myself and leaving my baby at home?

It's normal to be thrilled at the prospect of getting out of the house to participate in something that has given you pleasure and intellectual stimulation or something that can further your career. Sometimes knowing how much you enjoy an activity that takes you away from your baby makes you feel guilty. Leaving your baby voluntarily, for whatever reason, seems hard to swallow.

Go and enjoy yourself. As long as your baby is well taken care of while you will be gone, you are entitled to continue some of your previous pleasures. Whether you participate in a study group, go jogging, or sculpt lawn ornaments, pursuing your non-baby passions is good for you and your baby. You feel enriched and connected to other parts of yourself, and your baby learns that you are a complex person of value beyond your motherhood.

Feeling guilty for periodically following a hobby or professional pastime that doesn't include your baby is unproductive. Feeling guilty may indicate that you don't feel deserving of some fun for yourself, which may ultimately lead to your family agreeing that your place is firmly under their feet. Don't create a situation in which you are so devoted to your baby that you lose your ability to take care of yourself. You want to be a well-rounded role model for your children and you need to have activities you enjoy in your life. Provide excellent child care for your baby and then go!

Section Two
Your Relationships

During the course of my first year of motherhood, it became obvious to me that my baby's existence had prompted changes in more than just my personal life. My relationships with others shifted as well. Certain aspects of my marriage, like who did the laundry and cooking, changed visibly, while others, like how we spent our free time, or even if we had any, shifted more subtly. I remember feeling closer to my own mother in those first couple of weeks after giving birth than ever before, and surprised at the intensity of love expressed by my in-laws. I was probably most surprised at how much motherhood changed my friendships, as I eagerly sought out friendships with other new mothers, while some treasured lifelong friendships suffered as my new priorities and limited availability interfered with our former closeness.

In my years working with new mothers I've seen many women perplexed at the intensity and range of these shifting relationships. Obviously, having a baby makes a huge impact on a marriage, as two loving adults go from being a couple, caring only for themselves and each other, to being a family, taking care of a helpless infant. Finding time to devote to each other, to being a couple, after a baby enters a marriage can be difficult. Accepting that you and your husband may see this new experience very differently can be very stressful. But seeing your partner cradling your baby and sharing your love with this baby can also bring you closer.

Extended family relationships are similarly affected by your baby's birth. Many new mothers express delight that their relationships with their own mothers deepen. Some are frustrated to find their mothers-in-law becoming more critical or competitive. This new baby has made you a mother, but she has also made your parents and in-laws grandparents and any of your siblings aunts or uncles. Your baby's existence creates an awareness of where each family member is in his own life, as well as in relation to you and your baby, that might have gone unnoticed before. Having a baby and becoming a mother can change the way many women relate to even their closest relatives.

I also hear varied stories about how motherhood impacts a new mother's social life. While some first-time mothers are delighted to discover the more nurturing sides of their friends, others are saddened when their motherhood seems to cause impassable distances between them and their former best friends. Friendships come and go during the course of a lifetime, but seem especially precious when a woman becomes a mother for the first time, and can be particularly taxed or enhanced by the new mother's changing needs.

Section Two is devoted to how the most important relationships in a woman's life change when she becomes a mother for the first time. The first chapter in this section focuses on the marriage, the second chapter on the woman's extended family, and the third on her social life.

Chapter Five

The Marriage

〰

My husband and I believed we were more than ready to become parents together. We'd been married nearly five years; we had a number of nieces and nephews and between us a variety of professional experiences with parents and children. We very much wanted to become parents, and we *were* well prepared in many ways.

But just as I wasn't completely aware of the impact a baby would have on my sense of self, neither were we as fully alert to the impact she would have on our marriage. Although we worked well together and never had the least regret about becoming parents, our marriage needed to adapt in ways we hadn't anticipated. Assumptions we each made, sleep deprivation, and the shift from being two working, independent adults to having one adult working outside the home, one adult working (mostly) inside the home, and one previously nonexistent child in our lives demanded more dramatic adjustments than we'd expected. We needed to renegotiate many areas in our marriage. Some we did consciously, others sort of morphed over time. But the transition from couple to family was not as instantaneous or as smooth as we'd thought it would be.

This chapter addresses the issues that most couples experience when they become parents. Even when your relationship with your baby's father is fabulous, some change is unavoidable because you now have a third party to consider. How you spend your time together, how differently you spend your days, and differences in attitudes toward child rearing, sex, finances, and household chores all may create some tension between you as you adjust to being parents together. Having little time or energy for each other intensifies the struggle between you. And sleep deprivation may make both of you a little bit irrational.

Take heart, as these are normal and surmountable problems. Most marriages must go through a period of adjustment. Be patient, listen to each other, and take care of each other as well as you take care of your baby. If your irritations with each other do not diminish as you become more proficient at babycare (and you begin to get more sleep), seek professional help. Your baby deserves to have two parents who love each other as much as they love him. And you both deserve to feel loved and supported in your marriage.

What is a fair way to share the household chores? My husband and I *each* seem to think that I should be doing most of the housework, and yet that seems unfair.

If your goal is simply to get the tasks of living done, then, logically, it isn't so important who does them; if you're home more, maybe it makes sense for you to be the one to do them. But if you're seeking absolute equality in your relationship, who does what will seem crucial. It is rare to be able to have a totally "equal" marriage, but it is entirely possible to have an equitable one. You will each feel better about your contributions to your marriage and family if the tasks involved in your family's life are divided in such a way that you *both* feel is fair. When both of you feel that you're contributing substantially, then resentment will disappear.

First, make a list of all the things your family needs to survive comfortably, including clean clothes, an income, enough sleep, a clean place to live, food (both bought and prepared), someone to take care of the baby, leisure time, and so on. Take into account everything that can possibly be conceived as necessary to the family well-being. Assess honestly what each of you currently does to keep the family running.

If you're unhappy about how the housework is being handled, figure out what aspect is truly bothering you. Are you too overwhelmed by child care to keep up with the housework? Do you feel that if you do the bulk of the cleaning you are less of a modern woman? Does it distress you that even today, people still think that mothers should be the housekeepers? Do you feel unappreciated by your husband (or others)? If you are no longer working outside the home, does doing the housework make you feel less important than your husband? Or do you just hate housework and need some help?

Once you have sorted out what's troubling you about the new housekeeping balance, and you're clear about how you and your husband each contribute to your new family's comfort, you can try to remedy the situation. If you still feel overburdened, then you can more objectively and fairly adjust the division of labor. But keep in mind that whether you redistribute the jobs or find another approach should depend on how you define and experience the inequity.

I've seen a variety of useful and creative solutions. Here are three women with three different solutions who were equally satisfied that their marriages had regained the fairness they wanted.

- Betsy, a college professor, believed that housework was a political issue. She felt that if she did all, or even most, of the laundry or cooking, she was "selling out" or losing carefully won ground for women everywhere. She went back to work full-time, so she and her husband made a chart dividing all the chores as evenly as possible, allowing her to maintain her former standing in her marriage as well as in her social and professional circles.

- Dahlia, her good friend, had always wanted to be a stay-at-home mom; she acknowledged that it was simply more efficient for her to do the housekeeping while her husband worked full-time, thereby leaving weekends and evenings for family entertainment time. She accepted that her husband working outside the home while she worked within it was a fair division of labor.

- Neither Caroline nor her husband wanted to spend much time on the housework. Since she and her husband could afford it, they decided to hire someone to come in to clean.

If you sort out what truly feels uncomfortable to you and your husband about how the household chores get done, you will be much better equipped to find a compromise or solution to your problem. Housework is a necessary fact of life, but who does it is up to you and your husband. Consider your available resources and skills, and come up with a plan that suits your individual needs. You'll feel better, and the jobs will get done.

Who does how much housework is less important than having both you and your husband feel that the division is fair.

Why are my husband and I arguing over who has had the harder day?

Many couples I've known feel so overwhelmed with the responsibilities of work and babycare and are so exhausted from chronic sleep deprivation that they argue over all sorts of things. Arguing over which of you is the more exhausted and unable to cope at the end of the day has a perverse logic to it. If you are each stretched beyond your limits, there's a definite appeal to presenting yourself as more miserable than your mate is, because the happier or more energetic partner is the obvious choice to manage the end-of-day routines like dinner, cleanup, and bath. Although this is a surprisingly common scenario, it is not a great strategy in the long-run because you've created an incentive to be or seem less happy.

Once you've set up the precedent that whoever is closer to the end of his or her rope at 7 P.M. gets a reprieve from responsibility, there's a disadvantage to admitting when you've had a pleasant day. You might just get a baby thrust into your arms while your mate rushes off to take a two-hour bubble bath. Too often in the early months of parenthood, each of you feels so exhausted that it's hard to imagine that the other could possibly feel as bad as you do.

New mothers envision their husbands having a wonderful time at work while they are at home, unwashed, bored, and lonely. But at the same time, their husbands are conjuring up images of their wives cozy in their bathrobes, watching TV, relaxing over coffee, or going for walks in the sun with their adorable babies. *Neither* image is entirely true. You each have aspects of your days that are enjoyable, even enviable, but you each may also find aspects of your new lives stressful and, perhaps, unfulfilling.

You need a system that allows both of you to take needed breaks, relax, and enjoy each other and your baby. First, acknowledge that *each* of you needs rest, relaxation, and support in the early days of parenting. Conduct your relationship as if you are teammates working together toward the goal of mutual contentment, comfort, and enjoyment and you will be less inclined to compete to be the more put upon or the harder worker. Acknowledge that providing the primary economic support of a family is just as big a responsibility as taking care of the home and baby.

Second, be supportive of each other and attentive to each other's needs. If one of you has become the major wage earner and the other the main caregiver, your days are very different than they used to be and very different from each other's. Acknowledge that the balance in your relationship has changed and discuss how to make adjustments to accommodate those changes. If you can recognize that each of you is working hard and each of you has occasional lovely parts of your day, you may be able to assess better at day's end how to get through the evening to everyone's advantage.

Third, recognize that if you take care of your husband, he will take care of you. If your husband needs time to unwind when he gets home, for example, accept that and give him some time to make the transition from working man to working father! Plan that he will not have to help you until half an hour after his return home each evening. Similarly, if you miss being able to take a shower (have a cup of coffee, whatever) without worrying about your baby, set aside a time your husband will be in charge of the baby each evening. If possible, call on friends and extended family members to help you out with housework, child care, or companionship, so that you and your husband are not totally dependent on each other for emotional and practical support.

When either of you have had a particularly hard day, say so; your partner should then try to pick up the slack. But also be willing to admit when you've had a good day, and offer to do a bit more that night. You will find each other more enjoyable company when you focus on the pleasant aspects of your days. If you are each considerate of the other and respectful of the stresses in each of your lives, you won't feel the need to exaggerate the difficulties of your day just to get a bit of a reprieve. Focus on the positive, and help each other with the negatives. And don't keep score, because then neither of you wins.

If you and your husband have each had a hard day, then you each need attention, love, and support. Try not to set up a system in which the person with the more exhausting day gets released from the drearier duties.

What can I do to make my husband understand how hard I work and how difficult it is to stay home with the baby?

Talk to your husband about your feelings. Explain to him that adjusting to full-time motherhood is difficult not only because of the work itself, but because of the combination of changes in your life; it is the exhaustion, the isolation, the shift in identity, the lack of prestige, the loss of the familiar, and the repetitious nature of caring for a baby for days without end that wears you down. He probably doesn't realize how much energy and time it takes to keep a baby clean, dry, fed, and content all day, day after day. And if you feel he doesn't understand how hard you work, that means you are probably feeling unappreciated, and that feels very bad.

Many people will suggest that you have your husband spend a whole day or two taking care of the baby without any help from anyone. Many men will have a much greater appreciation for how long a day can be with an infant who cries, poops, and pees, but doesn't talk, laugh at his jokes, or help around the house. When he spends the day as you do, he will appreciate how tedious and exhausting child care can be and how efficient and saintly you are for taking care of your baby.

Having your husband get a taste firsthand of how you are spending your days will undoubtedly help him appreciate what you do. He will experience the struggles of one-handed activities, the inability to finish a task, the lack of structure, and the endless repetition. He will be glad to get back to his job and hand your baby back to your capable hands. But if your husband has a particularly easy day with your baby, as sometimes happens, do not despair. Be grateful that he and your baby had an opportunity to bond and you had a well-deserved break.

Above all, share with your husband how your experience of motherhood differs from his experience of fatherhood. When you have confidence that you both work equally hard to give your baby a good life, and when you both value your contributions to your family, you will be more confident and you won't worry if your husband doesn't completely comprehend how you spend your days. Both you *and* he need to value and appreciate the work you each do.

My husband is very critical of my mothering; why does he think that everything that goes wrong is my fault?

Having your first baby puts tremendous stress on a marriage. Although a baby can certainly bring a couple closer together, it can also magnify problems that probably already existed between you. When people are hypercritical of each other, the underlying issue often is more closely related to a lack of self-esteem than to an honest dissatisfaction with the other person. I've heard many women express similar concerns.

At this point in history, men have high expectations of themselves, and their women do, too. Fathers are supposed to provide for their families financially while also being lovingly involved in early child care. Many men express confusion and frustration about having to be all things to their wives and babies; others work hard to become "superdads." These superdads sometimes think that they are *the* experts at baby rearing and criticize their wives' mothering as proof of their superior knowledge.

Of course, this isn't very productive or satisfying. If you each feel confident as a parent only by making the other look bad, someone's feelings are going to be hurt, and your "confidence" becomes dependent on your mate's incompetence. It's ultimately pointless to try to compete with each other over who is the better parent, because objectively, you each want to be successful and do well by your children and each other. As soon and as kindly as you can, you need to try to change this behavior before it becomes a way of life between you.

❖ Find a stress-free time to talk to your husband about how his comments make you feel. Listen, without getting defensive, to what he has to say to you.

- Pay attention to how you talk with him about his parenting. Make sure you are supportive and loving and respectful of all that he does. Kindness breeds kindness.
- When he says something critical of you, try to avoid snapping back in a similarly critical way. Tell each other that your feelings are hurt rather than try to hurt each other in retaliation.
- Issues that existed before the baby was born do not disappear with the baby's arrival, and, in fact, often are exaggerated. If you were a control freak before the baby came, unless you learn to let go of that need for control, you will still be a control freak. The same goes for your husband.
- Solve the problems in your relationship as soon as possible. If you can't work things out between you on your own, seek professional help.
- Your goals as parents should be to establish a family in which all family members feel respected, loved, and valued. Remind yourselves to treat each other in ways you want to be treated.
- Try to remember that your marriage is as important as your parenthood. Make sure you listen to each other and care for each other as well as for the baby.

If your husband continues to be overly critical, seek help. You and your baby need to have the love and respect of your husband, and a father who constantly puts his baby's mother down is not doing anyone any favors. Adjusting to your new lives as parents can cause stress but it needn't be so painful.

How can I get regain my interest in lovemaking with my husband when I just want my body to myself after a day of holding the baby nonstop?

First, talk to your husband and tell him why you are a bit standoffish. Most non-mothers haven't a clue how much time new moms spend flesh to flesh with their babies. Your husband should be reassured to learn that you need physical distance because of your constant contact with the baby, not due to any lack of love for or interest in him. If it helps, keep a log of how much of your day you spend touching your baby and share that with him.

Second, recognize the difference between taking care of your baby and lovemaking. So many women who resist resuming a sexual relationship with their husbands tell me it's because they feel that they are giving physically all day to their babies and they want to be taken care of themselves or just left alone. They say, "I spend all day with a baby attached to me; the last thing I want is to fill *his* needs." Ideally, though, your getting into a more romantic mode with your husband should fill *your* needs, too. Again, talk to your husband and share your desire to have him nurture you for a while. Remind yourself that making love is meant to be enjoyable for you, too.

Third, find some time away from your baby. As valuable as it is for you to nurture your baby, you also deserve a break. If you truly feel that you have no time when your body is your own, make sure you take some time for yourself. Hire a baby-sitter for an hour or two; make a pact with your husband that every evening he takes total charge of your baby, maybe even being the designated bath-parent, for example, for a specified period; or swap baby-sitting with a friend. Getting away from the baby briefly may be all you need to make cuddling with your husband more appealing.

Last, both you and your husband will be reassured to discover that this stage of parenthood doesn't last forever. Time in the first year goes very fast, at least in retrospect. Your baby will need less and less of your physical attention and comfort, and before too long, your interest in a sensual marital relationship will return.

For a new mother, every day seems to take an eternity, but the weeks fly by before you know it.

Our sex life is just about nonexistent; he's interested, but I'm not. Is it normal to feel so out of sync?

Of course you feel out of sync; you are. Your body just finished nine months of pregnancy, labor, and delivery, with all the attendant emotional and hormonal changes, while your partner's body stayed the same. Your sexual appetite and comfort has been and may remain in transition for some time, while his desires have not changed one bit. Although having such noticeably different interest in sex isn't easy, it is *extremely* common.

There are several reasons women feel less interested in sex than their spouses do:

- If you went through pregnancy, labor, and delivery, your body needs to heal from the delivery and your hormones need to return to a non-pregnant state before you are likely to be as enthusiastic about lovemaking as your hormonally more stable husband is.

- Some women feel that when they spend all day taking care of their baby's physical and emotional needs, they have nothing left to give at the end of a long day.
- Others feel that they are "touched out": holding and cuddling a baby for twelve hours a day makes them want some physical distance from everyone, including their husbands.
- Lots of women, aware of the dramatic changes their bodies have experienced, feel unattractive after childbirth.
- Many new mothers are fearful of pain during intercourse.
- Some nursing mothers are uncomfortable with "sharing" their breasts with both their husbands and their babies.
- Another common deterrent to great sex after having a baby is the fear that your baby will need you at a particularly intimate moment, or that he will somehow hear you and *know* that mommy and daddy are "doing it."
- Some women (and men) have the idea that parents having sex is somehow inappropriate. It's hard for them to switch from mommy mode to sex kitten.
- And, as if all that weren't enough to put you off, sleep deprivation leads many women (and men, too) to prefer sleeping to lovemaking when there is the opportunity to choose.

Share your concerns with your husband. Talk about what it feels like to be out of sync with each other. Be patient with each other and read on.

How do we go about getting our sex life back on track?

New mothers are often less interested in being sexually intimate than their physically unchanged husbands are. You should also know that this discrepancy in desire is so common as to be almost ordinary; it is disconcerting, but it is also almost always short-lived. Patience, communication, and a sense of humor are very important at times like this; your husband needs to be patient, and you both need to communicate and maintain your sense of humor.

- First, be certain that you are physically ready to resume your sex life. Check with your doctor about whether or not you are fully healed, and describe any unusual pain or other sex-related concerns.
- Tell your husband what you are feeling. Sort out together what is preventing you from sharing the sex life you had enjoyed before.
- Assure him that new mothers often have a diminished libido for quite a while after giving birth; it is not uncommon for a woman's sexual appetite not to return fully until she has resumed menstruating and is regularly getting enough sleep. Help him understand that time will take care of most of the problems related to healing after childbirth.
- Make sure you and he both know that you miss your old level of easy intimacy, too.
- If you feel unsexy or worry that he no longer finds you sexually attractive, *tell him*: it might take him totally by surprise. Your husband might be the best person to reassure you that you are just as adorable as ever. And, remember, as more than one young mother has told me over the years, "Your husband loves you, and after all, he is a *guy;* he'll be thrilled to have sex with you no matter *what* you look like!"
- If you feel that your breasts should be off limits because they "belong" to your baby, let your partner know. And if you are

afraid that your breasts will be too leaky, share that as well. You may need to alter your usual sexual patterns for a while.

- ❀ Experiment with other methods of intimate behavior until you are more in the mood and to help you become more interested again.
- ❀ Make sure you have plenty of time. Because of all the hormone changes and chronic fatigue, you may require a little more time to become sexually aroused than in your baby-free days.
- ❀ Hire a sitter, go to a hotel, use your baby's one predictable nap time, or find some other way to be alone with your husband. You may need to feel safely baby-free to be as interested as your mate is.

In order for your sexual intimacy to return, you have to be physically healthy, emotionally ready, and have enough baby-free time together to want to be close again. When your body has recovered and your baby has a vaguely predictable sleep pattern, sex will become appealing once more. Talk with your husband, take your time, and work together to regain the closeness you both miss. Discussing your concerns openly should help to keep your guilt and his frustration to a minimum.

My husband and I used to have so much fun together. Now we can hardly relate to each other except as coparents. Is having only the baby in common enough?

In the first several months (and years) of parenthood, your life as a couple does change dramatically. But it is important to try to keep your marriage a marriage, not just a partnership in parenthood.

Unless you and your husband got together for the sole purpose of making great babies, it is probable that, hard as it may be to remember, you have lots of things in common besides your baby. You just have to remember what those were, and be open to discovering new shared interests as well.

One of the best pieces of advice I was ever given as a new mother was to schedule a regular date night with my husband as soon as possible after my baby's birth. It doesn't matter if it is once a week or once a month (though once a week is better) and it doesn't have to be at night, on a weekend, or cost a lot of money. From the time my first baby was an infant, my husband and I have been blessed with great baby-sitters, and we have gone out almost every Saturday night for years. It was hard at first to feel comfortable with even a very experienced baby-sitter, and a challenge to find economical things to do, but it's been wonderful for our relationship and even wonderful for our children.

If you have no access to a baby-sitter, you can have your date at home by renting a movie and ordering in from your favorite restaurant. (But you must plan your "date" for when your baby is likely to stay asleep for at least a couple of hours, and you must both vow to stay awake.) The point is to spend time awake and alone with your partner, and limit the time you talk about the baby. You will begin to remember what drew you together in the first place, and focusing on each other instead of the baby will enrich your relationship.

Although your husband may share your fascination with your baby, try to maintain a connection to those activities that interested you before motherhood took over your brain. Watch the news, read the newspaper, keep up with journals or articles related to your pre-baby work or hobbies, or develop new ones more conducive to life with baby. Yes, it can be difficult to pay attention these days, but broadening your range of interest is good for you; you will feel more like your old self and you and your husband will have more non-baby topics to discuss. In the short-term (the first several months), having only the baby in common can feel like plenty, but your marriage deserves to be nurtured as well as your baby, and keeping your marriage alive will reap great rewards over the next twenty or forty or more years.

Your marriage deserves to be nurtured as much as your baby does.

My husband and I used to be so spontaneous. We miss being able to just get up and go out. Will that ever come back?

Actually, you can be spontaneous now. Babies are really very portable. Most don't honestly care if you are holding them at home, at a ball game, or in a restaurant, as long as they are comfortable. While your freedom to drop everything and run off totally unencumbered is, obviously, more limited by the need to care for your baby, you can still be spontaneous; it just takes a little planning.

If spontaneity is important to you, don't try to put your baby on a schedule. Babies who can sleep only in their own beds at very specific times get very fussy when you disrupt their routines; babies without rigid schedules are more likely to tolerate a last-minute field trip during their usual nap time. (However, if you have a baby with a compelling need for a schedule or a baby with medical problems that require medication or more regular eating and sleeping patterns, your baby's health and schedule then must be considered first.)

Always have your diaper bag ready to go so that when the spirit moves you, you can leave quickly. Keep it well supplied with clean clothes and diapers in the current correct size. Some women leave extras in the trunks of their cars for added convenience.

Accept that having a baby requires some compromises; your spontaneity is limited, but it doesn't need to be eliminated. For example, *don't* pull a baby out of a deep sleep to go to a museum when you can reasonably predict this will make her very irritable, but do go to outdoor concerts or take walks or take advantage of those times when she is likely to be cheerful.

If you are the kind of people who like to get up and go, go! Enjoy your baby's willingness to go with you anywhere as long as you still meet her needs. Let's face it, the only problem with deciding to go out for ice cream at 9 P.M., now that you have a baby, is that you must either take your baby or get a sitter. You may get some icy stares or comments about taking a baby out late at night, but many babies are happily awake at odd hours. There's no rule against taking your baby out if it doesn't disrupt her life and it makes you happy. You can respect your baby's needs while taking care of your own.

I'm no longer bringing in a paycheck, and we have all these new expenses from the baby. Why do I find myself asking my husband for permission to spend our money?

No matter how hard you may try to detach your sense of worth from dollars and cents, we live in a society that clearly connects income with power and value. Many new stay-at-home mothers were accustomed to being paid for their work. No matter how highly you or your husband regard women who stay home, it can be a tough adjustment to no longer have a financial reward as proof of your importance and value to your family.

One new mother, Sally, spoke with great emotion about her realization that she had not been financially dependent on anyone since high school until she became a mother. She said, "Being self-supporting is the dividing line between being an adult and being a child." Giving up her income made her feel like a child again, like she didn't really have a voice in how her new family's money should be spent.

When Toni chose to stay home with her first baby, money was tight. Although she bought the baby a new little toy almost weekly, she denied herself some much-needed new clothes. Both these women, and many others I've known, felt that if they didn't contribute financially, somehow they weren't entitled to enjoy whatever money there was.

It might help you see how important you are if you calculate just what it would cost to hire someone to do all that you do for your family. Factor in the hours you spend daily and weekly doing housework, cooking, shopping, taking clothes to the cleaners, as well as keeping your baby happy. Consider your low-cost wardrobe needs as a stay-at-home mom.

If you were to work outside the home, your expenses would significantly increase. You would have to pay for child care, including hours of baby-sitting while you traveled to and from work (when you aren't paid), for food (lunches while at work, food for the sitter, and more frequent take-out for dinners), and for laundry or dry cleaning. You'd have to either hire a housekeeper, or do the work yourself on weekends and evenings. Your contribution to your family may not be visible as increased income, but it is vitally important, and it allows for decreased work-related expenses.

Also, talk to your husband. Have you decided *together* that his job is to earn the money while yours is to take care of the baby and home? You need to feel confident that staying home with the baby is your responsibility and your job. Then, if your not earning cash is genuinely OK with you both, the money he earns is the *family's* income. He earns the cash while you are the primary housekeeper and nurturer, and as such, you each have equal rights within the family and equal access to the cash.

When you both agree that your staying at home makes sense, and you both feel that what each of you does is important and vital to your family's well-being, it matters less who earns the pay. Make sure your husband sees the family income as belonging to both of you. When you recognize that you *really are* contributing to your family in critical ways, you will feel better about participating equally in the decisions about how to spend the income you have.

My husband and I decided that I would stay at home to raise our children and he would bring in the money. Why does he now act as if he is in charge of all financial decisions?

This situation is very different from the one before. The new mother in the previous question undervalues her own contribution to the family. You, however, may have a husband who undervalues you. Heidi had a similar problem. She worried, "Ever since I quit work to stay home with our baby, my husband acts as if he is entitled to decide how every penny is spent. I feel like what I do at home is very worthwhile, but my husband seems to think that if I'm not bringing in a paycheck, I don't deserve access to or influence over our money. I feel resentful and as if I have no say in our relationship anymore."

In an effort at achieving equality and maintaining a sense of independence, some couples, like Heidi and Jeremy, start their marriages with separate funds and assigned financial responsibilities. For example, before their baby was born, Jeremy took care of the mortgage while Heidi paid for the food and utilities, and each paid for his/her own clothes and entertainment. This can work out well as long as both agree to the arrangement and the expenses are fairly divided. When this couple had a baby and the wife quit her job, though, this setup no longer made sense. Some big adjustments, both to budget and attitudes, become necessary.

For a couple to make a successful transition from life as a double-income, child-less couple to life as a family in which the father works outside the home while the mother cares for the children, it helps if they have similar ideas about each of their roles. If you both agree that you are the one to stay home with your baby, then you also should agree that your work is equally important. You are no longer each earning for your separate selves; you are each contributing to the well-being of the family. Your husband is providing financial support while you are providing emotional and household support.

Your husband must learn that he could not go off to work so easily if you were not at home taking care of the baby, and the services you provide in so doing would be much more costly than he might realize. Your working would necessitate spending money on more than just child care; when both parents work they tend to spend more on clothes, dry cleaning, transportation, housekeeping, work lunches, and take-out dinners. Your staying at home provides a loving and close relationship with your child, but it also eliminates many other expenses.

If you are comfortable being given an allowance and having your husband make all your financial decisions, there is no problem. But if you are resentful of your husband's attitude, *tell your husband how you feel.* If, after sharing your feelings with him, he insists on controlling the finances and you continue to feel undervalued or treated like a child, you should seek professional help. Couples or individual counseling can help you and your husband become the partners and coparents you deserve to be. Don't just sit and stew about this: work with your husband to fix it.

The contributions of the homemaker are just as important as those of the breadwinner. Both deserve respect and appreciation.

My husband and I both work full-time, yet when we're both home, I am doing the majority of the child care and housework. How can I get him to help out more?

Unfortunately, you are not alone in this. Although women have made a lot of progress toward equality in the workplace, the majority of working mothers still do more housework and child care than their husbands, regardless of the number of hours either works outside the home. If you don't like how family jobs are divided between you, tell your husband.

He may not even be aware that you feel the responsibilities are unbalanced. If necessary, make a chart with all the tasks that need attention, including how long each job takes and how often each needs to be done. Discuss who should do which, keeping in mind each of your schedules, abilities, and interests, and be sure to agree that each chore is assigned fairly. Review the chart occasionally to make sure you each feel the assignments make sense, and adjust as needed.

Pay attention, though, to the possibility that you have unintentionally created the imbalance. Many new mothers, particularly those who work full-time, seem to put unreasonable demands on themselves. Your husband may be doing less than his share around the house or with the baby because you may be inadvertently setting it up that way. Because of archaic ideas about what it means to be a good mother, many couples slip into outdated patterns of behavior without being aware of it. For example, despite both parents believing that all jobs should be shared equally, the mom still does the bulk of the cooking and babycare, arranges for baby-sitters, and the like, because in her mind and heart, that's what it means to be a good mother. She may ask for help, but she actually hangs on to extra wifely or motherly duties to boost her confidence that she's a good mother.

There is nothing wrong with an imbalance as long as you are both comfortable with it; if you need to do more than your husband does to feel better connected to your baby, that's fine. But if you want a more equal distribution of labor, you must tell your husband and share the everyday jobs more fairly. Your marriage will be stronger if you feel satisfied that the responsibilities around your home are shared to your mutual satisfaction.

My husband is a stay-at-home dad while I'm working full-time. Is it normal that I'm sometimes jealous that he's home with our baby?

Every arrangement has its positive and negative aspects. While your being the family breadwinner may make a lot of sense from either a financial or a personality standpoint, that doesn't mean that you will always be happy. You may love being the parent in the workplace but still feel a twinge of jealousy as you see how close your husband and baby have become.

Your relationship with your baby can be every bit as close as your husband's. Naturally, when one parent works full-time and the other stays at home, their relationships with their baby will seem different. But that doesn't have to mean that you aren't close to your baby. You are still your baby's mother, your husband is still the baby's father, and you will relate to your baby each in your own way regardless of how much time you spend with him.

A stay-at-home parent certainly spends more time with the baby than the full-time working parent, but the working parent gets to provide the relief for both stay-at-home parent and baby. That means that at the end of the day, you are fresh and novel to your baby and to your husband, and that can be lovely.

If you are really worried about your relationship with your baby:

- When you come home from work, focus your attention directly on the baby for an extended period of time.
- Whenever you are with your baby, hold her, look into her eyes, talk to her, and play with her.
- If you breast-fed your baby before returning to work, keep it up. (See chapter on working for tips about breast-feeding as a working mom.)
- Call home from work during the day and talk to both your husband and your baby.
- Have your husband bring your baby to visit you at work or join you for lunch whenever possible.
- Spend time alone with the baby on your days off.

With minimal effort, you can maintain a wonderful relationship with your baby, and jealousy will no longer enter your mind. Enjoy the closeness your husband and baby have as well as your opportunity to work knowing that your baby is well cared for while you're gone.

You are the baby's mother and your husband is the baby's father, no matter who works and who stays home. Your baby will know and love you both.

Why does it drive me crazy every time my husband asks me, "What did you do all day?"

I remember hating that question myself. It made me feel like I needed to provide an accurate and complete accounting of all the wonderful things I was doing with our daughter, or else justify why the house was still a mess, dinner was not ready, and the baby and I were both crying. I often didn't know myself what I'd done all day. I felt unproductive, and it was hard to explain what, if anything, I'd accomplished other than creating more mess. I think I was simultaneously embarrassed and mystified about how little I had to show for how I spent my days.

Try to remember that in all likelihood your husband is asking about your day out of love and politeness. He is not trying to get you to admit that you've been watching soap operas all day (not that it would be so bad if you did) or to prove to you just how much more important his life is than yours has become. More likely, he loves you and your baby and genuinely wants to know what you've been up to all day—nothing more, nothing less. Your insecurities about your own competence may be aroused by his question, which is why you hate being asked, but that doesn't mean that *he* doesn't respect or admire you.

You don't need to feel defensive, search for creative answers, or pretend that your day was either easier or harder than it was. It's hard to feel efficient and proud when what you did all day was hold, feed, and change your baby over and over again, but that is what taking care of a little baby is all about for awhile, and it is more than enough. If you and the baby are both alive and healthy at the end of the day, you've done plenty. And if you've managed to get a little something else in, a walk, a phone call, a home-cooked meal, or a load of laundry, that's cause for celebration. Until you and your baby become more confident and efficient, loving your baby and maintaining your sanity is enough. You're doing a lot. Just tell him the truth.

I feel like I should be accomplishing more while I'm at home with the baby, and I feel like my husband thinks I should be doing more, too. Should I?

The goal here is to come to some agreement about what it means to be a productive parent in your family while being practical about what each of you can reasonably be expected to do. Most couples don't know what hit them when they bring a baby home; efficiency and organizational skills seem to evaporate. I can't tell you how many new mothers worry that their husbands don't understand why they can't get anything done and even more are baffled themselves. Both men and women often have unrealistic expectations of what their lives should be like when they first become parents. Relax: your energy and efficiency levels will increase enormously over time. What seems overwhelming now will become routine in a matter of a few months.

If you and/or your husband think you should be accomplishing more, you need to sort out what "more" means to each of you. What aren't you doing enough of, and for whom? Are you not able to keep up with the household chores, are you worried that you are not doing enough to stimulate your baby, or are you not taking care of your husband's needs? Do you or your husband feel that any time left over after feeding, changing, and playing with your baby should be spent exposing your baby to great art while listening to classical music, or are you expected to be scrubbing the toilets and organizing your closets? Maybe both? Are you still operating under the assumption that you should (or can) be as visibly productive as you were before your baby was born?

Assign specific tasks to each of you and determine together which ones are the highest priority and what is a *realistic* time frame in which to accomplish each job. Be reassured that caring for a baby takes all day and there often isn't time for much else. Understand that some days your baby will be more peaceful and your energy will be higher, and you will be more visibly industrious.

If you and your husband decide together what should receive your attention first (and you both accept that you are still learning how to function efficiently in your new role) you will feel more successful and less resentful about what you are expecting to accomplish. Go easy on yourself and each other, be grateful for whatever gets done, and you will accomplish more when you are able to.

My husband says he feels ignored. Could he be jealous of my relationship with our baby?

Yes, many new fathers feel jealous of their wives' close relationships with their babies, although they don't like to admit it, even to themselves. Before your baby was born, the most important other person in your life was likely to have been your husband. Now that you have a baby, he may not be too comfortable that the baby has suddenly taken that place of honor.

I remember Sandra's amazement when she discovered that her husband was jealous of her attentiveness to their baby. Although he was proud of what a wonderful mother she was, he sheepishly admitted that he felt left out. Many women become so totally focused on the new baby that they may be ignoring their husbands a bit. Some become so devoted to nurturing their babies that they have no more "nurture" left for their husbands. Even though your baby is also his baby, your husband may be missing being the center of your attentions. *Everyone* needs to feel important and valued; unless you value your husband only for his ability to procreate, you want your husband to know he's important to you, too.

While it is tempting to become very baby-centric when you're a new mother, and understandable to think that your husband should be able to cope with this shift in your focus (and to a certain extent, he should), your marriage deserves some attention, too.

If your husband feels left out, or that you only talk to him when you want to tell him what to do (a complaint I often hear from new fathers), try to remember that a little kindness and loving interest in his life can go a long way.

- Ask your husband about his day, and then carefully, genuinely listen to his answer.
- Talk to him about your day, sharing the interesting and fun moments as well as your frustrations.
- Help your husband become more involved with your baby when he is home.

- Find fun things to do as a family.
- Spend quality time together, even if that means just talking to each other.
- Socialize with old friends and continue to do things as a couple.
- Understand your husband's jealousy to be a sign of how highly he values you.
- Don't belittle your husband for missing your full concentration; rather, help him see that you are learning to care for your baby, and remind him that as the baby's needs decrease and you become more efficient, you will be more available to him once again.
- Tell your husband what you appreciate about him. Make a pact to say something appreciative of each other on a daily basis.
- Be supportive of each other. Your husband will be around long after the children have left home; maintain some couple closeness.
- If you are already highly attentive to your husband's needs, and you worry that his jealousy is a sign of his immaturity rather than reflective of your shift in focus, consider seeking therapy or counseling. Your husband deserves to have his needs met, but they must be realistic and reasonable. You don't want him to remain jealous of the baby or to make demands that you cannot or should not meet.

Remembering to be nice to your husband, finding out about his life and feelings, and sharing your day will not only make your husband feel less abandoned, it will improve his ability to be emotionally connected to you. So, even when you're overwhelmed, try to stay connected to your husband. He will then want to be attentive to you, and you will still know how to enjoy each other after the children grow up.

*Redefine quality time. Having a heart-to-heart talk
with your husband while washing dishes together can
be high quality time; pointing out the scenery to a
toddler while doing errands can be very satisfying.
An activity doesn't need to be high in cost or glamour
to be memorable.*

**My husband says he'll take care of the baby to give me a
break sometimes, but I don't think he can handle the baby
well enough. Should I let him take care of the baby by
himself, even when I know he won't do everything the
way I want him to?**

Of course you should. Your husband will take care of the baby his
way, and although *his* way may be different than *your* way, it is probably just fine. Although I've been asked this question many times, I've
yet to have one new mother tell me that leaving her baby in her husband's care would actually be dangerous. Unless your husband has a
physical or emotional problem that would render him unable to keep
your baby safe, both he and the baby will survive.

Usually, though, when a new mother worries that her husband (or
her mother-in-law, the baby-sitter, etc.) doesn't meet her standards, on
some level she *wants* to be the only one who can soothe, feed, rock,
burp, or comfort her baby. This sometimes translates into the belief
that, since she does it all *best*, everyone else, including the baby's
father, does it all wrong. It also means that this mother has decided
that she is essential to her baby's well-being, and therefore this mother

may never leave. Sometimes the new mother actually worries what it would mean if her husband *is* as capable as she is. That might make her feel like her skill at mothering isn't such a big deal.

Sadly, some new mothers, in an effort at being the best mother on earth, allow no one else to care for their baby, ever. While it feels good to be the best (and objectively, many mothers are truly the most successful at reading their baby's signals and keeping them content), being the *only* person capable of caring for your baby limits both you and your baby. You don't get any time to yourself, your husband remains less skilled than you are, and your baby doesn't develop the ability to be comfortable with anyone else, including his father.

Take an honest look at why don't you think your husband can take adequate care of your baby. If your husband doesn't put a diaper on your baby exactly *your* way, where's the harm? If you go out for a couple of hours and he can't get her to sleep, does it truly matter? Do you imagine that your baby will starve to death under your husband's eye? Do you really worry that your baby will be in danger? If not, then consider this: if your husband spends the day with your baby and they both do fine, will you feel a bit let down? The only way for your husband to become "better" or "good enough" is for him to have the experience of taking care of your baby; your fear of his supposed incompetence actually perpetuates it.

If your husband's clumsiness makes you feel more adept at child care, that's OK. But if being solely responsible for raising your baby is the basis of your self-esteem as a mother, your problem is not your husband's lack of parenting skills, it is your lack of self-confidence. Then you need to get some help.

On the other hand, if your goal is to get a bit of a break and/or have your husband develop a nurturing and close relationship with your baby, then go out, leave Dad with your baby, and handle the damage control later. You can wash clothes that have been pooped on, re-diaper, or feed an overhungry baby when you get home. If you don't let (or encourage) your husband to take charge of your baby when he offers, soon he will stop offering. Then you will have full responsibility for babycare, your husband will not develop as close a relationship with your baby, and your baby may not be as socially adaptable. You don't really want that, do you? If you will allow your husband to take care of your baby, he'll do just fine. So will your baby. And so will you.

My husband has never taken care of a baby before, so he leaves everything to me. How can I help him feel confident or relaxed enough to interact with her?

Lots of people are uncomfortable with babies if they have had no experience with them. Reassure your husband that although babies are delicate, they are pretty resilient creatures. Let him know you are confident he is and will be a great dad. And keep in mind that many people learn best by first watching and then doing; others need verbal instructions; some prefer to read what the experts have to say; and still others must learn by experience. Use whatever approach works for you and your husband.

- Show him the basics, like how to hold your baby, how to bathe her, diaper her, and the like.
- Talk with him about how you learned about child care.
- If you have been reading books about caring for infants, share them with him.
- When a friend or your pediatrician makes a suggestion, engage your husband in a discussion about it.

- On days when your husband spends little time with your baby, keep him informed about the baby's new tricks, habits, and interests.
- Point out what works for you and ask him for ideas when something doesn't.
- Finally, make sure your husband spends some time alone with your baby. Let him be in charge. In the beginning, he may want you in the next room (or on the next chair) rather than out of the house. Gradually, as you both feel ready, leave the baby in his care for longer periods of time.

Be loving and patient as your husband relaxes into fatherhood. It can be intimidating to take care of an infant if you never have before. And some people are just not baby people. Be supportive, be consistent, and above all, don't criticize. Have faith in him. He'll be a wonderful dad if he wants to be.

Since our baby was born, nothing in our relationship seems equal anymore. How do we get that sense of equality back?

You will have better luck aiming for fairness than for equality. Perhaps the most important thing to understand now is that fairness and equality are not the same, especially in a family. What is *fair* is that every member of the family feels respected, well cared for, and has what he or she needs; *equality* implies that everybody contributes in equal amounts and receives the same pleasures regardless of ability or need. Sometimes equality may not be possible even when fairness can easily be achieved.

When a couple becomes a family, the balance in the relationship changes. Who does which chores, who makes the money, how decisions are made, how the money is spent, and who decides it all, may need to shift. If equality rather than fairness is your goal, then you and your husband must earn similar amounts of money, work similar numbers of hours outside the home, and divide child care, household chores, and leisure time evenly. That's all possible, but very hard to do.

More likely, and often more achievable, you can sort out what chores need to be done and who has the time and skills to do them. Consider your family as a unit, and divide up the tasks of raising a family so each of you agrees upon who is responsible for what chores. Ideally, you will each take on what you do well and have time and inclination to accomplish. You will both value work within the home as much as earning money. If one of you is working outside the home many more hours than the other is, it may simply make a whole lot more sense to have the person who is home more do more of the household-related jobs.

I'm not suggesting that if you, as the mother, choose to stay home, that all the housework should fall to you. I *am* suggesting that you and your husband try to work out what jobs need to get done and who can do them, and keep in mind that housekeeping and child care are as important to family well-being as is income. You will feel you are in an equal marriage when you and your husband feel equally valued, and when you and your husband agree that *all* the work toward the common good of the family is equally important.

"Equal" does not always mean the same thing as "fair."

I want my husband to know what I want or need from him and for him to do it instantly. Why is it so hard for me to ask him directly for what I want?

Laura had a similar complaint: "My husband says he will do whatever I ask him to do, but I want him to know without my having to tell him what I want or need, and [for him to] do it." It's hard to ask for what you want when you first become a mother: on one hand, you really want assistance or support, while on the other, you want to be able to handle everything yourself. I've noticed a tendency among new mothers to feel that, because motherhood is "natural" and "common," they shouldn't need any help. You feel inadequate when you aren't your usual highly competent self, and you want so desperately to be efficient and motherly that you resist asking anyone to give you a hand. You think that not asking for help makes you seem less needy, but while you are trying to appear self-assured and independent, you are wistfully hoping for your husband to surprise you by doing *anything* to lighten your load.

Your husband is adjusting to fatherhood just as you're trying to adjust to motherhood. He may not know what you need, he may not want to step on your toes by taking over, or he may be too tired and overwhelmed himself to figure out that you could use some help. Neither of you is incompetent, but you are both novices at parenthood.

While you'd really like it if your husband could anticipate and fulfill your every whim without your ever having to open your mouth, it isn't realistic or fair to him. Even though you may have been incredibly tuned in to each other before, your lives have changed, and he may not be able to guess your needs as correctly as he did before the baby upset the marital apple cart. When you're feeling worn out, it would be lovely if your husband could spontaneously fulfill your every desire. But if you don't tell him, in words, especially in the beginning, what you want or need from him, he can't be expected to know what to do for you. Despite the disappointing fact that your husband can't read your mind, he still loves you and wants you to be happy.

So, if you need something, anything, from your husband, whether it is a full-time housekeeper or a foot massage, keep these thoughts in mind:

- Don't take offense that your beloved doesn't know what you need.
- Don't interpret his lack of insight or support as lack of caring or love.
- Don't assume that he is too awkward or incompetent to help you.
- Don't feel guilty or bad that you need help; everyone needs help!
- Don't assume that if he can't figure out how to help you without you telling him he is a bad husband or father or that you have a bad relationship.
- Do assume only that he doesn't know what he hasn't been told.
- Do tell him, clearly, when and how he can help you.
- Do ask for help rather than demand or complain.
- Do thank him when he is helpful, whether or not you had to ask.
- Do work on your ability to ask politely for help.
- Do think of your marriage as a partnership. If you can do something to make your husband's life better, do it, and he will do the same for you.

It's perfectly acceptable to ask or tell your husband what you want. If you can be direct, he will know when to help and when to back off.

You'll avoid resenting his lack of involvement, and even if he can't or won't do what you'd hoped, you'll have cleared the air. More likely, though, you'll get the help you need.

Although your spouse loves you, he can't read your mind. If you want or need something from someone else, ask for it. Even the most loving husband or friend may not know what you need or how to help you.

Often my husband asks me to do something but I don't seem able to get to it. Then he gets angry and I feel guilty, so why don't I do what he wants?

Maybe your husband's priorities and your priorities are not the same. When you find yourself consistently not meeting your husband's expectations, it could be caused by one of several possible underlying problems. Sort out what is preventing you from doing what your husband asks of you.

- First, you could be so overwhelmed by motherhood that you are barely scraping through the day as it is. In this case, you may want to see your doctor to be screened for postpartum depression or a physical problem, such as anemia, to get the help you may need to regain your energy and efficiency. If you have an emotional or physical problem, you owe it to yourself and your family to get the appropriate treatment.
- Second, your husband, as sleep deprived as you, may feel too

exhausted to take care of his usual tasks, and hopes that you, with your more flexible schedule, can pick up his slack. If you think your husband is overly stressed because of the new financial and family responsibilities, ask him how you can help him; realize that he may be struggling to adjust to fatherhood; and do what he asks in the spirit of love and partnership.

- Third, you may feel that he is not keeping up with *his* chores, so you begrudge his requests. Tell him that he still has responsibilities in the home. Make it clear to him that you still need and appreciate his help.
- Fourth, you may feel that since you've become a mother, he's begun treating you like his secretary or his mother, and you resent his new demands. If you feel the jobs he wants you to do are "beneath" you, discuss this with him.
- Fifth, since you are home more often than he is, he may think you have plenty of time to take care of what you may feel should be *his* jobs. Help him to understand that taking care of the baby takes up most of your day. Be direct about who should be doing what around the house.
- And last, you may just be so tired of filling you baby's needs all day that taking care of anyone or anything else seems like too big a burden. If you are simply overextended yourself, you may need to get some help around the house.

Once you have a better idea about what keeps you from fulfilling your husband's wishes, you can try to solve the problem. If you and your husband view your marriage as a partnership in which you are both working toward agreed-upon goals, then when he asks you to handle something for him, figure out what may be stopping you, discuss the problem, and then solve it.

My husband has decided that being a good father means earning a good living, so he now works constantly. How can I help him know that our baby and I need to spend time with him, too?

Let him know that, although you appreciate how hard he works for you and the baby, you both want to spend time with him, too. Many men feel that their most important contribution to the family is financial. Your partner may not realize that you value his companionship as much as his income.

As with so many situations in a relationship, be clear and direct with your mate.

- ❧ Tell him you miss him. Make sure he knows that you love him regardless of how much he earns, and suggest that, if possible, he take it easy at work for a while to get to know your baby.
- ❧ Ask him to make a realistic assessment of how many hours he needs to work to maintain his good standing, and to try hard to keep within that amount.
- ❧ If his job requires a lot of traveling, be supportive and tolerant, remembering that being on the road is difficult for him, too.
- ❧ Make a pact to speak to each other daily by telephone when he's away from home. Put the baby on the phone, too!
- ❧ If his schedule is unpredictable, become more flexible and creative yourself. For example, make dinners that can be easily reheated or finished at the last minute so you can eat together more often. Or take the baby and meet him for lunch occasionally.
- ❧ Don't rely on your husband for your sole social contact. Make a point to get out of the house and see your other friends or you'll resent his work even more.

❧ Make a schedule of times when you will make a special effort to be together. Dana and Alec agreed that they would have dinner together at least twice a week. Sometimes that meant eating at 9 P.M. and sometimes that meant putting it on Alec's work calendar, but it also meant Dana felt that she was still as important as his job.

Keep the lines of communication open between you. Show your husband you love him, appreciate his efforts, and recognize that his life has changed, too. Be supportive, don't whine, and enjoy his company when he's with you.

Since becoming parents, all we talk about is the baby. Are we always going to be this dull?

You're not dull; you're simply besotted with love for your new baby, maybe a bit obsessed with her, as are most first-time parents, and so busy with her that you have little else going on in your lives right now. As the novelty of being new parents wears off, as your baby becomes more independent, and as you begin to get enough sleep again, you will resume some of your old interests and hobbies and probably develop new ones. But in the early stages you talk endlessly about the baby because she is so fascinating and because your lives together are more narrowly focused than ever before. It's normal to be so baby-focused, but it can also be distressing to feel you and your husband have nothing else in common anymore.

If you can't wait for time and maturation to help you regain your wider range of interests, then making a conscious effort to expand your awareness of the world beyond baby may help. Make a point to do something unrelated to parenting or babies at least weekly and preferably daily, as an individual *and* as a couple. These ideas don't demand lots of time away from your baby, just your attention directed toward something more adult oriented.

- Ask your husband about his work, and really listen to his response.
- Join (or organize) a study or book group related to a topic that you've always wanted to explore.
- Go for walks in different neighborhoods with or without your baby along.
- Visit a museum, zoo, or arboretum together.
- Read the newspaper, read magazines, and listen to radio talk shows or watch the news.
- Go to a movie or rent a video or DVD to watch together so you have something to discuss besides your baby.
- Find an enjoyable project that you and your husband can work on together when he is home.

What's important is that you not lose yourself or your relationship just because you've become parents. Continue doing "couple" things. Enjoy life more and you'll enjoy each other more, too.

We have no time alone together anymore. We only take care of the baby. How can we become a couple again?

No matter how much you love your baby, you need time away from your baby to be a couple. You must make your relationship a priority. If you can hire a baby-sitter, do so. If you have no baby-sitter available and no family or friends willing to take care of your baby for a few hours, then you have to find a way to have couple time even if your baby is with you.

- Rent a movie and order in a meal. Discuss what you enjoyed, what was thought provoking. Analyze the characters, rate the meal, and talk about anything that isn't baby related.
- Plan that at least once a week you and your husband will spend some time together doing something you both enjoy that is not baby oriented, even if your baby is with you. Your baby won't mind if you talk about sports or the news while she's playing with her feet.
- Use your baby's nap time at least once every weekend to spend time with each other, giving each other back rubs, listening to music, or reading to each other.

Every relationship needs to be nurtured. Spend time doing things you enjoy as a couple, with or without the baby along. Having a baby may enrich a marriage, but only if you can maintain your life as a couple, too.

If you or your relationship are last on your own list of priorities, you will be last on everybody else's list, too.

Sometimes my husband can calm our baby down when I can't. Why do I feel like a failure if he can soothe him when I can't?

You are putting a lot of unnecessary pressure on yourself to be the perfect mother. It's *great* that your husband was able to soothe your baby, and it is certainly not an indication that your mothering is at all inferior! Nor is it useful to be competitive with your husband about who is the better parent. Your baby is lucky to have two loving parents.

Nancy, a stay-at-home mom, wanted to be the best mother ever. She worked hard all day to be appropriately stimulating and paid close attention to every movement and sound her baby made. She was an excellent caregiver, loving, patient, and kind. But when her husband came home from work, she sometimes felt deflated to discover that he could make their baby laugh and change diapers every bit as well as she did, even with only a few hours of active parenting a week. She felt that her husband's successes with their baby meant that her successes were less meaningful.

That's simply not the case. Many stay-at-home mothers feel that because they have chosen to be their baby's full-time caregiver, only they can do everything "right" or "best" for their babies. They feel that child care is a skill or an art, and they want to be acknowledged as the expert. They worry that if their husbands can do this job as well as they, with just a few hours at a stretch to learn, then maybe being a stay-at-home mom isn't as tough or as important as it feels.

Of course it is. You are with the baby all day long. You *are* the baby expert in the family. Your husband may be similarly good at child care, but you are the day-in, day-out caregiver. Sometimes being the one who's always around is exactly what allows your husband to succeed when you have not. He provides the novelty while you offer familiarity. That can be tremendously useful, as long as neither of you resents the other.

You are fortunate to have a husband who wants to care for your baby. If he is able to comfort your baby when you haven't been able to, that's lovely. His skill doesn't diminish the importance of your relationship with your baby nor does it indicate that you aren't good enough. Babies have two parents for a reason; sometimes you will be the only one your baby wants, and sometimes your husband will be. You can support each other, give each other breaks, and nurture an adaptable baby. That's good for all of you.

Remember that the goal here is to have a contented family. You don't really want to be in competition with your husband about who's the better parent, do you? If your husband takes excellent care of your baby, enjoy it. Your husband's successful fathering does not detract from your superb mothering.

Having someone else who can soothe your baby as easily as you can doesn't make you any less successful as a mother, it just means you can take a break more often!

Since our baby came, my husband and I snap at each other and argue over the silliest things. How can we get along better when we're so tired and cranky?

Many new parents are shocked to find themselves arguing instead of enjoying each other. Sleep deprivation, financial concerns, and the general upheaval in your life make it easy to take it all out on the one you love. When you're exhausted and your life seems so chaotic, you don't have the usual self-awareness and self-editing ability. You say things and use a tone of voice you might never have allowed yourself before. It's understandable why new parents bicker so much.

- Don't allow yourself to fall into the habit of saving your worst behavior for your spouse. Although many couples forget to be as thoughtful and nice to their loved ones as they are to strangers and casual acquaintances, your husband and you will benefit from showing each other kindness, understanding, and patience. You and your mate vowed to love and honor each other until death do you part, and honor refers to treating each other with respect. Just because you are confident in the love you share doesn't mean it's OK to be unkind or short-tempered. When snapping at each other is your primary mode of communication, it's hard to remember the loving feelings.
- When you or your husband is feeling particularly cranky, try to take a few extra seconds before you respond. Take a deep breath, drink a glass of water, walk away if necessary, but consider your words before they leave your mouth, and speak with love. Encourage your husband to do the same.
- Make sure you get enough sleep, at least every other day, even if that means you and your husband take turns being the parent on call. If you realize that you're too tired to get along with each other, get some rest and stay quiet or apart until you do.
- Take time to talk to each other, ask about the other's day, and truly listen.
- While becoming parents can bring a couple closer together, it often has the opposite effect, especially in the first months. You both must adjust to the increased demands on your time and

the decreased time alone together. The enormity of the responsibilities and permanence of having a baby can be pretty alarming, too. Problems between you seem magnified when you both feel stressed. When things get dicey between you, remind each other that this baby proves your love for each other; don't allow the transition to parenthood to drive you apart.

The hardest adjustment you may ever have to make as a couple is becoming parents for the first time. At no other time in your marriage will your life together change as abruptly or completely, and you may not be responding to parenthood similarly. Talk to each other, be thoughtful and considerate, and listen, nonjudgmentally, to the struggles and joys you each experience. If you are truly listening to each other, you are much less likely to be bickering and much more likely to be able to enjoy and support each other through this transformation from couple to family. Try to be patient with yourselves, maintain a sense of humor, and work toward collaboration. The extra effort will be worth it.

Chapter Six

Extended Family

Having your first baby is like dropping a stone into a pond. The ripple effect is greater than you ever imagined. The baby makes you and your husband parents, your parents and in-laws grandparents, and your brothers and sisters uncles and aunts. Your baby creates a deeper connection to all your relatives, and the process of caring for a baby stirs up all sorts of feelings about your own childhood, your relationships, and your hopes for your baby's relationships with his extended family. Sometimes the baby can make you all feel closer, which can be wonderful, but sometimes that closeness may feel a bit awkward, as individual expectations and styles conflict.

When you get married, you marry not only your mate but also his family. You become part of each other's families, and sometimes each of your original families has a very different style of communication or handling conflict. The culture of each clan, what it means to have angry words and hurt feelings, how to create and maintain comfortable boundaries and how to celebrate holidays, all need to be renegotiated when a new member is added. Rarely, though, do families make any conscious effort to accommodate a new spouse or a new baby. You may have preconceived ideas about what it means to be a family now that you have a baby, but your relatives may as well, and their ideas and expectations may not match or suit yours.

When you are a new mother, you are almost always sleep deprived and emotionally taxed beyond previous experience. When a new baby is born, some families become very close, as the new mother is warmly nurtured in her new role. But many new mothers are emotionally vulnerable, and sometimes, instead of feeling supported, a new mom experiences a relative's behaviors as intrusive, disinterested, or overly critical. You may find yourself angry and at odds with loved ones at a time when you most need their support.

Relationships with friends can be ended or limited by choice and immediate needs, but family members have or at least believe they have responsibilities and ties to each other that keep them in more constant and permanent contact, even if the parties involved just don't get along. Ideally, you, your husband, and your baby will have loving relatives who are self-confident and respectful of you and each other, loving and gracious, generous and considerate, and all in the amounts and styles you enjoy. If not, your job is to manage to get along well enough with the extended family so that your baby grows up loved by and loving toward them all.

While the previous chapters focused on you and your brand-new nuclear family, the issues in this chapter reflect the highs and lows of how relationships in your extended family change when a new baby is born. Some families accommodate a newcomer easily and intergenerational relationships flourish, while other families struggle to regain a comfortable new equilibrium. The questions and answers reflect the range of behaviors among relatives when there is a new baby, from joy to indifference and generosity to anger.

This chapter will help you know that your situation is not unique, and will offer some suggestions for increasing the positive connections between the generations.

I have so much more respect for my mother now that I have a baby. How did she do it all so well?

She did it all the way you are doing it, one day at a time. Maybe she had more help from family and friends, maybe not. Maybe she had different expectations of herself than you do, maybe not. Maybe it was easier for her, probably not. Most *non*-mothers think that mothers just *know* how to take care of children, and few realize that mothers are often overwhelmed, tearful, or lacking confidence. But every new mother learns as she goes along, even yours. It only appears easy to those who have never done it themselves.

As a brand-new, first-time mother, you understand in a deeper, more personal sense, the magnitude of effort it takes to care for a baby. You have a fuller awareness of the stress and physical discomfort as well as the profound love and enjoyment your mother likely experienced with you when you were an infant. It can be a beautiful and humbling realization.

I remember when my first daughter was born and my mother came to help me. Never before had I realized just how much time, energy, and love she had devoted to me and my brothers and sister all those years before. I know I was unable to fully appreciate all she had given to me, all her hard work, love, and sacrifices, before I became a mother myself. While I was a teary, awkward mess, her knowledge and calm attitude astounded me, taught me, and supported me. It was wonderful.

By all means, tell your mother that you appreciate her. You may feel closer to her now than at any other time in your adult relationship, and these are good feelings to share. Many women report developing a new level of love, appreciation, and respect for their mothers when they recognize the hard work involved in what they, before motherhood, thought were the straightforward, even brainless activities of child care. If you are one of those fortunate women, relish the moment. Enjoy and share those positive feelings with your mom. Becoming closer to your own mother can be one of the many great blessings of motherhood.

Learning to appreciate your own mother can be one of the many benefits of motherhood.

When my mother criticizes me, or challenges my mothering decisions, I fall apart. How can I get past this?

Recognition of your sensitivity is the first step. You may get upset when your mother criticizes you because you care so deeply that she thinks highly of you; maybe you're overly sensitive because of your newness and insecurity as a mother, or perhaps her criticism devastates you because you feel she has *always* been too critical of you. When one person's remarks have an unusually high impact, chances are that your response is not exclusively connected to the comment of the moment. Even as grown-ups, we all still want our mothers to be proud of us, and as a first-time mother, you may be especially defenseless.

First-time mothers are rarely very self-assured. It is quite common for a new mother to fall apart when she feels criticized or attacked, and her shaky self-confidence may lead her to interpret comments as faultfinding even if they weren't intended as such. When your belief in yourself as a mother becomes firmer, you will be able to share ideas and hear criticism from others, including your mother, with more objectivity.

If you are *particularly* sensitive to input from your mother (or your mother-in-law, sister, next-door neighbors) you need to become aware of that sensitivity. Knowing that anything she says takes on gigantic proportions in your mind may help both of you interact more appropriately and comfortably. If possible, tell your mother how her words can sting you.

Heather also found her mother's comments painful. She felt close enough to her mother that she was able to tell her quite directly, "Mom, I love you, but back off! When I need your opinion, I promise I'll ask," and that did the trick. Many other new moms have told the critical relative, "It's my turn to raise my baby, and while your suggestions may be well-intended, I need to do things my own way." In your own way, let your mother know that her "help" hurts your feelings and that while you cherish her involvement, you hope she will understand. Do your best to enjoy the closeness and to avoid the criticism. Hug her when she praises you and walk away or tell her when you feel put down.

Whether your mother is genuinely being hypercritical or you are actually hypersensitive to her, tell her that the slightest disapproval on her part undermines your confidence, and ask her to refrain from offering suggestions unless you've asked for her advice. Also, since you know that your mom's comments elicit a particularly strong reaction from you, learn to filter what she says through that knowledge. Don't be defensive: simply let her know that you are very sensitive these days, and politely tell her that when you need her, you'll be sure to ask for help.

My mother is older and not in good health. How can I help her to be more involved with my baby and me?

Talk to your mother. Many new mothers hope that their own experience with motherhood will bring them and their mothers closer than ever before. But for a variety of reasons, it doesn't always work out that way. If the new grandmother is not physically able to care for you and your baby, it can be a disappointment to each of you. She may wish that she could be more active in your life as much as you do.

- Face your disappointment together and you may be able to gain a different kind of closeness. Being honest about what you can do and be for each other can help you establish a very satisfying emotional involvement, even if your mom can't help you as much as you'd have liked. Maybe your mother can't help you bathe your baby, but perhaps she can still listen to you, offer support, or tell you stories of her early mothering days.
- Discuss her limitations openly but kindly and figure out what she can and can't do. She may be holding back because she doesn't want to burden you with her problems, or because she is afraid she is too weak or addled to help you. Unless you are open about her abilities, you can't know what to expect from her.
- Try not to resent your mother's failing health. Ask her about herself, understand her condition, and accept it with love. Chances are good that she'd rather be lively and spry, playing patty-cake, bringing you meals, and reminiscing about your babyhood with you just as much as you would.
- If your mother doesn't visit you as often as you would like, take the baby to visit her. Send pictures or movies and talk on the

telephone between visits so she can keep up with the baby's development.

- If your mother is hard of hearing, telephone contact may be too frustrating for each of you. Find out about hearing aids or special telephones designed for use by people with hearing problems. Use email or regular mail to keep in touch. Don't stand on ceremony and wait for a reply; write or call often. There is probably a whole lot more you have to share than she does.

- Accept your mother for who she is now, and remember the good times. Hold on to the qualities you cherish about her. Be grateful for what you have, and if her infirmities make her largely unavailable, be grateful for what you had.

No one really wants to see her mother aging and incapacitated, especially when you could really enjoy some good mothering yourself right now. But if your mother can't take as active a role as you'd like due to physical problems, you need to come to terms with that reality. Your having a baby means you are a grown-up now, and while all grown-ups still need a mommy sometimes, you may have to adjust your expectations to make the most of the time you have left with yours.

How do I get my parents to share their feelings about becoming parents, and show them how much I appreciate them now?

This should be easy. Be honest, loving, and direct; tell them about your newly discovered respect for them and ask them about their early parenting experiences. Most people are thrilled to have someone show an interest in them; your parents are likely to be more than delighted to reminisce about your infancy and their first exposure to parenthood.

Sharing your feelings and understanding (or lack thereof) about taking care of a newborn can open new avenues of conversation between you and your parents. If you are more needy now, you may be more willing to accept their advice and suggestions. If you desire more closeness now than before your baby was born, your parents may become more nurturing than they've been for quite awhile.

Having become a parent yourself, you have more clearly than ever entered the ranks of adulthood. Your parents may see you for the first time as an adult, and tell you stories they wouldn't have bothered with before. Be prepared to hear of events and emotions your parents have never related to you. As a result, you and your parents may see each other as more complete, genuine people than previously. Your relationship can become deeper and more satisfying.

Becoming a mother often helps a woman become aware of the tremendous emotional and financial investment her own parents made on her behalf. That, and the first-hand experience of caring for a newborn, can bring a clearer understanding and love to your relationship with your own parents. Tell them about your feelings, ask them about theirs, and you will all benefit.

I feel like my baby's grandmother is competitive with me about mothering. What can I do about this?

Unfortunately, I hear this all the time, and it feels terrible when it seems that your mother or mother-in-law is trying to show you up. Many new grandmothers, while ostensibly offering their wise advice or skills based on years of successful mothering, are, on some level, asserting themselves as the experts, and you, as the novice, are clearly not an expert yet. You're in a no-win situation. If you let her run the show, you feel powerless, resentful, child-like, or incompetent. But if you try to assert yourself, you feel petty, competitive, and worry about hurting *her*.

It sounds like you and Grandma are jockeying for position in your newly expanded family. There are lots of reasons for tension between the generations. Patricia, a first-time grandmother, felt old and uncomfortable being relegated to a role she saw as less vital than her daughter-in-law's, so she tried to show her how skillful she still was. Ruth's mother, who had devoted her whole life to motherhood, was, unintentionally, I'm sure, clearly competitive about who was the better mother, pulling the baby from her daughter's arms, redoing things around the house, giving constant instructions. When you're new at motherhood, you need to be taught and supported, though, not criticized and shown up.

Whenever you deal with loved ones, make sure to choose your battles; you don't want to feel bad about your mothering, but you also don't want to create a rift in the family unnecessarily. Develop some diplomacy, and learn to know when to assert yourself and when to let something go. These relationships are meant to last a lifetime; you need to find a way to coexist compatibly.

- Minimize the opportunity for competitive interactions. If the competition heats up most when the two of you are alone together, make sure you see each other only when your husband or sister (or anybody else) can be with you.
- When the competitive grandma offers to help, give her specific tasks with which you think she can honestly be helpful (organizing the baby's closet, cooking, gardening, or the like) and that you don't mind having her do her way.

- Have your mother baby-sit while you go out or take a nap. She'll be able to show her superior ability, and you'll get a break.
- Deflect or ignore the less irritating remarks (see the question and answer about unwanted advice in chapter 3).
- If your feelings are hurt, say so. If you calmly explain what bothers you about a particular interaction or remark, you'll feel less bullied, and your mom may have honestly had no idea how her comments made you feel. She may not have a clue that you interpreted her reorganizing your laundry room as being competitive with you.
- Mentally file away how difficult it is to have your loved one try to show off or try to prove her superiority to you, and resolve not to be this way yourself when the time comes.

When you and your mother or mother-in-law are both more comfortable in your new roles, the competitiveness between you should decrease. As best you can, remain calm, speak up when you feel actually insulted, and try to be grateful for whatever help comes your way.

When you deal with loved ones, choose your battles carefully.

I'm not too keen on my in-laws. How can I limit their involvement in our lives?

Occasionally, although not often, new parents feel that their parents or in-laws have such dramatically different attitudes and behaviors than those they wish to expose their own children to that they feel that too much contact could be damaging. In cases where there has been violence, sexual abuse, chronic substance abuse, or illegal activities, it makes clear and objective sense to limit a relative's contact with your baby. More often, though, adults simply don't like their in-laws (or sometimes their own family) all that much. Where do you think all those mother-in-law jokes come from?

When the problem is a matter of personality, style, or politics, keep in mind that your in-laws raised your husband, and your parents raised you. While nobody's perfect, and despite the fact that they drive you crazy, your in-laws (and your parents!) did a reasonably decent job, and therefore probably do have some redeeming qualities. Look for the good qualities they possess, the positive values they have instilled in your husband or you, and try to keep controversial subjects and behaviors to a minimum.

As your baby gets older, you can use visits with relatives as examples of how different people live and of how many choices and attitudes there are in this world. You can be respectful of your in-laws while explaining to your child how you choose to do things another way or understand the world differently than they do. Use the things they do that you don't approve of as a way of expanding your child's experience and awareness.

Your in-laws and your parents are blood relations of your baby. Unless there is real danger involved, limit *your* involvement with your in-laws, not your child's. Your child needs to get to know his extended family, their good points as well as their bad. What may seem unappealing to you may be enjoyable to your baby. Learn to be tolerant, accepting, and loving of your in-laws, and if they really drive you nuts, take a break, leave the baby with them and go for a walk, or absent yourself from a visit or two. Just don't criticize your in-laws in front of your baby, as criticizing his relatives may ulti-mately feel to him like a criticism of himself.

My in-laws are so irritating! How can I deal with them when I *do* have to be with them if I find them so unappealing?

Be polite and *don't* complain to your husband. Early in their marriage, Brian and Julie realized that no matter how delightful and charming (or annoying) they each felt their families were, they didn't always see them similarly. And while it seemed to be OK for one to voice his or her aggravation with his or her own biological relatives, even the gen-tlest criticism of an in-law made the other's blood boil. Early on, they agreed that criticism of an in-law is off-limits. I highly recommend this avoidance of conflict, as it is inevitable for irritations to occur, and you don't need marital stress compounding the in-law trouble.

Do your best to keep your irritation under control. Generally speak-ing, you have nothing to gain and much to lose by fighting with rela-tives. Now, I'm not saying that you should smile meekly while your sister-in-law hurls insults or dishes at you, but I am saying that if at all possible, manage your aggravation with dignity and grace. Accept that your in-laws love your husband and he loves them, and that they prob-ably mean well. Remind yourself that they produced your husband, so they must have done something right. Your in-laws are part of your life for the duration of your marriage, and they are as much your baby's grandparents, aunts, uncles, and cousins as your family members are. Try to tolerate the personality quirks that annoy you.

Recognize that over time, most people can be annoying, including you. Unless the family style is to have verbal brawls, if your irritation becomes uncontrollable and a bitter argument breaks out, everyone gets hurt. Your husband may feel pulled to choose sides, which would be painful to him, and to no one's advantage. Practice tolerance, a major virtue, and your family will not only benefit from the decreased tension, your children may learn about acceptance and unconditional love from your example.

Relatives are different than friends, and in-laws are different than blood relations. You and your mate chose each other; your blood relatives love you because they have to and because you share a life history. But you and your in-laws were connected initially through the mutual love of your husband and now through your baby. If you are lucky, you may learn to enjoy and love both sides of the family; if not, it is still in everyone's best interest to get along.

Whenever your in-laws are driving you crazy, remind yourself that they raised your husband, the man you love, the father of your baby. They must have done something right.

My mother-in-law insists on trying to take over my house and baby. How can I get her to let me be the mom without hurting her feelings?

Brenda had a similar concern, "My mother-in-law came to 'help out' when my baby was born. She reorganized all my kitchen cabinets (without asking me first) and made me feel like I wasn't in charge of my own home. My husband doesn't want to hurt her feelings, but I am seething. How can I tactfully tell her to keep her mitts off my spatulas?"

You must be polite but direct. Lots of mothers-in-law inadvertently (and sometimes intentionally) offend their daughters-in-law by coming on too strong, or "helping" in ways that undermine the new mother's confidence. Believe it or not, I've heard of new mothers having their living room furniture rearranged, their small appliances relocated, their closets cleaned, and even their husband's underwear replaced by meddlesome mothers-in-law. Whether your mother-in-law meant to take over your role or not, you feel she overstepped her bounds, and you need to find a way to politely but clearly regain your position.

- Once you have calmed down and you are well rested and ready, tell her kindly that you appreciate her willingness to help out, but that you want to take care of your home your way. Reassure her that you'll ask for her advice when you need it, and then do so, even if you only ask for her recipe for meatloaf, which you'll never make.
- When she offers to help you, be very clear about what help you actually need and want. Give her very specific jobs where how they are done doesn't matter to you or you won't care if she does them differently than you. Then let her do them.
- If she rearranges your things again, be more direct. Thank her for her efforts, but let her know that you have your own organizational methods, and when she moves your stuff around, you have trouble finding things.
- If you don't want her to touch or do anything, smile politely, saying sweetly, "Oh, Clara, thanks, I hate to see you working so hard, just enjoy yourself."
- Although this may be the chicken's way out, in some situations it may be best to enlist your husband's (or sister-in-law's) aid.

Ask a relative you trust to intervene on you behalf, suggesting to the offender that her efforts are appreciated but overwhelming.

- If she repeatedly ignores requests to leave your home intact, then you must learn to be even more direct. Try, "Clara, I know you want to ease my load here and participate in the baby's life, but I need you to back off. When you alphabetize my spices I feel like you are telling me I'm a terrible housekeeper; when you iron the underwear it feels just a tad bit intrusive." Or, "I'm still new at this motherhood thing and need to do things my way and develop a little confidence on my own. Your taking over makes me feel like I'm not in charge of my own house." Or, "I know I should be grateful for all the work you put into my kitchen, and I am, in a way, but when you reorganized everything without even asking me, I felt like I didn't matter. Next time, please ask me first. I'm sure there are lots of ways you can help me that would be great."

The idea is to be concise, kind, and grateful for her intentions (to which you give the benefit of the doubt), but also clear and to the point. Some women would be thrilled to have their mother-in-law come in and take charge, and you can even tell her that, but let her know that you're not one of them. Be nice about it, but set limits now, or you will be dealing with this again and again.

My mother seems crushed whenever I even hint that I might have my own, different ideas. How can I do things *my* way without her feeling insulted?

Motherhood is something that a lot of women are delighted to share with their daughters, but tension can arise when there are disagreements. You and your mother likely have to adjust to your new roles. Your mother is still your mother, and therefore more experienced than you, but this is your turn to make choices and decisions of your own.

Share with your mother your attitudes about motherhood. Explain to her why you place your baby in the crib in a particular way. Give her the articles that support your choice of toys, breast-feeding, whatever you are planning to do differently than she did. Invoke, when necessary, the "my doctor says we need to bathe her this way" approach. Talk about how research, the availability of information, and the array of babycare products have changed since your mother raised you. Share with her the thoughtful attitude you and your husband have toward parenthood. Include her in the way you have come to some of your ideas, and you should be able to maintain your closeness without compromising your ideas.

Your relationship with your mother is bound to change over time, and having your own baby is often a catalyst. You are able to make your own choices in part because your mother raised you to be an independent and careful thinker. Thank her for encouraging your curiosity and raising you to be a self-sufficient person, and remind her that it is not an insult to make different decisions than she did.

Trust your instincts. If someone you respect offers advice that seems outlandish to you, consider it carefully, and then do what seems to make sense to you.

My mother and I are very close, but she acts as if *she's* my baby's mother. How can I make it clear that I'm a capable woman and establish myself as a separate adult?

Carefully. If you and your mother have always been a bit too close, she may have looked forward to your motherhood as a time you will share even more. After all, now you are both mothers. But it's not only you who need you to be a separate adult now; your baby and your husband need you to be a grown-up, too. For your marriage and your baby's well-being, you must clarify boundaries and roles, and be firm in who you each are in your baby's life.

- As best you can, think through first what you need to feel separate. When you and your mother have always been a bit overly connected, it may be hard maintain the separateness you desire.
- Share with your mother how important your closeness is to you, and how her support has allowed you to become independent. Explain that you want to nurture that same independence in your baby.
- Give your mother "grandmotherly" ways to stay connected to you and your baby. Maybe she could make your baby (and each next grandchild) a blanket or sweater, put together a book of favorite family recipes, or make a collage of family photos.
- Create a regular time for visits, with you determining how often and where. Some women find it easier to be on their own turf with difficult relations, while others find that being in Grandma's home clarifies roles (she's more clearly in charge in her own home) and eases tensions.
- Develop new family traditions that acknowledge the next generation's existence.

❧ Offer (insist, if necessary) to host a holiday celebration or regular family get-together at your home, in which you do all the
planning. With a newborn in the house, you may need to keep
it simple or have something catered, but as you get more rest
and efficiency, hosting an event gives other family members a
break, establishes you as a grown-up, and allows your children
to enjoy hosting a family celebration.

Be kind to your mother and negotiate the shift in your relationship
lovingly. Make it clear to her that you want to keep your closeness
while at the same time enjoy your turn at being the mommy.

My mother gave up everything for her children, and I'm not sure I can or even want to do that. Can I still be as good a mother?

Of course you can. You can be a wonderfully giving mother to your
children without giving up everything for them. Being an excellent
mother isn't a matter of how much you give (or don't give) or whether
you make saint-like sacrifices; high-quality mothering isn't quantifi-
able. Great mothers give of themselves to their children, according to
their abilities and their children's needs. But giving of yourself until
the well is dry guarantees neither your baby's future well-being nor
undying gratitude.

Comparing yourself to your mother doesn't do either you or your
baby any good. I'm not suggesting that you don't try to be the best
mother you can, just that you will be most comfortable and probably
most successful if you mother your baby according to your own personal skills, interests, and style, adapting to the needs of your specific

baby. If your mother was a wonderful mother for you, that's fabulous. Feel free to be a wonderful mother to your baby in your own way, and don't worry about being as giving (or as creative or as good a cook or whatever).

Babies need to be loved and cared for and have mommies who are alert to their needs and who are emotionally available to them. They don't need to have mommies who feel like they must give up important parts of themselves (or "everything") to do that, as that kind of self-sacrifice may leave you lonely, empty, bored, overwhelmed, or resentful. You need to feel satisfied and complete and free to enjoy your life to be able also to give freely to your baby. If you are giving up your former life because you enjoy being a mom and prefer to devote your life to child rearing, that's fine. If you are giving everything up because your mother did, or because you think you should, even if you aren't suited to that kind of devotion, then you are not as likely to do it well.

Keep all of this in mind as you consider motherhood, sacrifices, and your own personality. Be loving and generous with your baby, spend time with her, set appropriate limits and goals for both you and her, and enjoy her. Be the kind of mother you are comfortable being, filling your baby's needs as best *you* can, and your baby will grow up feeling cared for without worrying that she must meet your standards rather than determine her own. That way, you lead a more satisfying adult life and your baby learns that while she is extraordinarily important, so are you, and it is OK for women to grow up and have ideas and lives of their own.

You can be a giving mother without giving up everything for your children.

Since my baby's birth my mother and I feel closer than ever. Will this last? Should it?

If you and your mother both enjoy and appreciate this regained closeness, it can certainly continue. Many new mothers experience this new connection to their mothers when they give birth for the first time. For lots of young women, particularly if they've been on their own for a while, having a new baby may be the first event in a long time that highlights the mother-daughter connection. It is also an area your mother is clearly more experienced in and knowledgeable about, so it feels more natural to each of you to have her take care of you than it may have felt for a very long time. This increased closeness can be lovely, and sharing the new baby, and having your mother nurture you as you learn to nurture your new baby, can be one of the joys of new motherhood.

It's hard to say how long the increased closeness will last, but it can go on for as long as you and your mother are both comfortable, and it can certainly add a new dimension to your relationship as adult women. You now have an experience to share, and few other people in the world (besides you and your husband and perhaps your in-laws) will care about your new baby's burps and smiles as much as your mother. Take pleasure in this heightened bond for as long as you wish. You are fortunate to have it and to be aware of it.

Every new mother is a little bit different; each woman has her own need for closeness and for independence. When Melissa had her first baby she wanted her mother to stay with her as long as possible. She and her mother adored those first few weeks together after the baby was born. The new grandma loved taking care of her, and Melissa shamelessly delighted in returning to those very clear mother-daughter roles, relishing being babied herself and learning about child care at her mother's side.

But don't worry if you are ready for some distance, despite loving being taken care of by your mom. After the first few days at home, Lori, another first-time mother, couldn't wait for her mother to leave. She was anxious to have her husband and baby to herself, as she felt that as long as her mother was around, real life, with Lori as the mother, hadn't yet begun. Lori needed to be on her own, to learn by doing, without a more knowledgeable woman around for her to rely on or to take charge of the baby.

Have fun with your mother while she is with you. Enjoy your enhanced relationship. If she needs to get back to her life before you are totally ready to relinquish her, take heart. Your emotional closeness can continue despite the greater physical distance and you and your husband and baby need to feel confident that you can create your family without her constant help. Just be sure to appreciate your mom while you can.

The mother-child relationship is special, primal, wonderful, and it is designed for the mother to be the giver much of the time.

Even though we have a brand-new baby, our parents still expect me to wait on them. What should I do to get our parents to pitch in?

You and your husband need to work out a plan. While you may never be able to count on these grandparents to help *you*, you should certainly be exempt from waiting on them when you have a newborn in the house. I know you don't want your in-laws or parents to think you're incompetent, but during the first several months of motherhood you just aren't up to running a bed-and-breakfast. You need to find a way to help them understand that your limitations as a hostess and as a loving daughter-in-law (or daughter) are temporary, and that their help would be appreciated.

- Before the next visit, set the ground rules. Be clear about who is to do the cooking and cleaning.
- Limit the number of hours or days of each visit to an amount of your choosing.
- If your relatives come from out of town, and you are reasonably certain that they will make your life harder, try to have them stay in a nearby hotel or motel instead of at your house, at least while you are so new to motherhood.
- Tell them you need help, and then give them specific and manageable tasks ("Please go to the grocery store and here is the shopping list," or "Would you mind starting the laundry?").
- Wear a nightgown and bathrobe if you are tired. Go to bed when you need to, saying politely that you haven't slept, and that you'll see them in the morning (or in an hour).
- Use your parents' or in-laws' skills to your advantage; if your mother makes a great tuna casserole, ask her to whip one up for you.
- If your parents or in-laws ignore your requests for help or don't seem to understand that their expectations of you are unrealistic, you will need to be very direct. Explain how overwhelmed you feel, and tell them that you love them, but that you will be a better hostess when you are more experienced and well rested.

- Avoid having them visit you in your home until you feel ready to be more accommodating. Visit them in their home instead.
- If they are offended by your inability to cater to them, try not to hold it against them. While you may never be able to live up to what they demand of you, it is their demands, not your short-comings, that are causing the problem. Once you accept that, you may be no less disappointed that you aren't getting the support you had hoped for, but you won't feel like there is anything wrong with you. Because there isn't.

My father seems so uncomfortable when I breast-feed the baby in front of him. What can I do?

You can talk to him about his discomfort to find out what exactly is bothering him; you can completely cover your baby and breasts when you're in his presence; or, if necessary, you can always breast-feed your baby in another room when Dad's around. Seeing you breast-feed your baby may be awkward for him for many reasons. Talk to him about what concerns him.

- Is he having trouble because he doesn't want to accept that now you, his little girl, are an adult?
- Does the whole idea of breast-feeding give him the willies? Maybe your mother never breast-fed you and your siblings in his presence and it's just weird for him.
- Of course, even though breast-feeding isn't sexual to you, giving birth and breast-feeding make it crystal clear that you are a sexual being. Is it his awareness of your sexuality that makes him

sweat? Or is it that he, like many other new grandfathers, just doesn't feel comfortable seeing (or at risk of seeing) your breasts?

If you can, talk with him openly about what makes him so edgy. Sharing his emotions about your new motherhood and his new status as a grandparent might bring you much closer to each other. Your motherhood firmly plants you in the land of adults; discussing what it means to each of you could provide a wonderful opportunity to enrich your father-daughter relationship. Once you know what about your breast-feeding troubles him, you can usually find a solution.

If you can't talk to him, either because of your personalities or history together, or if his discomfort is too great for conversation to overcome, you can try to be more inconspicuous when you do breast-feed in front of him. In my groups, I've seen many, many women breast-feed, some with everything hanging out and others who appeared to be simply cradling their babies in their arms. Those with smaller breasts have an easier time keeping their breasts out of view, but I've seen larger breasted women nurse their babies very discreetly, too.

- Many women use a lightweight receiving blanket to cover themselves and their babies while breast-feeding.
- Others have shown less skin by always wearing larger, looser tops. The baby latches on to the nipple, mostly under the shirt, and the mom drapes the extra fabric around her breast and the baby's mouth, minimizing exposure.
- Avoid wearing button-down shirts, as they make discreet breast-feeding more difficult.
- If you must wear a button-down (it's part of a uniform or a gift from your father), try unbuttoning the shirt from the *bottom*

rather than from the top, again using the loose material to camouflage what you're actually doing.

- Wearing an extra layer, like a jacket or vest, often helps block the view.
- If you're going to be breast-feeding, always wear two-piece clothing. Overalls work well with an appropriate shirt, but dresses don't lend themselves to maintaining your modesty.
- If your father remains too uncomfortable no matter what you do, you can always excuse yourself and go into another room for the feeding.

Just as you need to adjust to being a mother, your dad may be struggling to adjust to seeing his baby girl as a mother. Talking about your new roles and decreasing the visibility of your flesh will both help to lessen his embarrassment.

My baby is the first grandchild for my in-laws, and I don't think they were ready to be grandparents yet. How can I help them become more involved with my baby?

You will have to help them learn. You may have been absolutely thrilled to become a mother, but they may have had altogether different feelings when they realized that your baby makes them grandparents. It is lovely that you want them involved. If they are holding back out of respect for your independence, show and tell them that you want their more active presence in your baby's life. You may have to help your baby's grandparents become connected if it hasn't come naturally to them.

Recognize that grandparents come in all shapes, ages, and sizes, with different attitudes, interests, energy levels, and availability.

These days, women can become mothers for the first time at nearly any age from teens to middle forties. That means that these first-time grandparents may be youthful forty-year-olds, at the peak of their careers, or retired octogenarians, or any combination in between. If your in-laws are still working full-time or are otherwise still very active in their own lives, they may not be as emotionally available or as intricately involved in your life as you might have liked. Similarly, they may be less immersed in your life if they are elderly or in poor health. And given how much more mobile young adults are, if you do not live in close proximity to the grandparents, it may simply be geography that limits your closeness with your in-laws. There are a few things you may try to keep your in-laws connected:

- Tell them, lovingly, you want them to be more involved.
- Invite them over, suggesting specific times to visit with you in your home.
- Ask them if you can visit them in their house. Often visiting on one's own turf increases self-confidence. Your in-laws may be better able to be the supportive, involved grandparents you hoped they would be if they are on familiar ground, where they set the rules.
- Make frequent telephone calls sharing Baby's most recent charming tricks.
- Send photos often, by email or ordinary mail.
- Plan regular family gatherings and holiday get-togethers.
- Engage your husband in the campaign to include the grandparents in your family; while it's nice that you are extending yourself to them, having both of you encourage their involvement in your lives may make them more certain that they are wanted.

Never having been grandparents before, they don't automatically know what kind of rights and responsibilities you expect grandparenthood to entail. And becoming a grandparent isn't necessarily what they most wanted at this point in their lives. Be respectful of where they are in their lives; offer invitations to include them as often as you're comfortable, and be patient as you negotiate this family transition. And be assured that their level of involvement likely reflects more on their interest and ability than on their love for you or your baby.

Just as you are new to being a parent, your baby's grandparents are new to grandparenting.

I'm having trouble adapting to how differently my husband's family and mine solve disagreements. How can I bridge that gap so that there are no hurt feelings?

Families definitely have different ways of handling conflicts, difficult emotions, and relationships, and sometimes it's hard to blend those family patterns successfully. An occasional blowup, perhaps commonplace in the family in which you grew up, might be experienced as unbearably insulting to someone brought up in a house where no one expressed anger so directly. You will do well to be aware of each family's approaches to conflict and learn to adapt a bit. You want to keep peace among you for your baby's sake as well as your own, and showing your baby that there are many ways to express feelings and to get along will be valuable for you all. Whether you are right or wrong may often be irrelevant; what you do, though, if you're not careful, may be the cquivalent of breaking some serious code of etiquette in a foreign culture. For your relationship with your in-laws to survive, and to avoid making your husband feel as if he's being asked to take sides, you need to maintain open communication with your in-laws. Some people are wounded by behaviors that seem insignificant to others, so it is important to do what you can to clarify your differences and to make these relationships work.

When there is a conflict or the potential for hurt feelings:

- Talk to the person involved. If you have inadvertently hurt an in-law's feelings, for example, tell him that you are sorry. You don't actually need to apologize for whatever caused the problem in the first place and you shouldn't request an apology from him. Don't rehash the original problem here; just show you are sad that feelings were hurt and move ahead.
- If your family was accustomed to loud verbal fighting and your in-laws were not, tell your offended relative that arguing or yelling is normal for you. Apologize if she interpreted your outburst as a character assassination, explaining that you were simply treating her as you would have your own sister.
- Let your in-law know that your ability to let loose, while unintentionally hurtful to him, was actually a sign that you feel close enough to him to be your unedited true self.
- Tell the offended party that you are no longer angry, and that you still want to be friends. Reassure her that you don't hold a grudge against her and you hope she won't hold anything against you, either. Let her know that in the future, you'll try to be more sensitive to her way of dealing with disagreements or annoyances.

- If a disagreement causes your in-law to stop talking to you, show by your actions that you are sorry and that you want to regain a positive relationship. Be considerate; include the injured party often in your family events and the like.
- If you notice over time that a particular relative remains aloof, if he *still* won't talk to you, it may be that nothing you can do or say will break the ice. Sad as that is, you may have to accept that your way of handling a conflict may have done damage that you can't repair without a lot of time and effort.

If an in-law sincerely plans to break all ties to you, continue to be kind anyway, extend invitations, and whenever appropriate, send birthday and anniversary cards or gifts. Your husband will appreciate the attempt at civility, and it may slowly help mend the rift. Be careful when you attempt to solve conflicts with your husband's family in the future, and use this experience to help you raise your own children to interact efficiently with a variety of people and styles. Help your child learn that your husband's family's approach is not necessarily better or worse than your family's attitude—it's just different, and everyone would do well to learn to maneuver in each kind of family culture.

Sometimes who's right and who's wrong isn't as important as solving the problem.

My mother is often ill and her judgment is not too reliable. How can I gracefully let her know that I don't feel comfortable leaving my baby with her?

Focus on the positive. Lovingly tell her that you want her to visit as often as she'd like, but that she had her time to raise her children, and you don't want to burden her with helping you raise yours. Invite her over frequently and stress how important it is to you to have her be a part of the baby's life and yours. If her health (mental or physical) is really poor, she may actually be relieved that you aren't counting on her to baby-sit.

As much as you might need the help, your baby is your first priority. If you feel that your mom isn't capable of caring for her safely, then you must stand by your protective mother instincts. You need to feel secure that your baby is safe, but you also need not unduly insult your mother, and if you choose your words well and show your mother how much you appreciate her in other ways, you should be able to avoid hurt feelings.

Olivia's mom insisted that she wanted to baby-sit and that she was fully able, so Olivia let her mother baby-sit only after her baby was predictably sleeping through the night. She and her husband would put the baby to bed before her mother came over to sit, then they went out to dinner and came home before there could possibly be any problems. Sandi told her wheelchair-bound mom that they had decided not to use family members as baby-sitters at all, ever, and then stuck by that decision. Nina's mother-in-law, Sophia, was a bit too forgetful for her comfort, so Nina told her that they would rather visit with her than have her baby-sit. Sometimes they would hire a baby-sitter and take Sophia out, while other times they all stayed home to play with their baby.

Be firm in your conviction. If your mom tries to prove that you can trust her to care for your baby, take the conversation away from her ability and focus on your need. Tell her that you know she did a great job with you, you have other baby-sitters, and that you just don't want to tax her. Reassure her that you love and respect her and that she put in more than enough time taking care of *you*.

My sister-in-law's first baby is six weeks older than ours. How can I avoid the constant competition we're in?

Sibling rivalries die hard, don't they? As enticing as it is to some people to prove that they're still better than big brother Bob, competing with loved ones doesn't do anyone much good, and it can create awkward and unpleasant tension between you and your in-laws. When the competition begins, make a concerted effort to withdraw. If you won't play that game with them, then there is no game to be played.

- Whenever your brother-in-law points out an achievement or gift, respond with a sincere-sounding, "That's great!"
- If your sister-in-law asks you if your baby is walking (talking, crawling, doing calculus), just say, "He's doing everything on his own schedule, thanks."
- Change the conversation if comparisons between your family and theirs become pointed. If necessary, jump up, wide-eyed, exclaiming, "Oh, my gosh, I have to call Fred right now!" and excuse yourself.
- Don't add fuel to the competition between you. For example, don't mention that your father-in-law just gave you one thousand dollars to start a bank account for your baby, and don't

announce your baby's height or weight, teething, crawling, reading, or other tricks unless you know that they are exactly the same as your niece or nephew's.

- Develop an area of mutual interest with your brother-in-law, and then spend most of your time together pursuing or discussing it, whether it's painting, cooking, or talking about those Yankees.

- Limit your time together if the competition seems unavoidable. When you must be with these relatives, plan an activity that will take the focus away from your babies.

Competitiveness is sometimes contagious as well as annoying. Do your best to eliminate the opportunity and to back away when you find yourself engaging in comparison parenting.

My sister-in-law seems intent on proving to me that she knows better than I do about raising a baby. What can I do to avoid her criticism?

Steer clear of discussions about child rearing! Even if she is a child-development specialist, her opinions are not necessarily better than yours are. Parenting is not an exact science. Techniques and attitudes that work for some parents with some children don't work for others, and success is rarely directly related to specific techniques. Personality, natural attributes of both parent and child, and a lot of luck all contribute to how "well" a child is raised.

Some child-rearing "experts" promote ideas that other "experts" find appalling. And sometimes parents who do everything "right" or according to the parenting professionals still have problems with their kids, while other parents who ignore the current wisdom have children who grow up to be absolutely lovely. Unless the parenting approach either you or your sister-in-law employs puts the children in physical or emotional danger, chances are that you are both doing a fine job.

Lena's older sister was an early childhood educator, but despite (or maybe because of) her background and knowledge, she was also the most permissive parent Lena had ever seen. Lena's niece at two years old made other Terrible Two's seem Terrific. At seven, this niece expected adults to cater to her every wish and became petulant and defiant if she didn't get what she wanted. But at twenty-three, this young woman, now all grown-up, is a charming, pleasant, and agreeable person, defying all expectations to the contrary. Similarly, I know parents who appear to do everything "right," whose parenting exemplifies an excellent balance between permissiveness and rules, love and reason, limits and freedom, who have children grow up to become unpleasant and unproductive. Obviously, these situations are not the usual outcomes, but they illustrate that there are no guarantees in parenting or in life.

If your sister-in-law continues to offer advice on how you should care for your baby, limit your interaction with her. When you must see her, counter her criticisms with a pleasant "Thank you for your wisdom," and change the subject or leave the room. If your relationship will tolerate more directness, tell her that her pontificating on how much better her approach to parenting is than yours makes you feel bad. Remind her that while she may know how to take care of her children well, you know how to care for your children equally well. You each need to raise your children according to your specific personalities and strengths. And, if she continues to rag on you, it might not hurt to point out that parenting is not a competitive sport.

Raise your children according to their personalities, strengths, and needs as well as your own, not according to a formula.

My mother died several years ago. Is it normal that I miss her so much now that I have a baby?

Becoming a mother yourself is bound to make you think more about your mother; this is one of those times that most women want to share with their mothers. You may want to compare notes or thank her for her hard and loving work raising you. You'd like to be able to show off your baby to the new grandma, ask for her advice, share your experiences and emotions, and you can't. Many women find that their mothers are the only ones they can allow to see them at their most vulnerable, the only ones they can relax with enough to ask for help, and the only ones they want with them when their new baby is born. It's not at all surprising that having your first baby (and possibly each baby) reawakens both the awareness and the sadness that Mom is not here with you anymore.

What makes this time difficult is that you are missing both your mother as a specific person as well as the loving, mentoring relationship she provided. If you are lucky enough to have another older female relative, call her. Contact an aunt, a sister, or stepmother, or even your mother-in-law, and ask them about their early mothering days. Ask one of your relatives to remember details about your infant days and your mother's life. Most women will be delighted to talk with you, comfort you, support you, and share stories of their own experiences as a new mother. Developing a closer relationship with another female relative can be very satisfying for you both.

New mothers need to share their experiences with other women, both women going through the transitions and adjustments at the same time and those who have the wisdom and distance of being a generation ahead of them. Reach out, talk about those feelings, and understand how very normal they are. Chatting with someone older and more experienced than you can make missing your mother less painful. Talking with someone who knew your mother can make you feel less alone.

New mothers need to share their experiences with other women.

Both sets of our baby's grandparents live in other communities and expect us to spend our vacations and holidays with them. How can we make everybody, including us, happy?

Divide up the holidays between the relatives and start some new traditions of your own. If Christmas is the most important holiday in your husband's family, but Easter is more central to your family, you'll have it easy. If both families celebrate Passover and nothing else all year, you may have a bigger problem, but you can still solve it.

- Alternate the family with which you will celebrate each holiday. Celebrate Christmas and Easter at your parents' home in years that end with an even number, Thanksgiving and your baby's birthday with your husband's extended family, and reverse for odd years.

- ✤ Host the celebrations yourself and include both sides of the family.
- ✤ Stay home and celebrate important holidays as a nuclear family, and see each of your extended families at other times of the year, or a week later or earlier.
- ✤ Split Christmas and Christmas Eve or the first and last day of Hanukkah, celebrating one with one side, one with the other.
- ✤ Visit with relatives from each side often enough that holidays take on less significance.
- ✤ Create family reunion traditions. Meet the third weekend in April every year at a resort location with one side of the family, the second week in September with the other.

Be grateful that both families want you and your baby, but be steadfast in creating a plan that feels comfortable and manageable to you.

Is it possible that my in-laws and my parents are competing for "favorite grandparents" status?

Doesn't this sound like it is directly from a sitcom? Sad to say, this happens a lot. As Wendy, the first-time mother of a four-month-old said, "Not only are my parents and in-laws overwhelming us with visits and gifts, I worry about the potential for spoiling our baby, making her 'love' them for the gifts, not for themselves. How can I make them see that our baby will love all of them for who they are, and that their 'generosity' just isn't appropriate?"

Competitive grandparenting isn't easy to handle, but it's a common concern. The two sets of grandparents try to out-do each other in gift-giving, time spent with the grandkids, number and quality of photos, or affection received. It's one of the less unpleasant problems, but one that still needs attention.

Try to resolve this issue while the baby is still very young, before she is aware of the dueling loved ones and any spoiling can take place.

- Talk to each set of grandparents directly. Thank your parents and in-laws for their generosity but ask them to slow down a bit. Share your concern that their lavish giving will lead to your baby loving them for their tangible gifts, not for their wonderful personalities and relationships with her.
- Again, after thanking them, tell them you will appreciate their gifts for the baby more as she grows older, when gifts from friends and other relatives taper off.
- Tell them that you don't have the space or need for forty-seven stuffed toys or four party dresses in size six months right now. Suggest that if they really want to help you out, you'd prefer something more from their hearts.
- Don't tell one set of grandparents what the other set has given you. That might incite their jealousy and desire to outdo. If your in-laws admire a new toy or ask about its origins, simply thank them for the compliment, tell them what store it came from or what a great brand it is, and don't blurt out that your parents bought it for you.
- Plan activities that include both sets of grandparents so they can become friends rather than adversaries. Both sets then have equal time with the baby, and maybe friendship will eliminate the need to prove which grandparents are best.
- Tell your parents and in-laws how very much you appreciate and respect them, how important their presence is in their

grandchild's life, and that you don't want their gifts to over-
shadow the emotional closeness you know they can each have
with your baby.

- ❧ Reassure your in-laws and parents that you know that your
  baby will love each of them very much. Teach them that loving
  one of them will not diminish her love for the others.

If using the ideas above doesn't cause the new grandparents to scale
back the giving and feel more secure about their relationships with the
baby, accept that when your baby is old enough, you will need to teach
her about the value of giving yourself. As she grows up, tell her stories
about her wonderful grandparents. If the competitiveness between the
grandparents continues, help her to behave lovingly toward each
grandparent. Explain that sometimes even grandparents can act silly
and that it is OK to love them all very much.

How can my baby grow up feeling connected to our extended family members when we all live so far apart from each other?

It's wonderful when you and your families enjoy each other, and difficult when you don't get to be together very often. Despite the distances between you, you can have warm, close relationships with a
little extra effort.

- ❧ Take lots of pictures and share them shamelessly. Randi got a
  digital camera as a new baby gift and takes pictures nearly
  every day. She sends them to all her relatives via email to keep
  them updated as to the baby's progress.

- ❧ Ditto digital movies.
- ❧ Make frequent phone calls. If you worry about your phone bill, take advantage of the telephone service plan competition. Some telephone companies allow unlimited calls at certain hours or to groups of people who sign up together. Both in-home plans and cellular-phone plans are available and may save you lots of money while allowing hours of voice-to-voice communication.
- ❧ Visit in person as often as your schedules allow.
- ❧ Organize annual reunions with each side of the family.
- ❧ Plan to take vacations with family. Some of Tricia's favorite summer vacations have been when all the aunts and uncles and cousins went to the same beach town and rented a large house together. Even a long weekend will help cement those ties and create lovely memories.
- ❧ Speak fondly and often of your family members in front of your baby. Post pictures of Grandma and Aunt Lulu at your baby's eye level to keep them in your baby's memory until he is old enough to have memories himself.
- ❧ Appreciate your closeness despite the geographic distance. You and your family are blessed.

Chapter Seven

Your Social Life

Just because you've become a mother doesn't mean you have to give up your social life, and although maintaining a social life when you're taking care of a newborn can be a challenge, first-time mothers need their friends. Friendships, though, come in many guises. It may take a life-changing event (like becoming a mother) to make it clear to you which friends are your true soul mates, which friendships need common experiences to sustain them, and which friends you can always rely on for a cup of sugar or a bit of child-care advice. When friendships meet or surpass your expectations, it's terrific. When friendships fade or falter, it can be devastating, especially when you're in a time of need.

New mothers have all sorts of feelings about their social lives (or lack thereof). Often, a first-time mother will tearfully describe losing her best friend, who, unmarried and childless, is angry that she is no longer available for long telephone conversations or late weeknight club hopping. Other new moms express their pleasure when formerly casual acquaintances become incredibly generous and friendly now that all are mothers. Some women want to know how to meet other new mothers while others want to hear about what kinds of social things they can do with their babies along. Many want to talk about how to find a baby-sitter so that they can at least occasionally socialize in a baby-free zone.

The questions and answers in this chapter examine a range of concerns about how to have a satisfying social life after becoming a mother. Topics include how old friendships struggle to adapt to this new life phase, where to go to meet other new mothers, and how to maintain a social life at all while meeting the demands of a new baby. When you become a mother, your priorities, interests, and energy level may all change, but you still need a social outlet.

Even though it's hard to manage, you need friends. You need friends to validate your experiences and feelings, you need friends who share your non-baby interests, you need friends who can help you out in a pinch, and you need friends with whom you can just have fun. This chapter is intended to help you adapt to how motherhood changes how you socialize, and to develop and maintain a meaningful and satisfying social life.

I am so lonely since I've been home with my baby. How do I go about making new friends who have new babies, too?

First, you need to meet other women who also have young babies, and then you have to be willing to make the first gesture toward establishing a friendship. To meet other new mothers, you need to know where to find them, and to make that meeting turn into a friendship you need social skills and the willingness to try to connect with someone you don't already know.

There are a number of ways to find the other new moms in your neighborhood. Many new mothers feel isolated, and plenty will want to meet you just as much as you want to meet them; you just need to find each other.

- Look in your local newspaper for classes or groups for mothers and babies and join one.
- Call your local YMCA, church, synagogue, or community center and ask if they have classes or groups for young babies.
- Ask your neighbors or friends with older children if there were any groups or classes they particularly enjoyed, and then sign up.
- Take your baby out for a walk whenever weather permits, and bring your baby to a shopping mall, museum, grocery store, or local coffeehouse and strike up a conversation with other moms and babies you see.
- Be similarly friendly to other mothers with babies wherever you see them. Exchange phone numbers if you seem to hit it off, gather up your courage if you are a shy type, and call the other mom and suggest an outing together. This can be like a "coffee date": get to know the other person on neutral ground and see if you really like each other without much commitment. If you hit it off, you have a new friend!
- If you were in a birth preparation class, throw a reunion. Often the instructor will be more than happy to provide names and telephone numbers and will sometimes even help you organize it. Invite all the new moms, dads, and babies to a potluck dinner or just for tea and cookies, or to meet at a park or other public place. Take pictures, and then keep in touch with anyone you think might become a friend.
- If you didn't take a childbirth preparation class, ask your obstetrician or midwife if he or she would be willing to help you put

together a group of new mothers. Because of confidentiality concerns, you might only be allowed to post your name and number as an organizer of a group, but that might yield some great new friendships.

❧ If you are breast-feeding, LaLeche League is a great resource.

Be bold and willing to risk being turned down. I know many first-time mothers, including myself, who have made lasting friendships with other new parents they met at a coffeehouse, playground, or even a grocery store. Lots more new mothers have developed lifelong relationships with people they met in classes and groups. Go where the new mothers are, be open to any overtures toward friendship from another mother, and make the first move yourself if necessary.

When you see another new mother with a baby, chances are she would be as interested in becoming your friend as you are in becoming hers; say hello.

None of my friends from my former life have children yet. How can I maintain these friendships when our lives are so different now?

Some friendships will last forever, no matter how different your lives are from each other now, others need common interests and schedules to keep them going. Your life, your priorities, and the time you have available to sustain a friendship are very different than your childless friends'. The friendships that are based on close emotional connections, the soul mates among your friends, will stand by you, understand, and maybe even enjoy the differences between your lives. The friendships based on going out together or sharing work or hobby-related interests only may, sadly, dissolve gradually over time.

- ❦ If you very much want to remain friends with someone, tell her. Be honest and direct about feeling out of touch.
- ❦ Make an effort to see your friend without your baby.
- ❦ Make phone calls when your husband is around or when your baby is likely to sleep for a while so you aren't interrupted.
- ❦ Use email to stay in touch, as you can write whenever you have a free moment (and I know several new mothers who claim to be very adept at holding a baby while typing one-handed) so as to avoid interruptions.
- ❦ Share your concerns that your current life situations keep you from getting together as much as you'd like, and your desire to remain close despite the temporary differences in your energy, interests, and availability.
- ❦ Make sure that you are still listening to your friend even when you no longer share the same interests.

When a friendship does wane, though, take heart. Although lots of women are able to remain friends with their childless or single friends, many others experience exactly what you are describing. Some friendships require more effort, particularly if you were the more nurturing one before your baby was born, than you may have the energy to invest. Some friendships, less focused on an emotional connection, really need the shared activity or work to keep them going. You and your former friends may have very different needs and expectations now from each other, and that's just how life works sometimes.

It doesn't mean that there's anything wrong with either of you, nor is either of you actually to blame. You are just growing apart. When your lives take such a divergent course, remaining close can be difficult, although it can be very painful to lose touch with people you cared about and enjoyed. Do your best to stay close to those you truly care about or those with whom you have a long history, but don't dwell too long on the sadness about those you may have lost.

People in your life, including yourself, may resist the changes in your life that your motherhood provokes. Those who love the essential you, your soul mates and tried-and-true friends, will stand by you.

My friends had their first children years ago, and are totally unsympathetic to my needs. What can I do to get the support I need?

When a more experienced mother tells you, "You think *this* is hard, just wait until she's a teenager!" she's not trying to help you. As best you can, turn a deaf ear on those kinds of comments and do not complain to these "friends" about how difficult you find this stage of motherhood. I had one friend with older children who repeatedly told me that it only gets harder, and I remember thinking that whether or not her remarks were true, it was a particularly unhelpful thing to say. So what, if, in retrospect, changing diapers and nursing seem pretty simple and straightforward compared to deciding whether or not your fifteen-year-old should be allowed to go to a coed slumber party? What you're going through now is challenging and real and deserving of respect and support.

The emotional adjustment to motherhood is tremendously stressful for most women. At no other time in your life do you make so many changes so rapidly, taking on a new role, caring for a person who, just months ago, didn't even exist, shifting your priorities and responsibilities, altering your marriage, and for many, changing your position in the workplace. I can promise you that even though the child-care issues may become more complex as the children get older, the stress of the first year of motherhood is different and for many just as difficult and intense as any you will face in future parenting years. And for most women, being a mother (as opposed to parenting) gets easier, no matter what your friends say.

Find friends who are able to be supportive of you. You can still enjoy your old friends as you did before becoming a mother, but don't use these more experienced moms as your primary or only source of emotional support. Whether they are minimizing your struggles because they want to frighten you or to prove that they have it harder than you do, or simply because they don't remember their own discomforts, they are not helping you. Seek out women who *can* commiserate with you and/or remember their own personal conflicts and who will listen attentively and kindly to you. What you need are friends who have your interests in mind, not friends who, without meaning to, seem to need to prove that they are the better mothers or need more attention than they are capable of giving.

True friends are able to put aside their own issues and listen. Remember what it feels like to be a new mother, take note of what your more helpful friends say or do for you (or what you wish they would). Then, when the time comes for you to be the experienced and wise woman, and a first-time mother comes to you for some insight, remember that no one feels better when she's told that it's just going to get worse. Offer other new mothers the encouragement and support you all need.

True friends put aside their own issues and listen.

My friends don't understand when all I can talk about is my baby. Am I really dull now?

No, of course you're not dull; you've simply become a mother, engrossed in the details of child rearing. Many new mothers worry about becoming dull and uninteresting. But your friends' surprise at your newly narrowed focus doesn't mean you are boring; it's just that your interests and your old friends' are no longer the same.

If none of your former friends have children close to your baby's age, you probably have less in common with them now than you did before becoming a mother. New mothers are quite commonly completely absorbed by the novelty of their mothering experiences; they usually find few other topics as engaging as stretch marks, sleep deprivation, or their babies' latest tricks. Non-mothers are rarely capable of sustaining interest in someone else's baby for longer than the brief but polite reply of "Fine" to their "How's the baby?" Although diaper rash conversations may be exactly what *you* need, they may also leave your old buddies cold. But no one is to blame; you are simply in different places in your lives.

Being at a new life stage can consume your thoughts and command much of your attention. Assess whether your limited conversation is alienating your old pals and that's why they don't seem to understand. If your absorption with your baby really is excessive, if you no longer care about what happens to anyone but your baby, your husband, or yourself, you may need to make a conscious effort to broaden your ability to see beyond your immediate concerns.

On the other hand, despite the fact that caring for a new baby is pretty overwhelming at times, friendships based on a true meeting of the hearts will survive your temporarily narrow focus. If you feel that these formerly close friends aren't appropriately supportive of you or chastise you for your fascination with your baby, it may be that these friendships were based solely on engaging in similar activities. It's sad to lose the closeness you once shared, but if what you had in common no longer exists, a friendship that relied solely on sharing experiences may have run its course.

When friendship continues despite shifting life stages, job changes, and geographic distance, it will survive even if your discussions are a bit awkward for a while. All you need to do is talk to your friends about your changed interests and priorities, confess that you know your focus is limited right now, and learn to enjoy listening to what's going on in their lives. Really hear what your friends are saying about themselves, and talk to them not only about the various colors of your baby's poop, but also about the range of your emotions as you adjust to motherhood. Be open to shifting the attention away from your baby; remind yourself why you enjoyed these people before. When you share your feelings, not just the details of your day, your conversation will not be boring and your real friends will always be interested.

Some of my friends with babies have made very different choices about child rearing, breast-feeding, and work; why does it feel like these differences are driving us apart?

You can have friends who are doing things differently as long as you are all comfortable with your own choices and with the differences. Friends don't need to be duplicates of each other, making all the same decisions about how to be a mother, and variety can be enriching and interesting. Too often, though, discomfort and uncertainty accompany new mothers' choices, leading some women to become very defensive and almost militant about the rightness of their personal approaches to motherhood. If you don't feel remotely threatened by your friends' differences, their discomfort may seem kind of unnecessary to you. But some women feel that their decisions are being criticized when they are confronted with other new mothers who are doing things very differently.

If you are confident about having decided whether or not to breast-feed, to work outside the home, to let your baby cry at night, or to put her on a strict schedule, it is also likely that you will not feel defensive if your best friends make opposite choices. But if you or your friends are ambivalent about these important decisions, you may be uncomfortable when faced with someone who is doing things her own way.

- Understand that every mother and baby is unique, and that what works well for Carla may be disastrous for Claire.
- Discuss your choices with your family and friends. When there are differences, truly listen. You may learn something about child care or something about your friend. Either way, you will be better informed.

- Develop tolerance. Unless your child-rearing choices reflect wildly divergent life attitudes, values, and morals (and, honestly, these choices do not always reflect one's moral attitudes or values) a stay-at-home mom can generally still be friends with a woman who makes a different decision. And your best friend's comfort nursing her baby in public, while you retreat to the ladies' room, is not necessarily an indication that she's a psychotic exhibitionist you should avoid.

- There are many, many ways to be a good mother. Support your friends' differences as well as the similarities. Learn from each other why you each do what you do, and encourage each other to follow the approaches that work for each of you.

- If you are willing to accept that you and your friends may raise your children differently, but your friends are still intolerant of your opposing views, find out why. If they are worried that your approach to babycare is dangerous, at least assess if they have a valid point. Talk with your health-care professional and your husband about the differences in child-care techniques. If after exploring your friends' concerns you still feel confident that your ideas about motherhood are just as valid as theirs and that your attitudes reflect a difference in style rather than a lack of skill or knowledge, you may want to consider finding new friends.

Friends are supposed to bring you support and joy and love you for who you are. True friends accept each other's differences, learn from each other, and, when asked, offer advice tactfully and lovingly. They do not correct you when you are not incorrect. If your friends aren't tolerant of your divergent ideas, it may be time to find other sources of support.

> *What's right for you might not be right for someone else, but you each need to feel that your ideas are OK. You need to figure out what is right for you and your family, regardless of what your friends are doing.*

Sometimes, even when I'm with friends, I interrupt our conversations to make baby talk to my baby. Will all my non-mother friends think I've lost my connection to reality?

Lots of not-yet-mothers question their old chum's sanity when a formerly articulate and well-rounded friend becomes so baby-centered that she can't sustain an adult conversation without occasional baby chatter. Non-mothers rarely comprehend the depth of fascination a new baby holds for its mother. Neither do they "get" how sleep deprivation and the struggle to learn how to be a mother can temporarily change a bright woman's focus so completely. When you're new to motherhood, nothing else quite captures your interest as does that baby, and maintaining a train of thought that's unrelated to your primary focus is pretty difficult. So of course, your friends who haven't joined the motherhood club may wonder about you, too.

You could help them understand what's happening to you by anticipating their reactions and explaining to them that you haven't gone bonkers *before* you dissolve into baby talk. Explain that your world has changed, and so has your ability to converse. Reassure them that you are still interested in them and want to hear about their lives, but that it may be tricky for you to maintain an adult conversation for awhile.

Tell your childless friends that you remember well, before your baby was born, worrying about how much your friends seemed to change when they had their babies. Work hard to listen to your friends now, and apologize in advance for those lapses in concentration. And then call up your friends who became mothers before you did, and apologize for not having understood them!

I don't have the time or energy to devote to some friendships that I used to, and our lives are so different. Will I lose these friendships because I have a baby?

Whether or not a friendship can withstand the stresses created by major life changes really depends on the friendship itself and the level of commitment you each have to maintaining it. Some friendships really do last a lifetime, but others do not. It can be very sad when a friendship cannot transcend a major life-stage change, but it sometimes happens. Fortunately, usually other friendships develop to fill the void, but that doesn't always take away the sadness about the loss, especially when you thought that this relationship was special enough to continue no matter what.

There are different types of friendships, and not all survive the shifting interests and priorities that aren't shared:

- Friendships that can be described as two soul mates usually do survive one friend becoming a mother. Soul mates are friends because they care about each other in similar and deep ways. These friendships are supportive of each other's differences and choices even when they take the two friends on wildly different paths. There is affection and respect that exists beyond specific interests or lifestyles, and competitiveness is at a minimum. These friendships usually are able to withstand geographic and philosophical differences, and both people are willing to work on the friendship, to settle disputes, so that the closeness continues.

- ❧ Some friendships are based on enjoying common interests. While both parties are in a similar stage of life or on the same job, the friendship flourishes. When one person moves on, either to another location or job or life stage, when the common interests or hobbies disappear, they find little interest in each other. These relationships often do not survive when one member changes her focus.

- ❧ Another type of friendship depends on each friend helping out the other. Neighbors are often friends of this sort. They are great to carpool with or to borrow the proverbial cup of sugar, but once the mutual need is gone, if no other common interests exist, the connection fizzles.

- ❧ Some friendships are based on what one does for the other. I've seen many new mothers who, upon reflection, realize that they were the primary nurturers in a friendship. They enjoy listening to their friend's problems, being the supportive one. When they have their first baby, though, their nurturing needs are pretty well taken care of, and they may need some support themselves. It can be very disappointing to discover that when you are no longer capable of listening endlessly to your buddy's problems, that friend you thought would stick with you forever drops out of your life.

New mothers need their friends, and it feels very bad when a friend you thought was a friend forever does not stand by you as you make the transition to motherhood. Chances are that your friendship was not as solid as you had hoped, or that it meant something different to you than it did to her. But on a positive note, becoming a mother offers opportunities to learn about yourself and what you want and need from the people in your life, and while some friendships falter, others will develop and strengthen. Enjoy the friendships that stand the test of time and changing lifestyles, and accept that the life span of some close relationships may be briefer than you'd hoped.

Some friendships are not meant to last forever. They are tied to a specific period or function in one's life. It's sometimes painful, but OK, to let those friendships go.

My best friend is insulted when I'm distracted or even unable to talk on the phone with her. How can I make her understand that it isn't personal?

Tell her. It is totally normal to be distracted when you have a new baby, to always have an ear open to hear your baby's cry, or to be unable to get to the phone at all sometimes. You may not be able to devote the same kind of attention to your friends that you would like until your baby is a little more predictable and you are more confident as a mother.

- Explain to your friend that her friendship still means the world to you, but that you are responsible for keeping your baby content and alive. Ask her to understand that sometimes you may abruptly end a conversation, or at other times you may not be able to talk at all. Reassure her that this is a period of adjustment, and that your baby needing you in no way diminishes your wish to be a good friend.

- If at all possible, hire a sitter or leave your baby with your husband or trusted relative or neighbor and go out with your friend without your baby. Then you can focus on your conversation without worrying about the baby's needs.
- Invite your friend to your home. Sometimes seeing you with the baby may help your child-free best friend become aware of the effort involved in child care.
- Communicate via email. That way you can send messages when you have the time and respond with a bit more thought. If you're interrupted, you can save the message to finish and send later.
- If your friend doesn't accept your explanations and apologies for your distractibility, reconsider the value of the friendship. Good friends accept each other as they are, and if your distractibility is too annoying to your best friends, maybe they aren't such good friends after all.

Mary Lou used to love long and intense conversations, but after she had her baby, she wasn't able to remain as focused on her friends as she used to be. She also worried that her friends were upset with her, and struggled to keep everybody happy. When she realized that her ability to focus on her friends was compromised and that her friends were irritated and angry with her, she talked with them about her shifting priorities. Some friends completely understood and became very supportive, while a few slowly withdrew. Although she was sad to lose a few formerly close girlfriends, the ones who stuck by her were really committed to their friendship.

You and your friends need to accept that babies sometimes can't wait, and that your caring for your new baby is not intended as an insult to your friends. Your baby's needs, at least in the immediate future, come first. True friends will tolerate and even be proud of your ability to become a great mother.

I feel so isolated and sick of being at home with my baby. What are some fun things to do on days when I'm alone with my baby?

Being alone with a baby is wonderful, but it can also be boring after awhile. When you've sung "The Wheels on the Bus" thirty-four times, danced around the living room, and played with rattles, mobiles, and floor gyms until you can't stand it anymore, you have to get out, be with other people, and see something besides your own house. Take your baby on a field trip. Let your interests guide you.

- When my first daughter was a baby, we took advantage of our museums' free days. I'd pack her in the car, grab a lightweight stroller, and go. Public buildings all have wheelchair access now, and mothers with strollers are generally welcome to use them.
- Go to the zoo. As with museums, you will enjoy the exhibits while your baby enjoys the variety of sounds, temperatures, and sights.
- If the weather is bad, go to an indoor shopping mall or even a discount super store. Look at departments and stores you ordinarily wouldn't.
- Walk to a park or drive to one in a different neighborhood.
- If you can still carry your baby in a frontpack or backpack, or if

you are particularly adept at maneuvering your stroller, take a train or bus ride, even if you have no destination.

- ❧ Go to the library. Many libraries and some children's bookstores have story hours, but just being among the books may be enough of a novelty.
- ❧ Go to a local coffeehouse or ethnic restaurant, one that is friendly to mothers with babies. It's never too early to accustom your baby to restaurant manners. But be willing to leave if the baby becomes too fussy.
- ❧ Join a mother-baby class.

Most babies are actually very agreeable about going out, and whether or not your baby appreciates seeing a real van Gogh is irrelevant as long as you both enjoy the outing. You will feel better having shown your baby some of what the world has to offer and the much-needed change of scenery and pace will enrich you both.

With a little planning ahead, most babies will happily go anywhere. Take your baby out and have fun.

The only time I ever see my friends is when they come to my house. What can we do together besides sit in my living room?

Follow some of the suggestions in the preceding questions. You, your baby, and your friends can easily go to museums, shopping malls, zoos, or parks together, and your baby is likely to enjoy hearing your voices as you chat while strolling among the trees or boutiques. You may have to convince your friends that you and your baby will be good company, but it will be worth it as your friendships will thrive and so will you.

- Always travel well prepared, with extra clothes for each of you, plenty of diapers, and food.
- Time the outings for when your baby will be at his best—either asleep much of the time or cheerful.
- Do things you used to do with your friends. If you and your friends like eating out, find baby-friendly restaurants or bring a picnic lunch.
- Ask your friends when your baby is welcome and when he is not. Don't take your baby with you if the friend objects. Many friendships have been damaged when enthusiastic new mothers bring their new babies to everything, regardless of the friends' lack of interest in including them.

Your friends may be coming to your house because they think it is easier on you. Talk with them and tell them what you would rather do, and then do it.

I miss going to movies. Can I bring my new baby in under my coat without getting into trouble?

It's probably not a good idea to smuggle a baby into a movie theatre (or anywhere else) unless you know that the owners don't object, and you don't have to worry. Not only do you run the risk of getting into trouble, but should your baby cry, you might annoy your fellow audience members. In addition, it's never too early to consider living by example; if your sneaking-in behavior continues until the baby becomes aware of your lawbreaking, you inadvertently teach your child to break the rules when they aren't convenient to you.

There are other options for movie-loving new parents:

- Many television cable channels have wonderful movies. Your financial investment in cable or satellite hookups may ultimately save money otherwise spent on baby-sitting and entertainment (not to mention securing your emotional well-being). Copy movies shown at inconvenient times for future viewing, or to ensure that a fussy baby doesn't cause you to miss finding out if the boy finally gets the girl or whodunit.
- Similarly, VCRs and DVDs were invented for parents of young children. Get a reliable DVD or video machine and rent those great films you've always wanted to see. If your baby wakes up, you can stop the movie, attend to the baby, and no one will be irritated (except, maybe, you).
- Hire a baby-sitter, swap baby-sitting times, or ask a trusted and generous friend or relative to stay with your baby while you go to the multiplex.
- Call your local movie house and ask about their policy for bringing in a baby. Many theaters now have baby-welcome showings of first-run movies, often on weekdays or before a certain hour each day. If none near you allows infants to attend, urge them to add an occasional Mom's afternoon at the movies, and get your friends to write letters or make calls in support of this idea. Even once a month would be appreciated; if you attend regularly, you might become friendly with the other new mothers nursing babies while munching popcorn.

You don't have to give up your favorite forms of entertainment once a baby enters your life, but as evidenced above, you do sometimes need to be creative.

My closest friend has been unable to have a baby, and I think she has been avoiding me. I miss her friendship, but how should I deal with her jealousy and my guilt?

If your friendship is important to you, face the tension openly. You may or may not want to talk with your best friend about it, but if she's avoiding you, you have little to lose and lots to gain by trying to bridge the gap. I make no promises here; every friendship is different and every friend is, too. Your guilt may make you too uncomfortable to gush about your baby when you're with your old friend, while her pain at not being able to conceive yet may make her too uncomfortable to share in your joy. Some friendships can't survive the stress of one's achieving the happiness that eludes the other, but others, with a bit of effort and honesty, become stronger.

It is normal to feel at least a twinge of envy when your good pal succeeds at something you perceive yourself to be failing at. Before my first child was born, I suffered a miscarriage, and I must admit that for awhile it was very difficult for me to be around new mothers. I wanted to be enthusiastic for them, admire their babies, but my own sense of loss was too great. I didn't want to hear how happy they were, and I didn't want to hear any complaints, either. I was luckier than your chum was, though, in that only a few months later, I became pregnant with my firstborn. My experience with miscarrying certainly made me more sympathetic to those who were struggling as your friend has been, but my awareness of or sensitivity to another woman's sadness couldn't always help her to get beyond it. Sometimes friendships falter through no fault of either party.

If you have the sort of closeness that allows it, talk about it.

- Talk to your friend about feeling bad about having what she wants. Help her to be open with her feelings, too, so you really know what bothers her or how to adjust to this shift in your closeness.
- Ask her if she wants you to talk about the baby or about motherhood, or if she'd rather avoid the topic altogether. Respect her wishes, whether it be to continue seeing each other, but to avoid the subjects of motherhood and babies, or to distance herself from you. If she feels the need to take a break from your friendship for awhile, don't take it personally, and respect her needs.
- Express your disappointment for you both that you aren't sharing this new life stage together. Do your best to continue to enjoy activities or interests you shared before your baby was born.
- Make time to see her without your baby. Even though you may need her to listen to you, be particularly careful to listen to her.
- If you truly value this relationship, stay in touch with her. Don't stand on ceremony and wait for her to call you. Send emails, invite her over, and call her. She may love hearing from you, but she may not want to risk having to listen to your baby crying.
- On the other hand, don't drown her in your attention; allow her the time she needs to come to terms with not having a baby herself. She may not want to call you or visit if she fears that your preoccupation with the baby will emphasize to her what she is already missing. Accept graciously whatever happens between you.

Be as warm and supportive a friend as you know how, and chances are good that your friendship will ultimately become stronger. If the tension between you is too great, or if your friend cannot overcome her broken heart, the friendship may dissolve, at least until your friend has a baby of her own or resolves her emotions about not having what she really wanted. Do your best and good luck.

Some friendships can't survive one friend having what the other desperately desires, but some become stronger.

Whenever we get together, my friends always compare whose baby is doing best, sleeping most, growing fastest, etc. Can I socialize with them without all the comparisons?

You can certainly try. Competitive parenting has no positive value that I've been able to figure out, other than occasionally allowing the mother of the highest achieving baby to feel smugly superior.

When new parents focus on their baby's accomplishments (if you can call having the most teeth an accomplishment), they are usually just attempting to reassure themselves that they are doing a good job. While there's nothing wrong with comparing and contrasting parenting styles and babies' development for the sake of learning new approaches and eliminating one's fear that something is wrong, it can be very damaging to friendships and shake the confidence of a new parent. Babies who walk early or talk ahead of schedule are not necessarily going to be Olympic athletes or Rhodes Scholars, nor do their advanced skills indicate superior parenting. You can quote me on that. So, if all this comparing and competition makes you uncomfort-able, you have two choices.

First, you can try to eliminate the competitive spirit:

- ❧ Suggest that comparing and contrasting the babies' achieve-ments isn't such a good idea, and request that the competition be checked at the door. If your friends aren't trying to show each other up, they may appreciate becoming aware of how their behavior is experienced. End of problem.
- ❧ Use humor to deflect the unwanted ranking and rating. When another mother asks you if your three-month-old baby has turned over yet, respond with a joke, "Oh, he'll turn over by his wedding day." If you're grilled about your baby's height or weight, don't give specific numbers; say your pediatrician says she's just right for someone her size. Then change the subject to something unrelated to babies.
- ❧ If the contests continue, but you still like these women, social-ize with them only when there is an activity that will eliminate the focus on the children's accomplishments. Create a book club, go to the zoo together, or even run errands in a group, but don't just sit around comparing your Roscoe's first cold to her Marlena's superior sleeping patterns.

Second, you can avoid these people altogether:

- ❧ If it distresses you to be with them, stop seeing them, especially with your babies. Create a girls' night out, with the stipulation that there be no conversation about babies.
- ❧ Despite your fear of being isolated, try to get used to staying at home alone with your baby. Some women seek companionship

in the early days of parenthood because they get bored or lonely being alone all day with a baby and end up spending time with people they don't enjoy.

- ❧ Develop some interests or projects that you can do at home while caring for your baby. Reading, playing a musical instrument, cooking, gardening, and artistic and craft activities lend themselves well to time spent at home with a baby, especially if there is a way to put materials out of reach when the baby's up and about.
- ❧ Learning to live more at your baby's pace may also decrease the need for company you don't actually enjoy. Consciously relax; let go of the expectation of having something to show for all your efforts at child care. Have fun with your baby.
- ❧ If you are still desperate for company, schedule dates with women you meet in your childbirth class or at your doctor or midwife's office. Take up new hobbies with casual friends you'd like to get to know better.
- ❧ Sign up for a baby exercise class or group for new mothers, seek out other women with babies, and otherwise fill your social time with visits with less competitive women.

You don't have to be coerced into competitive parenting if it bothers you. Noting similarities and differences among babies and parents can be illuminating when the intention is to support and educate; it can be oppressive if it leaves you constantly on edge, or worried about whether or not you measure up. If you can't tolerate the competitive tension, find more compatible and agreeable friends.

> *Life is not a competitive sport; there are no clear winners or losers. Your value does not depend on how you or your baby compare to others.*

My friends and I have very different attitudes towards child rearing and discipline. It's starting to cause a lot of tension between us. What can I do?

It used to be that three topics were considered off-limits in polite company: sex, religion, and politics. In recent times, those three are often perfectly acceptable, especially among like-minded folks, but in your case, I'd think about putting parenting styles on the taboo list. When new or insecure parents share their parenting philosophy and it is diametrically opposed to how good friends would handle a similar situation, the tension sometimes mounts.

Acknowledge your differences, making it clear that both approaches are reasonable and valid, and move on to other topics. You may be disconcerted to learn that your neighbor allows her two-month-old to cry herself to sleep, but she may be equally certain that you shouldn't pick up your four-month-old every time you hear a little whimper. Child rearing is not an exact science; so-called experts disagree about everything from pacifiers to potty training. Your friendship should be able to tolerate some differences of opinion as long as those differences don't indicate an incompatible difference in life attitudes.

As long as you are comfortable that no one is actively endangering a child, learn to accept that there are many "correct" and acceptable ways to raise children. Your way may work for you and your baby, Robin's way may be just right for her family. Keeping an open mind allows your friendship to continue and may provide some insight into approaches to child-care issues you've not considered before.

If your friend's methods of handling her children are truly intolerable to you, that might indicate that your friendship hasn't enough of a foundation of mutual respect to survive. While democrats and republicans can certainly be pals, when their ideology is too vastly different, too rooted in incompatible outlooks on life, the friendship may stay on a more casual level or dissolve altogether.

Give yourself the opportunity to discover if these diverging opinions are solely about child rearing or if they reflect an unbridgeable gap between you. Look closely at your own ideas as well as those of your friends. Assess whether this friendship should have remained superficial, whether you or your friend needs to gain some parenting skills, or if it is time to let the relationship go. While it's interesting to have variety in your friendships, if you feel that your divergent child-rearing attitudes reflect unacceptably divergent life attitudes, let the friendship go.

The reason so many baby and child-care experts exist is that there are many, many right ways to raise a child.

If I go out with friends, I find I can't pay attention to the conversation. Can I possibly find my baby more interesting than my friends?

No insult to your friends is intended, but, yes, you may, for awhile, find your baby more interesting than you find your friends, particularly if they do not also have babies. You are a new mother, and it is a natural part of the process to become completely enchanted with your baby. When you are a new mother, it seems that the world revolves around your new baby, and all conversations should, too.

First-time mothers, due to a combination of sleep deprivation and intense fascination with their own lives, often find it hard to concentrate at all on any exchange that doesn't include references to spit up and diaper rash. Many worry that their new lives are so captivating to them that no one else's lives compare. Some fret that their old pals just don't get what having a baby is all about. And some lament that their own narrow focus may make them seem boring to others. No matter what aspect of your disconnected discussions upsets you, you and your friends can find common ground again. During the first several months of motherhood, baby-related topics dominate many first-time mothers' chatter; you will be able to sustain and enjoy adult dialogue after you've been getting enough sleep and your baby is old enough to allow you time and energy to resume some of your prior interests. You will very likely regain interest in your friends.

Don't panic. In time, your attention span is likely to resume its former, more mature length. Your world will expand to again include non-babies and mothers, and while your baby may always be fascinating to you, your friends' fine qualities will once again appeal.

Why is it that if a friend calls *me* on the phone, I'm thrilled and talk for a long time, yet it seems impossible for me to pick up the phone and make the call myself?

It not only makes sense, it happens all the time. Lucy was such a new mother. A first-time mom at age thirty-six, she had led an organized, structured, and predictable life before her baby was born. Motherhood hit hard; with chronic exhaustion and her house in a constant state of disarray, she hardly ever made a phone call that wasn't to a doctor's office those first several months. When her baby slept, which wasn't often, Lucy slept, did dishes, or just stared into space, and when the baby was awake, well, there weren't hands or energy available to call a friend.

But Lucy was also thrilled when a friend called. Like you, she couldn't manage to *make* the phone call, but she felt rescued when the phone rang for her just the same. Tell your friends that you still love them and need them in your life, and ask (or beg) them to understand if you aren't able to reach out to them for several months. Tell them clearly and directly how hard it is for you to initiate a call (or a visit or whatever), and also be sure they know how very much you appreciate it when they call or visit you. Repeat this to them as often as necessary, and when you are ready and able, you will be able to call them again.

When you are a new mother, it's a lot easier to accept a telephone call than it is to make one.

I am much older (or younger) than most of the other new mothers I've met. Will I always feel socially out of the mainstream?

A wise friend of mine, who just happened to be nine years older, having her first baby a year ahead of me, stated that once you have children, your children's age(s) determine your social life more than your chronological age does. I personally have found this to be true as well. The needs of your children often influence the time you have available for socializing and your kids' activities often dictate the adults you interact with most often. Being in the same parenting stage gives you a lot in common with the parents of your children's age-mates, as you can share similar struggles, concerns, and freedoms according to the level of independence of the children.

Don't worry that being in your forties (or early twenties) when your first baby is born will make you a social outcast. These days, women have their first babies at wildly varying ages. Not only will your current life events bring you closer to other new mothers regardless of your ages, you are likely to find other women who've made similar life choices. If you've waited until your late thirties or early forties to have your first baby, you will find increasingly significant numbers of other women who've done the same. If you've decided to get your family started early in adulthood, you'll also find women near your age to hang out and share ideas with.

Take advantage of the opportunity to expand your social connections. I've seen numerous enduring friendships blossom among women attending my groups who, on the surface at least, seem to have little besides their babies in common. Open yourself to the possibility of developing warm relationships with a variety of women.

- Looks can be deceiving. Don't assume anything about another person until you get to know her. Just because you wear designer suits and the new mother you met at the doctor's office wears nose and eyebrow rings and tattoos doesn't mean that you can't become fast friends.
- Enjoy getting to know a new mother who is not close to your age. Your different life circumstances can bring novel insights to each of you.
- Don't assume that simply having a first baby at approximately the same time guarantees friendliness or compatibility. You and that woman with a new baby in the park may be about the same age, but it's not a given that you will like each other.
- Having your first baby at the same age doesn't guarantee similar attitudes toward career, either. One forty-something new mother may have had her first baby late because she was completely focused on her professional advancement, while another may have desperately wanted to become a mother for years before finally adopting her newborn. Maybe you chose to have your kids early so that you could enjoy them in your youth, while your neighbor, also a twenty-one-year-old, may be trying to "get child rearing out of the way" so that she can pursue her vocation full-time.
- If you still want to find other new mothers who are closer to your age, do it. Join groups or ask a childbirth instructor, lactation consultant, or health-care professional to put you into contact with other new mothers, women you don't already know, who are closer to your age to commiserate on the joys and struggles of being an older (or younger) first-time mother.

Special Circumstances

This chapter addresses some concerns that are not as universal as many of the topics in the previous chapters, but still common enough to merit inclusion. Medical technology and social trends in recent decades have allowed women to become parents who might never have had the opportunity had they reached adulthood in an earlier period in history. When a woman becomes a mother by means other than the formerly "traditional" method (happily married man and woman have sex, get pregnant, and then deliver their own healthy, biological baby) she faces situations and concerns other women rarely encounter.

Becoming a mother is a complicated experience under the best of circumstances, and clearly not everyone has the best of circumstances. This chapter answers some of the most universal questions raised by these less-than-universal mothering situations. Since this book does not pretend to answer every question ever asked by a new mother (though I've tried to come up with the most pressing ones) I've grouped the questions according to emotional aspects of the problem.

For example, both single parents and adoptive couples may face the same questions about how and when to share information about the baby's biological beginnings. Gay and interracial couples may both experience discrimination or lack of acceptance. Couples with family histories of emotional or physical abuse need similar suggestions for maintaining their baby's safety. Situations that might seem very different on the surface may have very similar solutions.

The previous chapters answered questions that most new mothers will face at some point in the first year of motherhood, while this chapter explores answers to the most frequently asked questions from mothers whose somewhat unusual situations create rather different problems. This chapter addresses, in a broad way, how to handle your feelings and respond appropriately when your motherhood experience isn't quite so typical. These problems fall into roughly four categories:

- Women who achieve motherhood through nontraditional means: in vitro fertilization and egg, sperm, and embryo donors may allow a woman to carry a baby successfully to term. Adoption, although available for centuries, has undergone considerable changes in recent decades; people now adopt children of different races and backgrounds and have varying levels of involvement with birth mothers. Surrogate mothers offer parents the opportunity to adopt a child who has some biological connection to them.
- Women with different lifestyles: currently there is more awareness and, at least in some parts of the country, more acceptance, of alternative lifestyles. Gay people, biracial couples, and single women can all become parents; women may work while their husbands stay home to raise the baby. Couples may choose to raise a child together without getting married at all. Women can and do give birth to their first child at any age from their teens

to their late forties without even coming close to setting records.

- Unusual babies: babies are sometimes born with something iden-
tifiably different about them, ranging from multiple births to
minor cosmetic problems to serious medical concerns.
- Family problems: not all new mothers come from families in
which they feel comfortable. How to handle a potentially dangerous family situation comes up more frequently than most
people would wish.

There are national and local groups and associations available in
most communities that can offer support to new families in unusual situations. For more in-depth insights and to find companionship and
wisdom to help you with your individual concerns, seek them out. Go
to your library, search the Internet, call your state's social service department or your local community mental health center for referrals.
Sometimes what you will need most will be to compare stories with
someone who has experienced motherhood as you are experiencing it.

Nontypical Means to Motherhood

My baby was conceived with a lot of medical help. How much and when should we share information with the baby or our friends and family?

When having a baby involves months or years of medical interventions,
that process seems to take over your life for awhile. Once your healthy
baby is born the focus on getting and staying pregnant disappears and
you become a normal new mother with a normal new baby. Since you
were so consumed by the process of high-tech conception and then

being pregnant for such a long time, it may feel as if you need to share all the details of your attempts at conception with anyone who wants to know about your motherhood experience. And it feels reasonable to share those details with your baby as soon as possible.

I'm always interested when women want to tell their birth stories, and increasingly often, those stories include years of struggling to conceive and/or carry a baby successfully to term. Going through infertility tests and treatments colors some women's entire early mothering experience. For some, talking about the struggle to have a baby helps them make sense of it so that they can move on fully into parenting. Even when infertility treatments are successful, the new mother needs to be able to feel confident about her ability as a mother, and sometimes she may fear that her difficulty with the process of giving birth will mean that she will have trouble being a mother. I also think some women who need medical support to become pregnant feel a bit less worthy or capable, and letting others know that they needed help to get to motherhood helps them work through those feelings.

Tell people who ask whatever you want to tell them about how your baby came to be. While there are many, many women who rely on medical technology to have a baby, keep in mind that not all strangers will be as interested as you are in the specific details. Chances are the people closest to you already know how very much you wanted your baby, and how hard you worked to conceive.

If the baby is biologically yours and your husband's, your baby doesn't *need* to know any more about the circumstances of his birth (although when old enough to consider becoming a parent himself, the medical facts about his parents' trouble conceiving might be useful). Had your baby been conceived in a more romantic fashion, you probably wouldn't tell him about the candlelight and music playing;

similarly, you may choose not to share the story of the petri dish in which he was conceived.

On the other hand, if your child has the genetic background of someone other than you and/or your husband, your baby needs to know certain important facts about his origins. He may want medical information from each side of his biological family; beyond that, you will want to share facts about his origins as his curiosity and cognitive ability warrant. It is good that you are preparing now for helping your child know about his earliest beginnings. If you continue to be honest, clear, and forthright about how he came to be and give information as it is requested and in an understandable manner, it will be fine.

Our baby was adopted and looks nothing like us. How should we respond to the questions we get from strangers?

Answer polite inquiries politely. Respond simply and honestly and in a matter-of-fact tone. You don't owe a stranger a detailed explanation of why you adopted your child, but you also don't want to respond in such a way as to make your baby think that there is anything peculiar, wrong, or shameful about having been adopted. Most people mean well, and are asking you out of curiosity, not intrusiveness. Maybe they also have a child who seems to resemble no one in the family; maybe they are considering adopting a baby themselves; maybe they are just making conversation. Give the kind of information that the situation and your relationship with the questioner require. Assume that the question is well-intended, and answer it briefly and honestly.

When the person asking seems genuinely interested, pleasant, and receptive, just tell the truth.

- You may answer that your baby's hair is just like her birth mother, offering an opening, if you are both at ease, to discuss the circumstances of your baby's birth.
- As your baby gets older, when the question is posed in his presence, you can use this type of exchange to reinforce to your baby that you are thrilled that he is part of your family now, and that adopting him was the best thing that ever happened to you.
- Be upbeat in your explanation. For example, reply by saying, yes, she is exceptionally cute, isn't she? We adopted her—aren't we lucky?

If the situation doesn't warrant it, if you worry that the person asking is being rude or belligerent, or if you simply don't want to tell just anyone, don't. You don't need to give lots of details about how or why you chose to adopt or even that the baby was adopted at all.

- If the person asking is a stranger, or someone you don't want to share your baby's origins with, you can shrug and say, "Yes, isn't he cute?" or, "Thank goodness she's got her grandmother's nose!" You don't have to include the fact that you aren't related to her grandmother.
- If you do want to explain, but the timing isn't right, a brief "Aren't genetics interesting?" should stop the inquisition.

If someone is being actually impolite, you owe him or her no response at all. Just get up and move away. If your baby is old enough to understand, explain that some people don't know good manners or don't understand that a family is composed of people who love each other, and it's not necessary that they look alike.

Not all questions need to be answered.

Our baby was adopted (or carried by a surrogate mother). How should I respond when someone comments on how quickly I got my figure back, or asks me why I'm not breast-feeding?

You may say as much or little as seems comfortable. As the situation and your feelings indicate, you may smile and say thank you, or you may tell the longer version, that you were not the baby's birth mother. Either answer is acceptable; not telling someone that you didn't actually give birth to this baby is not dishonest. It's up to you to whom and under what circumstances you talk about your baby's origins, or about your body, for that matter. And it's up to you to decide how much detail you offer.

Just know that telling about how your baby came to be yours opens the topic for discussion, so be economical with whom you choose to share the facts. Relate the details you want to share with whom you want and when you want. You owe no explanation of how you've stayed in good shape to anyone. Be careful not to share too much information simply because you feel uncomfortable that you didn't have to work so hard physically to have this baby, but by all means feel free to tell the whole story of how you got your baby whenever you want to.

We adopted our baby. When should we start to talk about the adoption to our baby?

Now. You need to become comfortable with what you want your baby to know about his history and the sooner you are able to chat casually about how your baby came to be yours, the better. When the baby is old enough to understand, be direct and straightforward about how and why your baby became yours. Until then, get used to talking about his adoption with the people you love so that his adoption is as much a part of him as his name.

Generations ago, adoption was kept a secret. People worried that being adopted was somehow shameful or abnormal, and the less said about it the better. Some felt that the child needed to feel biologically connected to her family in order to feel emotionally secure; others felt that the child's birth parents were undoubtedly of poor family, moral, or mental backgrounds, and so wanted to shield the baby from the facts of his beginnings. Families refused to discuss the circumstances surrounding an adopted child's birth, often only to have the secret shared at some awkward or emotionally damaging time. In general, such secrets are a terrible idea: secrets actually gain power and importance by virtue of the need to maintain the silence. They rarely protect anyone, and they often result in feelings of betrayal when finally uncovered.

Current thinking suggests that the more relaxed you are about your child's adoption, the more relaxed your child will be. You need to be at peace with having adopted your baby and the arrangements you have made to be her parents, and your child needs to know how she became yours. Telling other people, politely, calmly, and lovingly, can make it very clear to them and ultimately to your baby, that you are proud to have chosen your baby, and that being adopted is wonderful for you all.

Our adopted baby is of a different race (or from another country) than ours. At what point should we begin to talk to him about his ethnic heritage?

Clearly I am a firm believer in honesty and clarity. Again, I'd say that your baby's origin and race should be natural topics for conversation. You may want to think about how to share information about your baby's biological and cultural background in two ways. One, how, what, and when do you share information with your child, and two, how do you deal with others, particularly non-family.

Before your child notices the differences between your features and hers, you can begin to help her understand and accept her uniqueness by commenting on how lovely her skin color or hair is. Introduce the concepts of adoption and racial differences, as well as the specific details of your child's history, as your child or others ask. Your child needs to know how much you wanted her and why she looks different than you. Maintain an atmosphere open to questions and give honest and appropriate answers.

If your child is unquestionably of a different race than either you or your husband, this issue will come up often. Steffa, a blonde, blue-eyed mother of an adopted black baby boy, was in a park feeding her baby from a bottle. A total stranger came up to her and asked if the baby's mother was breast-feeding him; she assumed that Steffa could not possibly be her baby's mother. Steffa tells numerous stories of this sort, of people who probably mean well but ask intrusive, presumptuous questions. If your baby is obviously not your biological child, you are likely to experience the same. You will need to learn, as she did, when and how to respond graciously to minimize your (or your child's) discomfort, and to maximize the possibility for a thoughtless remark to become a positive interaction.

- Seek support from other parents who have adopted children of other races or cultures. Ask, *before* your baby is old enough to understand what all the fuss is about, how other parents deal with questions about the racial discrepancy. Being prepared can allow you to consider your responses beforehand and alleviate some of the stress of trying to answer an emotionally complicated question.
- Those who adopt foreign-born babies often have gone through the experience with other adopting parents. Call them and ask how they've handled these situations.
- Contact the lawyers or social workers who helped you through the process for support.
- Become knowledgeable about transracial and international adoptions and apply that knowledge judiciously. Educate your friends and family and strangers when appropriate.
- Realize that because your baby is visibly of a different race, *her adoption is always evident.* This means you will work doubly hard to help her with issues of belonging and identity.
- Contact people in your community you respect, including teachers and clergy, educate them about your child's origins, and share your concerns with them. Help them to help your child feel she belongs and is accepted in your community.
- Always remember that your first loyalty is to your child, to loving her and to helping her feel thoroughly loved and accepted as part of your family and, ideally, the world.

My adopted baby looks nothing like me or my family, and I'm finding it really hard to feel bonded to her. Will I ever love this baby the way she deserves to be loved?

It may not be comfortable to admit to feeling less than thoroughly in love with your newborn, but it can be a normal part of becoming a mother in an adoption. For many new mothers, bonding begins during pregnancy, and adoptive parents don't have that opportunity. Also, part of maternal-infant bonding includes the recognition of the biological connection between the mother and her baby, the awareness that this baby is *her* baby, and the experience of gazing into the baby's eyes and knowing that you share a deep primal tie or biological history. When you and your baby are visually very different, the emotional bond may not come as quickly as you'd hoped; the bond then depends more on the experience of mothering than on the more primitive, visceral connection. It is normal, maybe even typical, for a mother to bond a bit less instantly with a baby who looks totally unlike herself.

In addition, the process of adoption itself may influence the bonding experience. Some couples who eventually adopt experience major disappointments before a successful adoption. If one or more potential adoptions have fallen through before you received this baby, you may be holding back your emotions for a while until you are certain that you really will get to keep her. When that fear of losing this baby subsides, you should be able to allow yourself to love your child fully. Also, if your baby arrived very quickly, which is sometimes the case, you may have had less time to prepare yourself emotionally for parenthood. Similar to a mother who delivers a premature baby, you may have simply had less time to get accustomed to the idea that you would soon become a mother.

Be patient with yourself and do not worry. Caring for your baby will lead to loving your baby. If it doesn't, after several months, talk to a professional to see what may be blocking you from feeling a more loving bond.

Our baby's birth mother was a drug addict (or alcoholic or prostitute), and as a result, our baby has medical problems. What and when should we tell our baby?

When there are problems, people often want to lay blame. Telling him that his learning problems are the result of his birth mother's poor choices makes it clear that he didn't get that way because of *you,* but I'm not sure what other benefits blaming the birth mother will have, particularly when he is very young. Your baby eventually will need to know about his birth mother's medical and genetic background. Telling him that he may have a biological predisposition to have problems with addictions, because of his mother's addiction, may help him to avoid such problems in his own life, and that has some value. But for now, you will need to figure out how much and what information should be shared with your baby.

Keep in mind that your baby's birth mother (even if she promises never to see your baby again or has died) will always have a place in your baby's life. She has a direct genetic link to your baby, and it will serve no positive purpose to paint her in an unnecessarily ugly light. Your goal is to raise your baby to be as healthy, successful, and content as possible, so consider that goal whenever you speak of his biological mother.

- As questions from your baby arise, answer them honestly but without lots of gruesome details. Your child will need to know the facts, but does not need to hear what a jerk his mother is.

- Make sure that any information you share with friends or family about your baby's birth mother is acceptable for your child to know, too. Other people do not need to know things about your child's biological mother's character or situation that you wouldn't want him to know himself. Whatever information you share with others can eventually, and possibly inappropriately, be passed on to your child.

Accentuate the positive. Your baby came to you because he deserves to be cared for well. You and he are both lucky that he is now your baby, and he needs to know that you will always be happy that his mother gave birth to him and gave him to you.

EMOTIONAL OR MEDICAL FAMILY PROBLEMS

One of my relatives was physically (or sexually) abusive to me while I was growing up. How can I keep my baby away from him without offending my baby's other family members?

Your first priority is the safety of your child. If you are committed to having no contact with the abusive relative, then including your children in this ban will be easy. Before any family event, check the guest list with the hosts and plan accordingly. Don't attend if you feel that you or your baby's safety is at risk. Chances are that if there will be many people at the gathering, and if you stay constantly in the company of others (ask your husband to escort you to the bathroom if necessary), you will not be at risk even if the offending relative shows up. But you have the right and perhaps also the responsibility to protect yourself and your baby.

If your family knows about the history between you and the abusive relative, your wishing not to see him shouldn't offend. Explaining your stand once or twice should be enough to clarify that you love your family, you want to participate in family get-togethers, but you won't put yourself in a position to be made fearful or uncomfortable unnecessarily. Make your requests for the guest list calmly; state your desire to remain out of the offender's company firmly and without undue emotion and your wishes should be respected.

If you feel that the abuser is still dangerous, and your family doesn't know about this part of his history, it may be time to share your story. Talk with a professional, a social worker or psychologist, preferably one with experience dealing with family abuse situations. You might want to have some family sessions to help your relatives accept and understand the seriousness of the problem, and to aid in getting the perpetrator to stop. If you've never dealt with your feelings about this part of your past, see about getting some counseling for yourself, as your new status as a mother may be stirring up many old and disturbing memories.

Despite the increased awareness of the prevalence of child abuse and sexual abuse in the world today, many families are still not too willing to accept that one of their own could have committed such a crime. This is true even when the former victim, now you, an adult, declares it to be true. If you fear that this relative is still a danger to others, it is your responsibility to talk about your concerns with any potential victims or their parents, regardless of your loved ones' resistance to facing this particular skeleton in the closet.

Telling family members that a loved one has been an abuser creates great stress and distrust, and it may be extremely awkward and uncomfortable, for both the former victim and for the accused. No one wants to believe that someone they love could abuse a child, or that a child could be abused without the knowledge of the adults in the home. Neither physical nor sexual abuse is extraordinarily commonplace, but both do happen. Abuse will continue unless it is prevented, and knowing about a potential danger, especially a former abuser in your midst, may be the best protection for your baby as well as other children.

Realize that as unpleasant as it may be to share the awful memories of your abuse, keeping the abuse a secret sometimes magnifies the problem. Silence is a burden, and the fear of telling is often worse than reality. What if the abuser tells a different version of what happened to you that puts him in a better light or spreads lies about you, making you seem like a liar or troublemaker? Tell your family what truly happened, protect your baby and other children with whom this person has contact, and work toward being able to come to terms with your own history of abuse. Focus less on not offending family members and more on healing. You and your baby are entitled to feel and be safe.

My husband is estranged from one side of his family. Is it reasonable to continue to deny contact now that we have a baby?

People grow and change and, given some maturity and luck, even learn from their mistakes. Some people who were lousy parents can be excellent grandparents. Sometimes, the same people who were pretty pathetic as parents can become close to their adult children once the burden of providing for a family and the chaos of living with young children is gone. They can become a wonderful addition to a growing grandchild's life as well as an unexpected support to you. Sometimes.

You'll have to evaluate all the circumstances and decide whether you believe it is best for your baby to cut off all contact with your husband's extended family. Certainly in some families, the less contact the better. When problematic behaviors continue or the hurt runs too deep, keeping your distance may make sense. When you feel you need to shield yourself or your husband or baby from potential damage, limiting contact may be necessary.

However, most families do have some redeeming characteristics. After all, your husband's family did raise him, and he's pretty great, right? It would be too bad to eliminate any possibility of you and your children having a positive relationship with these relatives who are, after all, also your baby's blood relations.

Do resume contact if:

- ❧ You feel that all your family members will be safe.
- ❧ You feel that establishing a new relationship with the formerly difficult relative can be healing to all parties.
- ❧ You and your husband want your baby (and any subsequent children) to know both sides of the family, regardless of past mistakes.
- ❧ You and your husband want to reconnect with his side of the family and relieve yourselves of the burden of hard feelings.
- ❧ The offending relative expresses the wish to mend the relationship.

Don't resume contact with these relatives if:

- ❧ You have reason to believe that whatever damage they caused your husband is likely to continue.
- ❧ You believe that contact with these relatives will harm your baby or you.

- Your husband's anger or pain will dominate the relationship to such an extent that it feels dangerous.
- You or your husband is unable to forgive and move forward.

Cautiously reestablishing an amiable relationship with the offending family member(s) can help everyone feel better about themselves and model to your children how to manage stressful relationships and forgive others. If the previously dangerous relative returns to his or her destructive ways, be prepared to break ties again. And if there is so much animosity between these people that they cannot be in the same room together without drawing blood, professional counseling may be in order.

My husband and I are blind (or deaf or otherwise physically impaired) and our child is not. How can we politely let people know that we have done the proper research and have appropriate support so that they stop worrying?

If you have the help you need so that your baby will be appropriately stimulated and nurtured, then all you need to do is to expand your repertoire of responses to well-meaning family and friends.

- Thank your worried loved ones for their concern and reassure them that you have considered all the implications of your situation, and have taken the necessary steps to educate and nurture your baby adequately.
- Have a schedule or plan for child care that you can share with your doubtful relatives.
- Don't be too defensive if the concerns expressed are simply the

same sorts of concerns expressed for all new parents. Nearly all first-time mothers put up with unsolicited comments and advice from well-meaning but irritating family and friends; this may have little to do with your disability.

- Accept help when it will be helpful and if it's offered lovingly. Every new parent needs help.
- And if you need more help, don't be afraid to ask. Contact support groups for similarly physically challenged adults to find the support you require. Be confident that many parents with various limitations are excellent parents who raise well-adjusted and talented children.

I had a serious postpartum depression. I'm much better now, but I worry about my relationship with my baby. Can we still have a good mother-baby connection?

Yes, you can. As you start to feel better and return to your old self, you will regain the energy and emotional presence to connect with your baby; the bond will develop. Postpartum depression and postpartum psychosis are both relatively rare but significant, sometimes-devastating problems that have gotten a lot of media attention in recent years. Fortunately, this attention should lead to better understanding and treatment of the disease, and therefore, the dire problems caused by these terrible disorders should be minimized. Once you are treated and recover, your lives and relationships can return to normal.

- Continue your treatment for as long as your doctors deem necessary, including taking your medication as prescribed and following through with any psychotherapy or other programs suggested. If something isn't working or if you feel your depression increasing or returning, call your doctor immediately.

- ❧ Don't be afraid to ask for help with the baby and the house as you need it. Asking for what you need is a sign of strength, not weakness.
- ❧ Take care of yourself so that you can take care of your baby. Eat properly and get enough rest. If that means that you ask your mother-in-law to baby-sit while you nap, or you find a good friend to supply you with occasional meals until you're fully recovered, so be it.
- ❧ Find a support group, either in your community or online, to share your feelings and concerns.
- ❧ Take your time and get to know and love your baby. Once you are fully recovered you will have a lifetime to bond.

Our baby has developmental delays, so our experience is unlike any of our friends. How can we feel less alone?

While some of your experiences are similar to your friends' (sleepless nights, lack of free time, changes in priorities, etc.), others are decidedly not. Depending upon the severity of the problems you face, you might have more contact with a variety of professionals, greater financial demands, different expectations of your baby's future, and perhaps unexpected emotions as you become accustomed to having a baby that is unlike the baby you'd fantasized about.

- ❧ Ask your pediatrician to refer you to professionals experienced in working with families of children with similar problems. Get support for yourself as well as for your baby.

- Teach old friends that you are still the same person, and tell them that you will let them know how much or how little you want to share about your baby's problems. They may be keeping their distance because they don't know what to say to you.
- Even if you are feeling overwhelmed (especially if you are feeling overwhelmed), call your best friend.
- Make sure you and your husband devote time to yourselves and your marriage in addition to caring for your baby. Talk to each other about the changes in your social life.
- Find a support group (or start one if there is none is your area) for mothers or parents of children with similar disabilities. Establish friendships with people who do know what you're going through.

You are right that your friends may not know what you're going through, but that doesn't mean that you can't still be friends. Get support where and when you can and hold on to your dear friends at the same time.

Our baby was born with some physical anomalies (or is developmentally delayed). What should I do when someone asks what is wrong with her?

Again, you do not need to answer any question that you do not wish to answer. If you want to respond respectfully, give a brief and clear response. Answering simply that your baby has a developmental delay or describing the nature of your baby's physical anomaly should suffice in most situations. Sometimes you'll find that the questioner has a child with a similar disability and wants to offer suggestions or support; sometimes you'll find that he just has poor manners or no impulse control and just blurts out whatever crosses his mind. Answering simply allows you to maintain your dignity without lowering yourself to unnecessary rudeness.

When someone asks you what is wrong with your baby, especially when in your baby's presence, they usually have no idea that you or your baby might be hurt by the question. Most people are well-intentioned: their questions most likely come from curiosity or the desire to connect with you. People rarely want to hurt you or to point out to you, in case you've forgotten, that your baby is somehow not normal. While your baby is too young to understand the specific words you use, as long as you remain calm and polite, however you answer these questions will be OK.

Once your baby is old enough to know that the curiosity is directed at him, how you respond to his disabilities and the stares or questions they elicit will strongly influence how he feels about himself and you. You have a few months before your baby will pick up on the specific words you use and less time before he will be aware of your emotions.

- Talk with professionals who understand your baby's condition and contact other families who have children with similar developmental or physical problems. Find out about appropriate support groups and treatment programs.
- Learn whatever you can about the specific diagnosis and your child's prognosis.
- Be prepared to answer questions from well-meaning strangers and deflect those from rude people.
- Love your baby and include him in family life in whatever ways you can. If you need help in adjusting to life with a child

who is unlike what you'd expected, get it. There is no shame in feeling sad or disappointed that your baby may not have the future you'd once imagined, but you need to come to terms with the child you have, learn to love him, and offer him the best life you can.

All children deserve to be treated with love and respect. And all children deserve to have the opportunity to learn and grow to the best of their abilities. Knowing what to expect can help your whole family plan for this child's future while nurturing and supporting each other in the present. Responding calmly to occasional inappropriate remarks from others will help your child know that you are not embarrassed or uncomfortable with who he is, that you accept his possible limitations, and that you love him. The words you use will be less critical than the spirit in which you and your child face the world together.

My baby has physical abnormalities that are pretty obvious to anyone within a few feet of her. What can I do to deal with the stares and questions?

If your baby has obvious physical problems, people will occasionally stare and even ask some impolite or at least uncomfortable questions. As with any question, you are under no obligation to answer, but it is wise to be prepared and to consider when and how you want to respond so that you and your child can minimize the awkward or unpleasant moments. Unlike questions about a child's origins, which may imply some prejudice or social condescension, questions about a child's physical abnormalities may be driven by simple curiosity.

Regardless of the intent of the questioner, you want to protect your child from unnecessary embarrassment, rudeness, or stress.

- ❦ Answer questions briefly and honestly. Who knows, the person wondering about your baby may know someone with similar problems and be able to offer you ideas or support.
- ❦ As your baby grows up, you can use these awkward situations to teach him about polite behavior, such as not staring at others.
- ❦ Whenever possible, you can educate the person asking by suggesting that his questions make you uncomfortable (if they do) or that people staring makes your baby feel bad (if that's true). Tell the curious that, while you know she means well, her stares or comments about your baby's appearance make you feel bad, and politely ask the person to leave you alone.
- ❦ Focus on your baby's positive attributes, and help others see them. When someone asks what's wrong, you can say that he has cerebral palsy, and that you feel blessed to have him in your life because he is such a loving, bright, and fun person.
- ❦ If your baby has permanent visible problems, he will need to learn to tolerate unwanted attention. Help him understand that some people just want to know why he looks different than other babies, that there are many different kinds of kids, and that he is wonderful.

My baby is just big (or small) for her age, and people keep commenting on her size. What should I say?

OK, I have to say this. Sometimes people, without meaning to be, are just plain stupid. I know a lovely family whose first baby was very small for her age. Whenever someone asked how old she was, the mother would answer, and then they would exclaim, "But she's so tiny!" By the time this little girl was two years old, she'd heard this routine so often that, if someone asked her age, she would pipe up, "I'm two and tiny!" Although it seemed cute, she felt that "tiny" was part of her age, and it became part of her identity, and not always a good part. Most people want to be known for the whole of themselves, not just the visible and unusual parts

People love to comment about babies but often have nothing to say. So usually the first thing they notice is what pops out of their mouths. Most of the time this isn't much of a problem, but you and your child may become pretty tired of the disbelief that she could be so small at her age. Small stature isn't a real problem; eventually, most preemies catch up developmentally, and genetically small people can do just fine in life as long as they don't become insecure or awkward *because* of their size. Other than occasionally influencing whether one tries out for basketball or gymnastics, size really doesn't play a major role in one's life; size doesn't affect intelligence, determination, creativity, dexterity, or interpersonal skills. But the constant attention to size can present problems eventually; the frequent mention of a child's size, whether "too" large or small, can chip away at her self-esteem.

- When asked about your child's size, you can explain that she is little because she was premature or large because both her grandfathers and one great aunt were all over six feet tall.
- Some parents, in an effort to take the focus away from their baby's appearance tell the person commenting that looks are just not that important.
- Some parents simply nod, or say yes, she is a good size, and change the subject altogether.

- Depending on your personality and your baby's, you could instead respond by any number of cute or clever remarks. You can tell the questioner that she's just the right size to be her, remind the questioner that good things come in small packages, or joke that she's tall enough that her feet will reach the ground.

As your child gets older, especially if she remains extremely small or large, she may need to develop a thick skin. Not only do adults comment on unusual size, other children do also. Help your child to develop social skills and a positive sense of herself so that when others question or tease her about her size, she feels confident that her size is not who she is. Make sure that she knows that she has value besides being able to hide in small places, or being able to reach the highest shelf without help.

UNCONVENTIONAL LIFESTYLE CHOICES

My partner and I are gay. How should we answer some of the rude questions we get?

Whenever you are asked a question that seems rude, you have the option of not answering. You may welcome the questions asked by a close friend yet bristle at the idea of a casual acquaintance or stranger asking the same thing. If you are an openly gay couple, you have probably already been inundated with rude comments from some and complete acceptance from others. Having a baby may give rude people more ammunition with which to try to hurt you, but real friends and people who know the importance of love and friendship will continue to offer support and understanding.

Answer whichever questions you want to answer in as much detail as you feel comfortable answering. Although I rarely advocate withholding important information, there may be valid reasons not to reveal who fathered your child. If you want to keep the identity of the baby's biological father a secret, *keep it completely secret*. Often, telling one person, no matter how well-meaning he or she is, can lead to problems, either because that person tells another, or assumes that someone else already knows, or shares the information in a way you do not like.

If you don't want to tell somebody something, don't. There are many ways to deflect or avoid answering unwanted questions. If you still want to be polite about it:

- You may respond, "I appreciate your interest, but that's really a private matter," and change the subject.
- Tell them that what's most important to you is that your baby is here now.
- You can say, "Oh, I don't want to bore you with that old story."

If you want to use humor and reply somewhat rudely:

- Answer by saying, "I never asked you who *your* father was."
- Tell them that you don't plan to have the specifics of your baby's conception discussed any more than you would want to discuss the night their parents conceived them.
- Ask them if their question means they are considering having a baby the same way.

If you want to share the story of your baby's beginnings, go ahead. As with all questions, you may answer as fully or simply as you wish and it's a good idea to answer the question with an answer suitable to the person, place, and time.

I'm a single mother by choice. How much am I expected to say to people who question my decision to raise my child alone?

What you are expected to say doesn't necessarily dictate what you do say. You may answer as fully or as simply as you wish. If you feel that the person is well meaning, explain that you know raising a child alone is hard, but that you are up to the task. If you feel that the person asking is judgmental or intrusive, you may choose to point out that your choice is a personal one.

Although technically none of anyone else's business, people worry that raising a child as a single mom can be very stressful. In their efforts to warn or prepare you about the troubles that may lie ahead, many people don't realize or care that their questions may hurt or anger you. Begin by expecting the best, but be ready to cut any unpleasant conversation short.

- Remember that you owe no answer at all to rude questions. Tell as much or as little as you want about the baby's origins or the existence or whereabouts of the father.
- Remember that what's important is that your baby has a mother and other relatives who adore her, that you will provide sufficiently for her both emotionally and financially, and you can tell *that* to the nosy neighbor who asks what happened to the baby's father.
- Find other single mothers for support. Many community mental-health centers and organizations that help families or

women offer support groups or can make appropriate referrals. Knowing how other single women handle rude remarks and other stresses particular to your situation can help a lot.

- ❧ Know that while single motherhood can be stressful, it can also be very successful. Be clear to others and to your baby that this is what you want to be doing. Get help when you need it, but don't waste your time trying to justify your choice.

I am working and my husband is the stay-at-home parent. How do we respond when people challenge us on our choice?

The truth is often the easiest response. Saying directly, "Having Joe stay at home with Cindy just works out best for us," "I earn more money than my husband," or, "My husband is more nurturing than I am," is usually all you need. If curiosity actually turns to criticism, nip it in the bud.

- ❧ When that first criticism comes, you may be able to cut off the potential disapproval by extolling the many virtues of your child-care plan.
- ❧ Some people just have a preconceived idea of how to raise children, and no other way will do for them. If someone criticizes you for being "unfeminine" or "not motherly," your explanation of why your husband is the stay-at-home parent may never make sense to her. Tell her that while you appreciate her concern, her remarks hurt your feelings. Request that your child care and work arrangements no longer be discussed, and change the subject.

- If someone criticizes your husband for being "unmanly," respond similarly. You don't have to start a fight; you simply limit your contact and conversation to more neutral and manageable topics.
- Start or join a group for families with stay-at-home dads so that you and your husband will have the support of other couples making similar choices.
- Agree to have periodic discussions with your husband about how the arrangement is working for each of you. Make adjustments to your schedules if either of you is dissatisfied.
- Relax. If you are content with being the breadwinner while your husband is the bread baker, it will be fine, your child will be fine, and before long, no one will bother you about any of this.

BLENDED FAMILIES

This is my first baby, but my husband has two kids from a previous relationship. How can I be sure to be as good a mom as his first wife was?

Be the kind of mother you want to be and put your efforts not into competition but into making your marriage and your family experiences nurturing and comfortable. Your marriage will succeed if you and your husband love and are committed to each other, and if you help each other grow and feel content. Being good parents together can certainly enrich your marriage, but comparing and contrasting your parenting styles to anyone, especially an ex-spouse, can only cause trouble.

- Try to remember that there are many aspects to being a mother, and that everyone does it slightly differently. Try not to worry about how you and his first wife differ.

- You have enough to fret about just being a first-time mother. If you are overly concerned about whether you measure up to your husband's expectations, you may have marital issues that need attention, rather than parenting issues. Marriages break up for complicated reasons; similarly, they succeed for complicated reasons. It would be rare for your marriage to falter simply because you aren't the same kind of mother your husband's ex was.

- If you feel that your husband is comparing his ex-wife's parenting skills to yours, remind him that you are new to motherhood and that you are still learning the job. And tell him to keep those particular thoughts to himself. If he wants to help, then he should help, but telling you that you don't meet his standards will only hurt you both.

- If you are worried that he will not love you as much if you aren't as good a mom (as if that can be measured) talk to him about it. Have him reassure you that you are together for a multitude of reasons, and that your mothering skills are excellent.

- If you worry about meeting the standards set by your husband's earlier wife in any area, especially if these worries are unfounded, you may need to work through these feelings. Initiate heartfelt conversations with your husband about your concerns. If his reassurances don't alleviate your anxiety, seek professional help. Becoming a mother for the first time when your husband has already had children creates a set of problems other new mothers don't face. Talk with each other openly about your insecurity; if that doesn't relieve the pressure you feel, get outside assistance.

- If you are clearly a better mother than your husband's ex, it's OK to be pleased with yourself, but don't gloat or announce your superiority. Boasting or even pointing out in which ways you are a better mother won't elevate your status, and you, your stepchildren, and your relationship with them will benefit by treating their mother with respect. Your good mothering will be evident without any unnecessary showboating and your acceptance of them and their mother will nourish their self-esteem as well as their love for you.

- If your husband's ex was/is a good mother, be grateful. Children of divorce need all the positive parenting they can get; be appreciative that you don't need to worry about undoing any peculiar or damaging mothering your stepchildren have experienced. Make peace with the ex if at all possible; if you're lucky, she could even become an ally.

How can I be a good stepmother when I am so much more in love with my own baby?

New mothers who are also stepmothers are increasingly common, but that doesn't change the fact that being a new mother and a stepmother can be confusing and stressful. Of course you love your own baby enormously, and good for you that you are a bit worried about that love being uncomfortable for your stepkids! You can be both a good mother and a good stepmother, even if you love your biological baby differently.

When your husband has had children before, you confront many issues that first-time mothers having children with first-time fathers don't. Your baby's father's first children may become jealous of the new baby, they may already be jealous of you, and you may envy or resent your husband's relationships with his older offspring. Depending on the custody arrangements and the ages of his kids, you may enter motherhood with some experience raising older children, but little with raising a baby, while for your husband, this is old hat. Your new baby is both a little brother and an only child; you are the mother of one but also a stepmother of more. Every couple's household is disrupted when a new baby arrives, but, if you have occasional custody of your stepkids, your home is disrupted repeatedly. So, what to do?

- Accept that your feelings for your new baby are bound to be different from your feelings toward your stepchildren. You don't want to flaunt the fact that you love your baby inordinately, but you don't need to hide it.
- Try not to use words like "my own baby" or to compare your baby to your husband's kids.
- If you had positive relationships with your stepchildren before, expect that to continue.
- Be aware that this new baby may cause your stepchildren to fear losing their dad's attention and affection. Help your husband to love this new baby while still loving his other kids. Plan times for you all to be together as well as times for your husband to be with his older children.
- If your relationships were tense before, expect that to continue, but try to make this new baby part of the extended family. If the older children offer, accept their help. Include them in appropriate celebrations and ceremonies. Keep working to improve your communication and remember that these children didn't choose to be your stepchildren, but they are part of

the package of your marriage. Treating them well is always a good idea.

- ❧ You don't *have* to love your stepchildren in the same way you love your biological child. But be mindful that they will always be a part of your husband's and your baby's lives and, therefore, yours as well. Think of your love for each child as different, not as better or worse, more or less. Loving each of your children differently, step-, adopted, or biological, is appropriate, realistic, and constructive. Expecting anything else of yourself is not.

My first baby is my husband's third. How can I be a good mother when he knows so much more about taking care of a baby than I do?

Lucky you! Where did we ever get the idea that women should just spontaneously know everything there is to know about caring for a baby or know more than the baby's father? Of course, if your husband was at all involved in his first children's upbringing, he is bound to know more than you do. He has first-hand experience while you don't. That's just fine.

Accept that he knows more about babycare because he is experienced and you are not. That's all there is to it. If he has a few good baby-calming techniques or is handier with a diaper, consider yourself blessed. Learn from him, and be grateful that his skill means that you may take an occasional break without anxiety while he takes over the child care.

Your concern, however, indicates a bit of that old insecure-mother syndrome. You may feel that since you are the mother, you *should* be the family expert on your baby. If you worry that his higher parenting IQ diminishes your stature in his (or your own) eyes, you have a whole different problem.

- Relax. While your husband has been through this stage of parenthood before, he has no more experience in this marriage and with this particular baby than you do.
- In a very short time, you will catch up to your husband's skill level. Particularly if you are a stay-at-home mother, in a matter of weeks you will be the expert about *this* baby.
- Try to give up the idea that either you or your husband is better at parenthood. It doesn't really matter which of you can make the baby smile faster or clean spit up more efficiently. Support each other's parenting attempts and teach each other what your personal experience has taught you to be true about your particular baby.
- Remember that the goal in a marriage is not to be better than your spouse but to support each other's talents and skills as well as to help each other through tough times. Comparing your skills to his, regardless of who comes up short, can be very destructive to your relationship and doesn't help you feel better about yourself anyway.

My husband feels that he wasn't a very good father to his older children. How can I help him feel better about parenting this new baby of ours?

Show him you trust him with your baby, and tell him that you are thrilled that he wants to be a great dad to your child. Often, men who had first families in their early adulthood spent far more time nurturing their careers or themselves than their families or children. Some of these same men, when they have children in subsequent marriages, feel they have a second chance at parenthood. But they worry that they won't be up to the task.

- Your husband needs your support and encouragement. Consult with him about any and all questions and concerns you have about child care. Listen to his ideas and use them whenever possible.
- Leave him alone with your baby for periods of time so that he becomes comfortable. If your husband is one of those people who learns best by experience, hand him the baby and get out of the house. If he learns best by watching first, show him how you do things, and *then* let him take over. Then praise how well he took care of everything.
- Even if you think your husband did something dumb with your baby, as long as the baby isn't in danger, be positive and complimentary about his child-care attempts.
- Tell him in so many words that you are proud that he intends to be involved in this baby's upbringing.
- Do not criticize his methods and approaches to child care.
- Do not offer advice unless you fear for the safety of your child. Let him do things his way. Does it truly matter if he puts on the diaper differently than you?

Be supportive and loving and show him you are confident he will be a great father.

Mothers of Multiples

We have triplets (or quadruplets, quintuplets, etc.). Is there a nice way to avoid strangers' staring and inappropriate comments?

As with any unusual situation, multiples draw attention; sometimes that's a good thing, but sometimes it isn't. Toting around lots of toddlers will generally get you a bit of extra help, as friendly folks rush to hold doors open for you or let you go ahead of them in line. But just as often, the novelty of your multiples may erase the ability to be polite from the minds of passersby, and your three babies are greeted with stares that would otherwise be thought of as rude.

- Understand that your babies are uncommon, and therefore interesting. Most of the stares mean no harm.
- If you dress the babies alike, their multiplicity becomes even more obvious. If you want them to have distinct and separate identities and obscure, however minimally, the fact of their twin-hood, dress them differently.
- Adopt the nod-politely-and-move-on approach to unwanted attention from strangers. When someone asks you, as if it weren't obvious, if your babies are quads, nod nicely and keep moving.
- If further questioning persists ("Did you use fertility drugs?"), your personality and patience will dictate whether or not you answer.
- Remember that your children will learn from you. If you are pleasant to these rude people, they will be too. But in addition, if you describe their existence as a gift from God, they will feel that you cherish them, and if you talk about how much trouble

they cause, they will know that they are a burden. Choose your words carefully even before your babies speak.

We have twins. Many people compare them to each other, in front of them and us. How might I help them not say things that hurt one or the other of my babies' feelings?

People compare children all the time, even when they aren't twins. Grandma notices that Luke is walking much earlier than his cousin Frannie; your neighbor brags that her children slept through the night much earlier than yours; or your third-grade teacher remarks that your brother was much better behaved than you were. Rarely is this a valuable or constructive comment. If you or your child is the "better" one, it may feel good for the moment, but you also know that your turn to fall short will come soon.

Many people seeing twins (or other multiples) can't seem to help themselves from commenting on the resemblance, asking which one is sweeter, or even if you know which is which. Although some families enjoy the attention, these observations and questions can be harmful. If you choose to respond to inquisitiveness, you may find yourself unintentionally declaring which child has which traits, and such labeling often limits your children's ability to explore the whole range of their abilities and interests. You don't have to succumb to other people's wishes to pigeonhole your kids.

- ❧ If asked which one is better at anything (sleeping, eating, disposition, etc.) don't choose one or the other. Assure the curious that *both* your babies are totally charming and that they are behaving just as other babies do.

- If your twins are fraternal (and for larger multiples), you can educate the inquisitive. Tell them that one is bigger than the other because fraternal twins are no more alike than any non-multiple brothers or sisters, and that they will have many similar and different traits as a result.
- Always treat your babies as individuals. Encourage their strengths, admire and appreciate their individuality.
- Do not, however, push your children into specifically distinct roles. Don't assume that because Ashley is a quiet baby she won't like sports or that Don's ability to turn over at three weeks means you should start gymnastics lessons for him but not for his sister. Allow each child to try lots of activities and encourage each child to develop in many areas.
- When asked if you can tell them apart, show how you do it! Point out the freckle on one's chin or the fact that you always dress Margaret in blue.
- Once your babies are old enough to decide for themselves, support a variety of interests and even some "out of character" activities.

Index